BOOK 3

Y0-AGF-894

TEACHING GUIDE

*For Hard-cover
and Paperbound Editions*

WRITING:

UNIT-LESSONS

IN COMPOSITION

Prepared by

JAMES L. PIERCE

*Director of Instruction
Tamalpais Union High School District
Larkspur, California*

With the assistance of

DON P. BROWN, *San Carlos High School
San Carlos, California*

ALBERT L. LAVIN, *Supervisor of English
Tamalpais Union High School District
Larkspur, California*

MELVIN J. TUOHEY, *formerly of Cabrillo College
Watsonville, California*

MRS. LOUISE VELTE, *Redwood High School
Larkspur, California*

GINN AND COMPANY

© Copyright, 1965, by Ginn and Company
Copyright, 1964, by Ginn and Company
All Rights Reserved

Home Office, Boston, Massachusetts 02117

ACKNOWLEDGMENTS

HARCOURT, BRACE & WORLD, INC.: From the preface by Andre Gide of *Night Flight*, by Antoine de Saint-Exupery, translated by Stuart Gilbert.

THE SOCIETY OF AUTHORS: From "The Revolutionist's Handbook," by Bernard Shaw. Reprinted by permission of The Public Trustee of Bernard Shaw and The Society of Authors.

CONTENTS

INTRODUCTION

The Approach to Composition

The basic assumption of WRITING: *Unit-Lessons in Composition* is that the student will improve his writing by closely analyzing the writer's craft in a reading selection and then practicing the fundamental rhetorical skill revealed through this analysis. The emphasis is on the how and why of writing, on technique, yes, but on technique in a particular context. In other words, the student not only practices composition skills, but also explores the relationship between the skills and the writer's intention. He does not merely define and practice, for example, subordination; he does analyze the varieties and purposes of subordinate construction in specific writing situations; then given a similar writing problem, he uses those skills appropriate to the effect he wishes to create for his reader. He sees how the professional does it; he realizes that he differs from the professional only in degree, not in kind. That form is inseparably wedded to content becomes part of his compositional consciousness. Also part of this consciousness is the awareness that each writing situation implies a specific purpose and a specific audience. The aimlessness of the "Friday theme" disappears.

The experienced teacher of composition will quickly realize that such an approach is not unique; it is used in a number of college rhetorics. (The generic book is J. C. Dent's *Thought in English Prose*.) Yet WRITING: *Unit-Lessons in Composition* differs from the typical college text in at least three significant respects. In the first place, the reading selection on which each unit is based, rather than being invariably a complete essay, is as short or as long as the skill of the unit requires. For example, it may be a brief excerpt, as in Unit 25, where the first six sentences of Stephen Crane's "The Open Boat" are sufficient for the students' understanding of the aspects of point of view taught in this unit. On the other hand, it may be a passage of more than twelve hundred words, as in Unit 4 and Unit 21, where the complete original selection is used as a basis for helping the student to combine fact and feeling or use source materials responsibly. The advantages of this practice are readily apparent: the student does not diffuse his energies trying to analyze at the same time all the complexities of form and content found in an entire essay; he is able to focus his attention on a fundamental rhetorical skill exemplified in the passage and to analyze closely the relationship between the skill and the intention and meaning of the passage.*

In the second place, the rhetorical skills are defined more specifically and more concretely than they usually are in composition textbooks. This is accomplished primarily in two ways: (1) the questions lead the student beyond mere injunctions that he practice subordination or vary sentence beginnings or use image-forming words—he is asked to determine just what forms these

---

*Obviously, close analysis of a long essay is valuable training, but such analysis usually stresses understanding thought at the expense of comprehending form. The point being made here is that a high school student is more likely to master a skill if he can examine its use in a passage of manageable length.

skills take in specific contexts; (2) because the method of analysis is largely inductive in its application to his writing, the student makes the discovery himself instead of trying only to verify what the teacher or the text has already told him.

In the third place, WRITING: *Unit-Lessons in Composition* recognizes not only differences in grade level but also a fact long ignored in composition texts: that the varying abilities of students within a grade present a serious teaching problem. Each unit, therefore is prepared on three levels: one for the superior student, one for the average student, and one for the below-average student. Although the reading selection remains the same for all three levels, the amount of information supplied and the intensity of analysis required vary according to the ability group for which the unit is written.

Built-in Sequence—Built-in Flexibility

The 25 unit-lessons in Book 3 are arranged purposely in a definite order so that any instructor following this order uninterruptedly will build a sequence of skills progressing from simple to complex, from the more concrete to the more abstract; from skills developing primarily economy and preciseness in word choice to skills involving problems of organization based on critical thinking; from skills that involve direct sensory responses to skills that require the student to practice subtleties of emphasis, tone, and underlying purpose. (The specific interrelations of this sequence are pointed out in the unit-by-unit treatments that follow this general introduction.)

But, to provide the teacher the flexibility in choice of content that a class or a teaching situation may demand, each unit in this book is prepared so that it may be taught out of sequence—in any order—with minimum dependence on any other unit and with maximum profit to the student. There is no cross-referencing whatsoever in any unit; no unit presupposes completion of a previous unit. Taught in a regular sequence from 1 to 25, the units will help the student refine his skills in word choice, in building sentences, and in organizing his ideas and feelings primarily from a logical stance or from the stance of an increasing sensitivity to problems of emphasis, rhythm, figurative language, and voice. Nevertheless, a teacher who wishes to go directly to any particular skill at any time may do so with the knowledge that the unit is completely self-contained. All basic terms are defined in the unit; the progress of learning is developed from the initial Practice to the final Problem without reference to—or stated dependence on—any other unit. Similarly, if a crowded or interrupted schedule makes it impossible to teach all or most of the 25 unit-lessons during the school year, a teacher may choose any smaller number of units, and in any sequence, knowing that the integrated, self-contained quality of each unit supports a conclusive, forceful, and student-participative treatment of a fundamental or imaginative aspect of writing. Each unit is designed to have a definite impact on a student's writing, regardless of the order in which it is taught.

Flexibility of Teaching Method

Each unit-lesson in this book is to a large degree self-instructional; the teacher, therefore, may vary his or her presentation all the way from a closely controlled whole-class development to the assigning of any unit as individual homework to be completed entirely outside of class time. The authors of these unit-lessons—all classroom teachers—know at first hand the pressures of class load, of paper correcting, and of trying to cope with individual differences in student ability, interest, and inclination. These authors have therefore attempted to prepare unit-lessons that will not only help relieve the teacher of the unnecessary, busy-work pressures which often abound in the teaching of our native language but will also help the teacher concentrate on the positive, creative, and individual aspects of the writing act. Writing is essentially personal. Therefore, the ideal teaching situation in composition should be, as much as school conditions allow, a personal relation between student and teacher. The unit-lessons permit this kind of teaching. Probably an effective general way to teach any unit would be as follows:

1. Follow the *Teaching Guide* suggestions for motivating the unit in a whole-class presentation. Read the selection aloud—discuss it thoroughly—elicit inductively arrived-at comments on the techniques the selection displays.
2. As soon as the class has a basis for attacking the unit skill, set up a writing laboratory situation, each student working individually. Move around the class, helping individual students as they need help.
3. From time to time draw the class back into a whole-group situation. Have the students write a group composition on the board. The students might contribute individually a phrase or sentence from the Practice 1 or Practice 2 work they have already completed. Conduct the writing and the revision at one time. Have students evaluate the group composition.
4. Return to the individual writing situation. Keep the emphasis on the individual's responsibilities as a writer.

The preceding approach, of course, should be varied as each class demands. The point is that WRITING: *Unit-Lessons in Composition* permits this flexibility of approach, always freeing the teacher to pace his teaching according to the needs of the class. Furthermore, the unit-lessons put the burden of performance on the student rather than on the teacher.

Scheduling the Units—Time allotments

Book 3 contains 25 unit-lessons. Normally each unit requires from three to seven class periods to complete.

SEMESTER: Teachers planning to use WRITING: *Unit-Lessons in Composition* in a semester course might teach one unit-lesson per week, thus covering a selection of 15-18 units, with the remaining units held in reserve for special emphasis, extra student-contact work, or individual or small-group projects.

YEAR: For a year course in writing, the teacher can also plan to teach

15-18 units—one unit every two weeks (allowing a week for literature emphasis in each two-week period) with the remaining composition units in reserve, as in the semester course.

EACH UNIT: In general, plan one day for the preteaching and motivational aspects of the unit; one to two days for working through the Practices; and two days for writing and revision of the Problems. As you progress, less time can be devoted to the motivational phases of each unit-lesson, more time to the end-writing phases.

What About the Four Forms of Discourse?

Most of the units develop skills from selections that are primarily expository (see Unit 22, "Combine the Forms of Writing," for a two-level definition of exposition). But none of the units treat any of the four forms of discourse as separate entities, as goals for student writers to achieve—for the following reasons:

1. In normal writing, description, narration, and exposition are usually inextricably intermingled. Moreover, the success of a passage that is primarily descriptive or narrative or expository is often enhanced by the writer's use of one or more of the remaining two forms.

2. All serious writing is persuasive in intent; all successful writing is persuasive in accomplishment—the writer has persuaded the reader to share the world the writer knows. E. B. White's "From Sea to Shining Sea" (Unit 4) is an example of a passage that would ordinarily not have been called "persuasive" in the classical rhetorics, but which probably persuades many readers to share White's joy in the romance of tracing a path across the continent in a Model T. H. L. Mencken's "The Hope of Abolishing War" (Unit 20) is an example of a passage that would ordinarily have been labeled "persuasive writing, intended to convince" in the classical rhetorics. The label may fit Mencken's intent; it would be difficult to prove or even identify his accomplishment. Successful writing is more than labels applied to the source; successful writing involves the reader.

3. A word is a word, a sentence is a sentence, and a paragraph is a paragraph, whether the writer emphasizes exposition, narration, or description; restricts himself to one of the three forms; or combines all three. The main end in writing is to convey ideas and feelings in the most effective manner possible. If the student has worth-while content and a sincere purpose, and if he directs this content and this purpose to a specific audience, his final success will be determined by how well he chooses his words, structures them in sentences, and puts his sentences together—not on whether he tries to write narration, description, exposition, or argumentation.

As Perrin says in *The Writer's Guide and Index to English:* "People do not sit down to write 'exposition'; the word is convenient for grouping various articles that convey information." (p. 514, 1942 ed.)

4

Student Responsibility

In teaching WRITING: *Unit-Lessons in Composition*, it will be advisable to handle the important matters of revision and evaluation wholly within the atmosphere of holding the student responsible for what he writes. Perhaps one of our major weaknesses in our teaching of writing in schools is that we have let the student believe he is writing only for the teacher, that the only "correct" writing he need do is in the English class, and that "composition" is some strange form of endeavor required by English teachers for a grade, having no relation to the writing the student does in history, algebra, science, or elsewhere.

REVISING: If at the outset you wish to turn to the Appendix ("Revise What You Write") and work through it with each class, you will find help in setting up for the student a positive attitude toward the writing of first drafts, revising, preparing the final draft, keeping a specific audience in mind, and, above all, assuming a personal responsibility for what he writes.

To spare yourself endless correcting of mechanical errors and elementary structural errors, emphasize early in the year that every paper turned in for evaluation, whether or not it is to be graded, must be a "fair copy." In other words, the student guarantees that his paper has been proofread. To help instill this attitude, set up group procedures for proofreading (see Appendix, p. 171, level A; p. 169, level B; p. 163, level C), or appoint five or six students as proofreaders to whom the other students will submit their papers before preparing the final copy. This practice can free you from the minutiae of correcting so that you are free to help students improve their basic skills in rhetoric.

Evaluating

In the testing the authors have done, students reacted favorably to the idea of learning one skill at a time and having their papers evaluated for their proficiency with the one skill in the unit. This approach to evaluation permits more positive judgment of the student work by the teacher as well as by the readers. It also makes it possible to hold the student responsible for maintaining each previously taught skill as he proceeds through the units.

To acquaint students with concrete examples of the standards of careful accuracy that will be followed in your class, duplicate and distribute early in the year some representative examples of student papers. Lead the class through an evaluative analysis of these papers. By the time the students finish their analyses, they should have fairly well in mind the standards by which a paper is judged.

THE UNIT-BY-UNIT TREATMENT

The unit-by-unit treatments in this manual attempt to give the teacher as much specific practical help as possible in teaching each unit. The framework which follows is organized so that the teacher can become oriented to the unit in the shortest possible time:

I. Preparing to Teach the Unit
   A. Purposes of the Unit
   B. Skills Students Will Practice
   C. Scheduling the Unit
II. Motivating the Unit
   A. Background: Author and Selection
   B. Setting the Stage
III. Teaching the Unit
   A. General Points of Emphasis and Interest
   B. Special Observations for Levels A, B, and C
IV. Evaluating the Unit
V. Additional Writing Topics

Within this framework, we suggest that the following principles guide the teaching of each unit:

A. In introducing the unit:
   1. Attempt to connect the material to be studied to the student's personal experience—his habits, his writing, his reading, and his understanding of contemporary events.
   2. Relate the material in the unit to the previous composition work of the class and to the work which will follow the unit.
   3. Enliven and vivify the unit selection by setting it in context, relating it to the author, and reading it aloud.
B. In working through the unit:
   1. Vary the approach to the Practices, sometimes working them on the board, sometimes doing them orally, at other times having the students doing them in groups or individually.
   2. Bring in current material where appropriate.
   3. Use student writing for discussion and analysis as much as possible.
   4. Make the Problems the capstone of the unit.
   5. Instill in the students a feeling of personal responsibility for everything they write.
   6. Create, wherever possible, an audience for the students' writing.
C. In evaluating the unit:
   1. Hold students responsible for all skills learned previously.
   2. Accept papers only after they have been proofread, and, if necessary, revised by the students.
   3. Judge primarily the skills taught in the unit.

Because WRITING: Unit-Lessons in Composition is a pioneering approach to the teaching of writing on the secondary level, the authors will appreciate receiving your reactions to any aspect of this program. Please address your comments to Author, **WRITING: Unit-Lessons in Composition,** in care of the nearest office of Ginn and Company.

UNIT 1 — CHOOSE WORDS HONESTLY

Selections from ''*Politics and the English Language*''in
SHOOTING AN ELEPHANT AND OTHER ESSAYS
by George Orwell and
THE HOLY BIBLE, King James version,
Ecclesiastes, Chapter 9, Verse 11

(Student Text—A-Level, p. 1; B-Level, p. 2; C-Level, p. 2)

I. PREPARING TO TEACH THE UNIT

A. Purposes of the Unit

1. To help students understand that jargon impedes clarity.
2. To illustrate the characteristic features of jargon.
3. To illustrate that objectivity need not depend on an ornate, roundabout, artificially impersonal and polysyllabic diction.
4. To urge students to prefer the specific and the concrete to the general and the abstract.

B. Skills Students Will Practice

1. Identifying and criticizing the jargonistic elements in selected prose passages.
2. Revising unnecessarily complex passages into readable, direct prose.
3. Translating jargon into familiar diction.
4. Using specific illustrations and concrete images to clarify a description of a typical happening or a discussion of a general proposition.

C. Scheduling the Unit

1. The students might well begin their composition work for the semester with this unit, for it will help to establish a no-nonsense attitude toward composition, and it is certainly intended to help dispel the notion, often erroneously held by students, that effective writing is largely a matter of possessing a large fund of Latinate, polysyllabic words. Focusing on the importance of word choice, the unit emphasizes the relationship between clear thinking and forceful expression—a principle wisely established at the outset of the semester. Moreover, a major intention of the unit is to engender in the students a respect for precise thinking and writing. Finally, the unit will prepare the students for much of the work they will undertake in the remainder of the book.
2. As your students are apt to study either an essay or a novel by Orwell during the course of the year, they could, indeed, study this unit in conjunction with the essay or novel. The unit would reinforce Orwell's interest in language, especially in the political use of language, and

would give the students an opportunity to practice Orwell's principles of clear expression.

II. MOTIVATING THE UNIT

A. Background—Author and Selection

1. AUTHOR: Students will undoubtedly recognize George Orwell (pseudonym of Eric Blair) (1903-1950) as the author of *Nineteen Eighty-Four* (1949) and, possibly, as the author of *Animal Farm* (1946) (this satire in the Swiftian vein is still widely read by students, even though the specific satire on Russian communism seems to escape most of them). It may come as a surprise to them, however, to learn that Orwell started his career as a British civil servant in Burma, quit that post when he realized the futility of imperialism (see *Burmese Days*, 1934, and the essay "Shooting an Elephant"), became part, purposely, he says, of the "underworld" of the poverty-stricken during the Depression (*Down and Out in Paris and London, 1933)*, fought and was almost killed in the Spanish Civil War (*Homage to Catalonia*, 1939), and was a Socialist of a very tough-minded sort (*The Road to Wigan Pier*, 1937). His early death from tuberculosis cut short a brilliant career as a political and social critic and as an imaginative writer of the first rank.

His view of literature as propaganda ("All art is propaganda. . . . On the other hand, not all propaganda is art," he says in his long essay on Dickens) sets him somewhat apart from the main literary currents of the first half of the 20th century. Nevertheless, V. S. Pritchett has called him "the conscience of his generation," and Lionel Trilling has paid tribute to him in "George Orwell and the Politics of Truth" (in *The Opposing Self*, Viking, 1955). Full-length studies of Orwell are John A. Atkins's *George Orwell: A Literary and Biographical Study* (Ungar, 1955), Laurence Brander's *George Orwell* (Longmans, 1954), and Christopher Hollis's *A Study of George Orwell: The Man and His Works* (Regnery, 1956)—unique titles all!

2. SELECTIONS: "Politics and the English Language" was first published in 1946 and has since become a favorite anthology piece. It has become a very popular essay because in it Orwell attacks the debased use of language to conceal thought or lack of thought. High-sounding empty phrases, clichés, circumlocutions, are the stock-in-trade of those who have not thought through an idea or of those who want to conceal the unpalatable from an unsuspecting public. Orwell uses specimens from contemporary writers to illustrate his thesis that not only does sloppy thinking corrupt writing—sloppy writing corrupts thinking: The hackneyed and the roundabout modes of expression can become automatic responses; once they do, there is little chance for a clear and precise examination of an idea.

The unit selections—the passage from Ecclesiastes and the corrupt modern version—form part of Orwell's demonstration that official language is imprecise and vague. He pursues his analysis to illustrate that official diction is not only fuzzy but also often purposely misleading. (Modern political campaigns will confirm this charge.) Reading the essay should help the student become conscious of his expository lapses and should help him become a more critical reader.

B. Setting the Stage

A few suggestions for starting this unit are:

1. Confront the class with an official pronouncement of some sort—from a government agency, from an educational institution, from a large business organization—explaining an action or a policy (e.g., why taxes must be raised, why students drop out, why executives' salaries must be raised). Ask the students to write explanations of the meaning of the pronouncement. Use their explanations as the basis for a discussion in which the ambiguities and uncertainties of the pronouncement are illustrated. Ask them to account for the vagueness of the pronouncement and to suggest how its lack of clarity might be rectified. Tie this exercise to the concern for jargon in the unit.

2. Duplicate a student's paper that suffers from pretentious diction. Ask the students to evaluate the paper. They will disagree about its worth. Those who see it as pretentious will probably lack principles by which to judge it. Ask the class to suggest standards; then have the students turn to the unit to determine, among other things, how their suggested standards compare with those recommended by the unit.

3. Put on the board this dictum: "The language of politics is the language of deceit." Lead a discussion on the meaning of the statement. Some students will understand it in the Orwellian sense; others will not. Elicit the different meanings of "politics" held by the students. Try to get them to supply specific examples to illustrate their conceptions. Use their confusions and uncertainties as reasons for examining what is meant by precise and specific diction.

4. Use the essay itself, "Politics and the English Language," as a lead-in to the unit. (However, the essay might be read with more profit *after* the students have studied the unit.) If the essay is not available, use some other work by Orwell to generate interest. A number of anthologies now contain his essay "Shooting an Elephant." Some students will have read *Animal Farm* or *Nineteen Eighty-Four*. Use their knowledge of these works to generate a discussion on the corrupt uses of language. In *Animal Farm* what happens to the democratic principles that served as rallying points for the revolution? ("All animals are equal, but some are more equal than others.") How is Newspeak, in *Nineteen Eighty-Four*, used to control thought? What are the principles of Newspeak?

III. TEACHING THE UNIT

A. General Points of Interest and Emphasis

1. The main point of the unit is that ready-made phrases and pretentious diction usually hide thought rather than reveal it. You can stress this point at the outset by reading the corrupt version of the passage from Ecclesiastes to the students before they study it in the text. Ask them what it means; conduct a preliminary analysis of its diction. Then read the original from Ecclesiastes to the students. Ask them which version they prefer. Why? This preliminary analysis will prepare the students for some of the exercises in the text. (For Level C, see item 5 below.)

2. Help the students understand the context of the unit selections by reading to them the first two paragraphs of Orwell's essay. Stress his point that the specific, precise word will help to make the thought clearer—to the writer as well as to the reader. Also read to the class the questions Orwell suggests a writer should ask himself in order to improve the clarity of his writing. You might also wish to place the passage from Ecclesiastes for the students. There should be at least one or two students in the class who have read this work from the Old Testament. Perhaps they can help the rest of the class understand why both its style and content appeal to modern writers like Orwell and Hemingway.

3. Suggest that while the class is studying the unit the students search for examples of jargon or pretentious diction in regular news stories, in advertisements, and in letters to the editor (a rich source). Have them bring their examples to class for discussion and for written analysis.

4. You may wish to have the students examine the use of precise, yet familiar and unpretentious diction to convey difficult and complex thoughts in the excerpt from Bertrand Russell's "Touch and Sight: The Earth and Heavens" (Unit 10), the excerpt from E. M. Forster's *Aspects of the Novel* (Unit 18), and the excerpt from Loren Eiseley's *The Immense Journey* (Unit 22).

5. *Level C Only:* The preliminary analysis of the "officialese" version of the passage from Ecclesiastes, suggested in item 1 above, will not be very productive with Level C students unless they know the meaning of the words listed in "Words as Used in the Selection." Teach these words as vocabulary words (opportunity to do some inductive teaching of prefixes and suffixes here) before you ask the students to react to Orwell's paragraph.

B. Special Observations for Levels A, B, and C

1. *Introductory Material:* You may wish to give the students a somewhat fuller explanation of jargon than the text provides. How does it, or does it, differ from, for example, cant, argot, parlance, patois, slang? Orwell is primarily interested in "official" language, hence the term *officialese.* Margaret Nicholson's *A Dictionary of American English Usage* (Oxford University Press, 1957) contains an informative article on jargon.

- 2. *Practice 1. Levels A and B:* To help the students get started, you may wish to list the four characteristics of jargon as column headings on the board; then have the students suggest items to list under one of the headings, say, "abstract nouns."

  Level C: Here you may want to introduce the concept of the "abstraction ladder," going from the specific to the general, from the concrete to the abstract. Hayakawa's example of the cow could serve as an illustration: Bessie, a guernsey, a cow, livestock, wealth. Have them work out their own ladders with such familiar articles as a chair, a book, a car. This activity will help prepare them to make the judgments about the specific and the general required by the Practice.
- 3. *Practice 2. Level A:* The students will likely have difficulty with this exercise; it is deceptively simple (confirmation of Orwell's thesis that once you get into the habit, it is easier to write roundabout, textbookish prose than it is to write clear, simple prose). Help the students get started by working out with them a revision of the first sentence. First, suggest they change to the active voice. Then, is "Recent studies" informative; is it necessary? Can we change the abstract "urbanized culture" to a more personalized level? Is "City dwellers feel lonely" too drastic a change? Why?

  Level B: Translations: (*a*) "Honesty is the best policy"; (*b*) "A little learning is a dangerous thing."

  Level C: The board technique is appropriate here. Using the students' suggestions for completing the sentences, work out the first two items on the board. (The students may have some ingenious suggestions. Bear with them.) Have them read to the class their completions of the other items. The class could discuss whether or not the qualities ("good nature," "loyalty") are adequately illustrated.
- 4. *Practice 3. Level A:* Translations: (*a*) "Honesty is the best policy"; (*b*) "To each his own"; (*c*) "A little learning is a dangerous thing."

  Level B: The class can have fun with this exercise. Give the students enough time to work out their "officialese" versions. Some may wish to translate other adages. Duplicate some of the best translations, then ask students to identify the original sayings. Or use the exercise to compile an anthology of horrible examples.
- 5. *Practice 4. Level A:* See suggestions for Level B under Practice 3.

  Level C: Point out that abstract nouns have certain characteristic endings (e.g., -*tion*, -*ity*, -*ment*, -*ness*, -*ance*). Explain the difference between the active and passive voices. You might suggest that the students use columns to do the analysis:

NOUNS		VERBS	
Original	*Modern*	*Original*	*Modern*

- 6. *Practice 5. Levels A and B:* This Practice is a warm-up for the Problems. Use it to help the students develop specific examples. What, for example, would be suitable specific examples to illustrate "Nothing is enough for the man to whom enough is too little"? How specific need the examples be? Have the students read and evaluate one another's paragraphs.

- **7. *Problem 1:*** Use the review before Problem 1 to remind the students of the principles stressed in the unit and to give them specific guidance for accomplishing the work assigned in the Problems.

   Level A: You could use the latest edition of the school newspaper to suggest other topics for this assignment. What articles would lend themselves to the kind of specific, from-the-insider-to-the-uninitiated development suggested by the assignment? Some of the reporters will likely be in your class. Ask them how they would revise their articles to fit the assignment.

   Level B: This is not an easy assignment; give the students as much help as you can to get them started. See the suggestions for Practice 2, Level A above.

   Level C: Some students may resist the goody-goody, school oriented implications of this assignment. You might wish to suggest topics that draw on outside-of-school experiences: problems on the job, an insipid movie, the antiheroic hero, hubcaps along the highway—what you will. You might suggest that these students do *either* Problem 1 or Problem 2.

- **8. *Problem 2. Level A:*** This could be an optional assignment.

   Level B: See the suggestions for Problem 1, Level A above.

   Level C: You may want to hold a class discussion before the students write in order to identify suitable principles and reasonable supporting details. Those who choose persons to write about may want to keep their subjects anonymous.

IV. EVALUATING THE UNIT

Use one of the compositions written in response to the Problems as the principal item for evaluation in the unit. Allow the students plenty of opportunity to proofread and revise their papers so that you will not have to concentrate on mechanical errors when you evaluate the papers. (See the suggestions for revision in the Appendix: "Revise What You Write.") Perhaps the students could write their first drafts in class, criticize and proofread them in groups, then write their final drafts at home.

Tell the students that their papers will be judged on their clarity and precision; the criteria will be those listed in the review before Problem 1. In his essay Orwell suggests other caveats that you might want to use to guide your students in their writing:

(i) Never use a metaphor, simile or other figure of speech which you are used to seeing in print.
(ii) Never use a long word where a short one will do.
(iii) If it is possible to cut a word out, always cut it out.
(iv) Never use the passive where you can use the active.
(v) Never use a foreign phrase, a scientific word or a jargon word if you can think of an everyday English equivalent.

Have the students revise their papers after you have evaluated them. Hold the students responsible for the revisions. Read some of the better papers to the class. Conduct a group evaluation of one or more papers, if you wish. Do all you can to create a climate in which good writing is respected.

ADDITIONAL WRITING TOPICS

A. Read the lead review in a current edition of *The New York Times Book Review*. Select a representative passage from the review; copy it. Then write a critique of the passage, using as your standards the principles of clear writing you have studied in this unit.

B. Copy a short expository passage (one or two paragraphs) from Orwell's essay "Shooting an Elephant." Write a critique of the passage, using as your standards the principles of clear writing you have studied in this unit. In your introductory paragraph, explain the context of the passage and indicate what influence, if any, the context seems to have on the diction of the passage. Does your analysis lead you to suggest any qualifications to Orwell's guides to clear writing? Why or why not?

C. Your student council has decided *not* to allow representatives of partisan political organizations to advocate their views on your campus. You are asked to write a defense of this decision. Do so, making the position of the council as clear as possible by supplying specific examples in support of the council's reasons for taking the action. Or, if you wish, write an attack on the decision. First, give a fair summary of the reasons for the council's action; then, attack these reasons in as specific a manner as you are able.

UNIT 2 — USE NECESSARY WORDS ONLY

Selection from "Soldier's Home" in *IN OUR TIME*
by Ernest Hemingway

(Student Text—A-Level, p. 7; B-Level, p. 7; C-Level, p. 7)

I. PREPARING TO TEACH THE UNIT

A. Purposes of the Unit

1. To show students how to achieve simplicity in their writing by (*a*) eliminating unnecessary words, (*b*) selecting the best word or phrase for the purpose, and (*c*) tightening sentence structure.
2. To illustrate how meaning governs economy.

B. Skills Students Will Practice

1. Eliminating unnecessary words and phrases.
2. Choosing the precise word for a particular effect.
3. Tightening sentence structure to achieve clarity and economy.
4. Studying the relationship between meaning and economy.
5. Writing with an eye on economy.

C. Scheduling the Unit

1. This unit continues and supplements the content of Unit 1. If your class has become interested in style and how writers achieve clarity and simplicity, you may want to move directly into this unit after they finish Unit 1. Sometimes, however, getting students to work for an honest, direct style becomes such a difficult task that it is better handled in two sessions that are spaced by several weeks or months. This gives time for what is learned on the first assault to be assimilated.
2. This unit could be taught to students at any time their writing tends to become overblown and artificial.

II. MOTIVATING THE UNIT

A. Background—Author and Selection

1. AUTHOR: Ernest Hemingway (1899-1961) was born in Oak Park, Illinois. In high school he began to write—light verse, humor, serious fiction. After graduating, he tried to get into the army, failed, worked briefly on the Kansas City *Star*. But he was soon in Italy, where he drove

ambulances for the Red Cross during World War I. His literary career began when he settled in Paris several years after the war and became acquainted with Gertrude Stein, Ezra Pound, and Sherwood Anderson. In his late twenties he returned to the United States, but by 1937 he was back in Europe as a war correspondent covering the Spanish Civil War and then World War II. For his active participation in World War II, he was awarded a Bronze Star. After the war he lived in Cuba and in the United States—writing, following the bullfights, hunting in Africa and in other parts of the world. He died from a blast from his own shotgun on July 2, 1961, at his mountain home in Idaho.

His best-known novels include *The Sun Also Rises* (1926), *A Farewell to Arms* (1929), *Death in the Afternoon* (1932), *For Whom the Bell Tolls* (1940), and *The Old Man and the Sea* (1952). For the last novel he was awarded a Pulitzer prize in 1953; then, in 1954, he won the Nobel Prize for literature. His style has had wide influence in the literary world. His prose is clear, full of detail, simple in structure. He packed the maximum content into the minimum space; yet, because of his extraordinary feeling for rhythm and his keen sense of word value, his prose often has the emotional impact of poetry. Hemingway was a master in the art of understatement.

2. SELECTION: "Soldier's Home" is one of the fifteen sketches and short stories collected in *In Our Time*, Hemingway's first book, published in 1925. Several of the stories concern a boy growing up in the American Northwest; others touch briefly the brutal happenings of war. The collection has the strange mixture of beauty and pain one finds everywhere in Hemingway's work.

"Soldier's Home" (the selection comprises the first four paragraphs of the story) is about Krebs's first weeks at home after his return from war. It is typical of Hemingway's later work: the author makes no judgment of Krebs's attitudes; he simply allows the reader to know them. Krebs wants to live, as the last sentence in the selection implies, in the cool, clear, easy, natural way that he knows he can live—without involvement, consequences, intrigue, lies, or commitment. However, the nearness of sisters, father, and mother make detachment impossible. Whether he lies or speaks the truth, whether he remains detached or becomes involved, he cannot find his ease, and the reader sees the despair of a lost man.

B. Setting the Stage

1. Hemingway's entire story, and it is rather short, illustrates very well the principles of economy this unit proposes to teach. A careful analysis of the story would provide an excellent introduction to the unit.

2. The phrase "economy of statement" is used frequently in this unit, and the word *economy* may be a fortunate choice. A discussion of this term may help introduce an important point this unit hopes to make: Meaning governs economy. Sometimes the best economy is to spend money (buying expensive clothes may mean buying fewer clothes; investing in a new

pair of reading glasses may prevent future medical expenses). So it is with one's prose: sometimes the writer achieves his purpose best by using many words, and occasionally he *wants* an elaborate style. One has to know what he is doing, what his purpose is, if he is to be economical with money or with words.

A discussion of the term *economy* may prove to be a good way to begin this unit.

I. TEACHING THE UNIT

A. General Points of Interest and Emphasis

1. The rationale that lies behind unnecessarily difficult or ornate language makes an interesting study. Why do people waste words? Perhaps again the economy metaphor is useful: People find it easier to spend money indiscriminately than to budget carefully. So it is with language. Language economy requires precision—in thinking, in word choices, in sentence structure, in organization.

2. But it is not merely laziness that causes extravagance in language. There are causes that lie deep in human nature. You might pose some questions: Is one's language a status symbol? If so, what do most people want their use of language to "prove"? Is language ever used as a cover—for ignorance or guilt, for example? Why do languages contain euphemistic words and phrases (often wordy)? Is jargon an aid to economy sometimes? When? Are there times when one is grateful that language offers a chance for circumlocution? If there is time, an investigation of the psychology of language would be useful here. We can, however, perhaps conclude that a person may not write honestly unless his attitude makes him want to.

● 3. *Practice 1. Levels A, B, and C:* The value of this Practice lies entirely in the reasons the students offer for the variations from Hemingway's sentence. The exercise is easy, but if it teaches students to appreciate the leanness of Hemingway's language, it will have been worth while. Challenge any student to reduce the original without losing meaning.

● 4. *Practice 2. Levels A and B:* A possible very lean version: "Machines have revolutionized modern living. Always, as civilization advances, it changes." Students will notice that the original statement does not make much sense. "As the history of the world advances" is not accurate: Civilizations advance, and history merely records this progress. This example passage reveals that often when a writer realizes he has not said much, he keeps adding, hoping that he can make his point if he piles on enough words. It is better to take the opposite direction. When wordiness appears, tear up the paper and start again—but only after the necessary thinking that should precede writing.

Level C: Ask some students to write their revisions on the chalkboard. For those students who still think there is "one right way" to say something, this may serve as another illustration that there are many good choices available to the writer. Here is a lean version of the passage: "In modern times, automation has eliminated many jobs. But history should remind us that through the ages inventions have continually replaced human hands."

- 5. *Practice 3. Level A:* Using the right word for a particular job is essential to economy, but this is something that one cannot teach easily. Students may benefit from looking at other Hemingway stories and finding examples of "one right word." Here are examples to work around:

    a. He was in one of those hopeless spots.

    b. I was miffed when I saw people in the back acting zany while I tried to give my report.

    c. We weeded out all the obstacles to victory.

    Level B: In comparing sentences students may discover that their changes have altered the effect of the sentence. Saying "She directed the fur robbery" *does* change the meaning of the original, and students should understand that "Which sentence is right?" is not the question here, but rather: "Which sentence is better for a particular purpose?" "It was she" rather than "She directed" is a waste unless it is needed because of the information in an earlier sentence. The value of the Practice lies in the thinking and reactions that accompany "tightening" these sentences.

    Level C: These students particularly need to understand that "right or wrong" is not the question. What many of them need is awareness of the many possibilities writers encounter when they fashion sentences. In these sentences they see pairs of possibilities, one in each pair more direct than the other. Which words obstruct or determine the degree of directness?

- 6. *Practice 4. Level A:* A possible revision: "Some people think Conrad is a better novelist than Hardy. Both novelists use setting to reveal character. In Hardy's novels character *is* fate; in Conrad's novels characters are *victims* of fate." As soon as you receive a creditable version, you may want to read it to the class with the question, "What does this improved version reveal that was perhaps hidden in the original?" These students will already have discovered that the writer of the textbook passage has no central point. The value of the tightened sentence structure is in the quickness with which this fact is revealed. The Practice thus gives evidence once more that incomplete or murky thinking can hide, or at least play hide-and-seek, behind murky language.

    Level B: Have students compare their versions. You will hope that many of them will feel the sincerity and honesty of the original and will consent to change only the obvious: "chair which was in front of me." Other changes will be personal and will have to be defended.

    Level C: In this Practice clarity governs economy. The student whose directions are most easily understood has written the best sentences.

- 7. *Practice 5. Level A:* An oral discussion may be more interesting here. Every student will see some different kind of artistic damage that has occurred in the reduction. If the students write, you may want many of them to read their paragraphs aloud.

Level B: Here, also, discussion and reading of paragraphs will be more profitable than writing only.

Level C: Students will need help with this Practice. You might ask them: Does Hemingway waste words when he says "easily and naturally," or is there a difference between these words that makes both of them necessary? What is the nature of Krebs's unhappiness that this sentence describes? Students will agree that Krebs's reaction is complex, and that perhaps Hemingway has given it the most "economical" description. He had to make sure his readers would feel the contrast and the deterioration in Krebs's world.

- 8. *Problem 1. Level A:* A possible revision: "A man has two ways of knowing his world—scientifically and poetically. As a scientist he examines the structure of things: He understands a rose by analyzing its parts—stem, root, bud, leaves. As a poet he understands objects in their total meaning: he responds to a rose in its entirety—its smell, touch, shape, color...."

Level B: Is there any advantage, you might ask, in combining the first two sentences? Or does the repetition of "I worked" serve an artistic purpose? You may find no wasted words in the passage, but there may be some interesting disagreement among the students.

Level C: The first four sentences in this passage are cluttered with redundancies. But the last four contain repetitions which may be purposeful. One cannot be sure how this passage should read unless he knows its full context. A possible version:

> The first time I saw the elephant
> hunter, a large, lean old man, he
> was carrying a U. S. Army rifle
> and a canteen. He seemed friendly
> and honest, but rather awkward,
> and somehow not a typical hunter.
> All the time I was with him he
> talked only about hunting, hunting,
> hunting. But I learned something
> from this old man: Hunters do not
> judge a hunt by the take—they judge it by the
> excitement.

- 9. *Problem 2. Levels A, B, and C:* The topics for all three levels require primarily descriptive prose. The writer who is after economy in description must have a clear picture in his mind; if he does not, he will probably be vague and wordy. The writer's task is (*a*) to visualize a scene clearly and (*b*) find the most economical way to write about it so that the reader can see it, too.

ʼ. EVALUATING THE UNIT

Problem 2 is perhaps the only work in this unit that should be graded, and the grade should depend on the success with which the students have achieved economy. You might give them the criterion for evaluation before they write: *Does the paper use only the words that are necessary?* (Have all deadwood, redundancy, and unnecessary repetition been eliminated in the final draft? Does the word choice aid economy? Are the sentences tightly structured?)

V. ADDITIONAL WRITING TOPICS

A. Select a newspaper or magazine article that needs tightening. (If you have difficulty finding one, consult the letters-to-the-editor sections in periodicals and newspapers.) Make a revision, eliminating unnecessary words and restructuring sentences. Hand in the original with your revision.

B. Select a statement that you would like to support or refute—an adage, the theme sentence in an article, or a judgment someone made in a conversation. Write your support or refutations in clear, concise prose, so that anyone who can read will be able to understand it. Make every word serve your purpose.

Here are some statements you may use: (1) Married women should not have full-time jobs outside their homes. (2) High school students should not own cars. (3) Children grow into better adults if they have been raised in permissive atmospheres. (4) Parents should exercise control over the books and magazines their children read.

UNIT 3 — RENDER SENSORY EXPERIENCES

Selection from *LOVE'S LABOUR'S LOST*
by William Shakespeare

(Student Text—A-Level, p. 14; B-Level, p. 14; C-Level, p. 14)

I. PREPARING TO TEACH THE UNIT

A. Purpose of the Unit

1. To encourage students to vitalize their writing through sensory language.
2. To help students recognize the value of direct, economical writing.
3. To illustrate the effectiveness of specific verbs in expressing motion.

B. Skills Students Will Practice

1. Selecting language that appeals to the senses and relates experience directly to the reader.
2. Condensing description through the use of concrete nouns and specific verbs.
3. Expressing motion and action through verbs which specify the relationship between nouns.

C. Scheduling the Unit

1. *Position of Unit in Sequence of Skills:* The emphasis in the preceding unit is on economy in writing; this unit, focusing as it does on concrete and specific wording, emphasizes a means of achieving economy. If this unit is taught in its present position, the attention given to the relationship between language and experience should reinforce the student's concept of economy introduced in Unit 2 and at the same time add to his skill in writing direct, clear prose.
2. Unit 3 can be a useful complement for a number of lessons. For example, an appreciation of Ernest Hemingway's prose depends in good part on the reader's understanding of the difference between concrete and abstract language. As an introduction to a poetry unit, this study of the effectiveness of sensory language, condensation, and particularization should be valuable in fastening the student's attention on some of the important aspects of any poem. Also, Unit 3 may be used to illustrate a truth about an effective vocabulary: Good writers and speakers depend not so much on a great number of elegant words as on making careful distinctions among ordinary words.

II. MOTIVATING THE UNIT

A. Background—Author and Selection

1. AUTHOR: William Shakespeare (1564-1616) was a man of diverse talents and interests; we know him primarily as a playwright and a poet, but he was also an actor, a director, and an uncommonly successful business-man. There seems to be considerable evidence that he, like his father, was an ambitious man, who put his talents into the general effort to raise himself and his family in Stratford society. Shakespeare's grandfather had been a farmer, his father a Stratford merchant, guild member and landowner; by the time of his death, Shakespeare had raised his family further, becoming himself a wealthy man and a member of the gentry—a position which gave him the privilege of holding a coat of arms. According to tradition (supported by some documentary evidence), young Shakespeare attended Latin grammar school in Stratford, where he was instructed by university graduates; having completed the seven-year course, he was apprenticed to a butcher. His early marriage and fatherhood may have sharpened his ambition, for sometime around 1587 Shakespeare appeared in London, where he was to make his fortune. From this time until a brief time before his death, at fifty-two, in Stratford, he wrote or collaborated in about three dozen plays (the exact number is disputed). The brilliance of this body of work is even more remarkable when we consider how very short that period of production was, and when we recognize that had Shakespeare written nothing more than his one hundred and fifty-four sonnets, published in 1609, he still would have been judged one of England's greatest literary figures.

   Thomas Marc Parrott's *William Shakespeare: A Handbook* (Scribner, 1955) is an excellent scholarly and highly readable account of Shakespeare's life and work. An unusually good piece of speculation based upon what is known of Shakespeare's character is Edwin Arlington Robinson's fine dramatic poem "Ben Jonson Entertains a Man from Stratford."

2. SELECTION: *Love's Labour's Lost*, from which our selection is taken, was probably first written in 1594 or 1595, but the text we know is a revision prepared in 1597. The play is a kind of social satire, in which the playwright employs common sense, chiefly through the character Berowne, to ridicule social absurdities of the day—the extravagance of language common to the time, many aspects of courtly love, and even pretentious displays of learning found among fashionable circles. Both the setting and the common sense are rural in derivation, reflecting a good deal of Shakespeare's own background and accounting (at least in part) for the popularity this play enjoyed among the lower classes as well as among the bright men and women surrounding the sensible, cool-headed Elizabeth I.

   The song "Winter" comes at the very end of the play, immediately following a companion piece, "Spring." It is a strongly realistic poem and stands in sharp contrast to the usual romanticized pictures of winter's joys (the line "'Tu-whit, Tu-who!' a merry note" is a bit of verbal irony, jarring as it does with the sensory experience the poet relates—the word *merry* bordering on sarcasm). The realism is based on the writer's experience with the actualities of dark, cold English winters. In this respect the song underscores the play's ridicule of the artificial.

Also, from this brief song, we get insight into Shakespeare's skill in characterization. The use of common names and the reference to ordinary occupations tend to dramatize the nature of winter by relating the season to the people who experience it most fully in its rudest forms; at the same time, the naming of people, the specifying of activities and effects, and the particularizing of setting constitute the beginning of characterization. It is this relationship between people and season that gives the poem its strength.

B. Setting the Stage

1. A good way to introduce this unit would be to conduct a brief discussion of how we experience the world—through our five senses, through sight, sound, touch, taste, and smell. These are the links between our minds and the world. How does one know a woman is beautiful, a fire is hot, vinegar is bitter? How does one know that the man at the next table has burned his hand on a baked potato? It is possible, though unlikely, that the man will make a general announcement; but his muted howl, his dropping the potato onto his plate or silverware, his fingers thrust into his mouth have already made the situation clear.

   A few questions of this kind will focus the students' attention on the importance of the senses in our understanding of what goes on about us. The mind processes the information coming through the senses, sometimes so rapidly we tend to think we have experienced only a conclusion (that poor man has burned himself), when in fact the conclusion depended on the information supplied by the senses (one or more).

2. Another step leading to this unit would be to discuss briefly the possibility of sharing an experience with someone who was not present during the experience. What kinds of words will help the listener or reader to "sense" the experience and bring him to the same conclusion the speaker or writer has drawn? A brief consideration of the possibility, even if not wholly accurate or satisfying, will prepare the student for points to be made in the unit itself.

3. It is often useful to draw on newspapers and magazines to illustrate the effective use of sensory language. A comparison of two articles—or passages—may lead to some useful observations, both as preparation for the unit and as reference points in the course of the study. Also, short stories provide passages rendering sensory experience (e.g., Steinbeck's "Flight," Hemingway's "Big Two-Hearted River," and Faulkner's "Two Soldiers").

III. TEACHING THE UNIT

A. General Points of Interest and Emphasis

1. Read the song aloud, with each student following his copy. The initial reading should be done at the instructor's usual speed, without exaggeration. A second reading, at a slower rate, should anticipate possible misunderstanding (e.g., "ways be foul," "keel the pot," "parson's saw," "roasted crabs"), so that when the student begins working on the practice sections he will be sure of the language he is asked to work with. Once it is evident that each line is clear to the class, another reading, like the first, should follow. to bring attention back to the whole.

2. It might be helpful, before actually turning to "The Craft of Writing," to get individual reactions to the mood or "feel" of the song. What impression of winter does one get from this poem? Very likely, many responses will be vague or narrow (cold, terrible), but a few may help point the way (physical discomfort, antagonistic nature). The instructor may have the opportunity to emphasize the importance of relying on the evidence in the poem to support the reader's impression. Too, at points during the study of the unit and once it has been completed, the class may compare their reactions to the mood with their original impressions. Such discussion will offer the instructor a gauge to measure the class's grasp of the part played by sensory language in creating mood.

3. The instructor may see value in emphasizing the peculiar effectiveness of a few of the "double-duty" words in the poem, as a means of indicating that a careful selection of words can lead to suggesting a little more than the writing actually says. (A few words with the class about *denotation* and *connotation* would be relevant to this unit.) The word *hiss*, for example, suggests more than the escape of steam through cracks in the skin of roasted crab apples; the words *greasy, brooding, foul,* and *merry,* in the context of the poem, have more than a single meaning each.

4. The following prose models in this text may be useful illustrations of skills analyzed in this unit:
   a. Unit 5—excerpt from "The Eighty-Yard Run" (words expressing motion)
   b. Unit 9—excerpt from "On the Difference Between Wit and Humor" (condensation)
   c. Unit 17—excerpt from *You Can't Go Home Again* (language of the senses)

B. Special Observations for Levels A, B, and C

● 1. *Practice 1. Levels A, B, and C:* There should be little trouble for the student in finding three visual images, but it is worth while to make distinctions as to sharpness, clarity (the frozen milk, the icicles, Marian's nose)—there will not be full agreement, of course, but there will be concentration on the matter of visual images. References to the sense of touch may vary surprisingly; while the emphasis should be on a direct appeal to the sense of touch, recognition should be given to the imaginative reader who "feels" the weight of the logs Tom bears or the discomfort of a raw nose.

- 2. *Practice 2 Level A:* Use the chalkboard for two or three examples, drawn from members of the class, before setting the students to individual work—this, in order to preclude hazy images. When the class has completed the Practice, select a few examples of each (sight and sound), discuss, and compare them with the examples from Coleridge and Arnold— and, of course, with Shakespeare's song.

  Level B: In this Practice the student is asked to go immediately into the application of the skill. Many efforts may be weak. Using the board, select a few samples from the class for general discussion of merit and for comparison with the examples from Coleridge and Chesterton. Those students who feel their first efforts to be inadequate should rewrite their sentences.

  Level C: A few examples drawn from the class and placed on the chalkboard before individual work will give direction to the uncertain. It might be best to concentrate on sight, including discussion of the students' efforts, before going on to sound. Since it is likely there will be considerable variation in merit, some discussion of why this or that sentence is effective or hazy would be worth while.

- 3. *Practice 3. Levels A and B:* Most students will see the need for concrete, specific nouns to improve these sentences, but they should be reminded that the verbs have need of attention as well. If there is time or apparent need, discussion of student samples for the first sentence will help discover the means for attacking the other sentences. "Gobbledygook" usually challenges students.

  Level C: It is important to anticipate the difficulty some students may have with various words included in this Practice. A clarifying discussion of vocabulary should precede the working on sentence improvement. Note, in the "roundabout" versions the number of words replaced by "keel" and "pot" in the original.

- 4. *Practice 4. Levels A, B, and C:* The variation of choice here may be great; the important aspect of the Practice is not so much the line selected as the explanation offered. It would be wise to remind the students of the author's discussion of Shakespeare's skills, so that they will be clear about elements which contribute to compactness. At the same time, students should be encouraged to analyze their chosen lines to show in detail what and how much comes out of the wording. It is not enough to say that the image of icicles hanging by a wall is lifelike and tells a lot about winter. The writer should explain what is lifelike about it, what makes it lifelike, and what senses are played on.

- 5. *Practice 5. Levels A and B:* The explanations, again, are of more importance than the words chosen. But the class should be urged to make choices which offer them the best opportunity to demonstrate their understanding of sensory language, without straining the effectiveness of the images. (There is always danger, of course, that the eager student will force his analysis, and in the effort to see it all, will see more than is there. It is a delicate balance to keep.)

Level C: It is probably best to follow **a.** with a discussion of students' accomplishment before going on to **b.** One student might read his sentence for *blows*, and the rest of the class comment on his explanation. It might also be helpful, for emphasis, to replace each of the underlined words with a synonym. ("And Dick the shepherd *breathes on* his nail" is less effective not only poetically but also sensuously—but why?)

- 6. *Practice 6. Levels A and B:* This practice might be fitting for small-group work (say, four or five students to a group). Each student should read his work draft to the rest of the group, who then offer comments on his use of sensory language; each writer then rewrites his draft, making whatever improvement his group's comments suggested to him. Another method is the simple exchange of papers for comment. The point is to get the student to evaluate another's writing on a similar subject; what he sees in the writing he criticizes may help him in improving his own work. It is suggested that these writings be evaluated (as far as the instructor's temperament will allow) only for the effective use of the skills called for in the practice; spelling, punctuation, even minor grammatical problems, should be kept out of the center of attention.

- 7. *Problem 1. Levels A, B, and C:* Review all skills treated in this unit before students take on this writing. Discuss the point of view from which the narrative is to be written and what kinds of action are likely to occur—what has to be seen, heard, felt (possibly even tasted and smelled, as blood, grit, clothing, perspiration) to make the scene come alive for the reader? Stress condensation: Struggles of this kind are rarely long. It might be suggested to the class that while there must be a *sense* of confusion in the narrative, the writing itself must be direct, economical, orderly. The instructor might consider encouraging the writers to write rapidly, in phrases and fragments, during the first draft, coming back to more conventional construction during revision. Small-group work might be convenient and meaningful for this problem—up to the final draft.

- 8. *Problem 2. Levels A, B, and C:* The best preparation for this Problem is class reading of the results of the preceding Problem. Four or five of the best efforts can be dittoed or simply read aloud, and discussed in whatever detail the instructor finds beneficial to the group. Following class discussion, a review of the skills practiced in this unit should be useful as summary and preparation.

  The question of point of view should be discussed with each level. So should the means of transportation. What difference will there be in the kinds of detail related by an observer in a train, on horseback, or on a boat? The students should be urged to select their own settings. If individual students have trouble making a choice, the instructor should have a few suggestions, general enough to allow the writer to rely on his own experience, but specific enough to tap that experience—local scenes, for example, the color or the actions seen from the window of the school bus, the sounds in a neighborhood block at a certain hour, the smells that come from a row of stores as we walk through the city or from different crops as we walk along a country road.

IV. EVALUATING THE UNIT

The usual evaluation procedures should be followed, but grading should emphasize the skills treated in the unit—the use of effective sensory language, condensation through concrete diction, and the use of words expressing motion (or energy words). The student will appreciate being evaluated on his application of the skills he is supposed to have learned.

V. ADDITIONAL WRITING TOPICS

A. Ask students to write a brief description of the school cafeteria during the last few minutes of the lunch period, of the assembly place at the moment a rally begins, or of the last play of an exciting sporting event.

B. Read aloud (or distribute dittos of) a dull passage in a newspaper account of some physical event (a game, a runaway car, a rescue), and ask the class to enliven the piece.

C. A reproduction of a painting (say, a Hogarth), or a magazine photograph (or several) can be used to initiate a writing assignment to employ the skills practiced in this unit.

D. Ask the students to recall a mood they have recently experienced, but one produced or stimulated by a setting or a situation, and have them explain that mood in terms of their environment. Caution them to avoid moods brought about by such obvious occurrences as cutting remarks, straight-A report cards, increased allowances; the writings should emphasize the "feel" of the setting, since the feel is dependent on well-chosen particulars.

UNIT 4 — COMBINE FACT AND FEELING

Selection, *"From Sea to Shining Sea"*
by E. B. White

(Student Text—A-Level, p. 19; B-Level, p. 19; C-Level, p. 19)

PREPARING TO TEACH THE UNIT

A. Purposes of the Unit

1. To help students understand that feeling may effectively be combined with fact in expository writing.
2. To illustrate how one's response to an event invests the event with meaning.
3. To illustrate the effective use of personification.
4. To caution against the writer's direct presentation of his feelings.

B. Skills Students Will Practice

1. Analyzing the combining of emotional statements with information in White's essay.
2. Using emotional responses to characterize objects.
3. Using personification as a technique to keep the writer's self in the background.
4. Investing the written account of a memorable experience with the proper balance of information and emotion.

C. Scheduling the Unit

1. This unit serves as an apt summary unit for the three units that precede it. The first two units in the text encourage the student to use a specific, unadorned diction, to develop a straightforward, economical style. The third unit, while emphasizing concrete diction, encourages the student to create an emotional or sensuous response in the reader. The two injunctions are effectively combined in this, the fourth, unit. The objective and the subjective, the expressive and the informative, are happily fused in White's essay, and the unit encourages the student to emulate the fine balance White has achieved.
2. This unit may be used to complement the study of the essay as a literary form. The unit selection would serve as an example of the modern informal essay at its best. By studying the unit, the students would gain specific insight into the components of this form and its stylistic features.
3. You may wish to have your students study this unit in conjunction with their reading of other essays by E. B. White. Studying this unit would help give the students a clear understanding of his stylistic ease, and

the students could, moreover, draw examples of his grace and his blending of the impersonal and the personal from the other essays.

II. MOTIVATING THE UNIT

A. Background—Author and Selection

1. AUTHOR: The students will, of course, gain some understanding of E. B. White (1899-   ) from reading the unit selection. His delight in experience, his attachment to the land, his sense of wonder are all revealed in "From Sea to Shining Sea." The students may find it interesting to learn that White did start his writing career after the cross-country trip, working on a newspaper in Seattle until, so the legend goes, he quit because a copy editor changed his reporting of a man's saying, "My God, it's her!" to "My God, it is she!" White's career began in earnest when he went to work for *The New Yorker* in the 1920's. He stayed with *The New Yorker* for eleven years, helped set the tone of the magazine with his commentary in the "Talk of the Town" column, and developed his deceptively easy style, a style which is the envy and admiration of professional writers. James Thurber, who also worked on *The New Yorker*, credits White with teaching him how to write an effective English sentence.

   Among White's works are *One Man's Meat*, (1942) a collection of essays he wrote for *Harper's*; *Here Is New York*, (1949) another collection of essays; *The Second Tree from the Corner*, (1954) a collection of essays, reminiscences, and short stories written over a period of twenty years; *The Elements of Style*, (1959) a revision of William Strunk, Jr.'s textbook; and *Stuart Little* (1945) and *Charlotte's Web* (1952), two enduring children's books.

   Preferring the country to the city, White has lived for many years on a farm in Maine. His aim, like Thoreau's, has been to simplify, to get down to essences. His superlatively clear style reflects this aim. Perhaps the best expression of his intention as a writer is this statement from *The Second Tree from the Corner:* "The hope and aim of a word-handler is that he may communicate a thought or an impression to his reader without the reader's realizing that he has been dragged through a series of hazardous or grotesque syntactical situations."

2. SELECTION: "From Sea to Shining Sea" was first published in *Ford Times* as a tribute to the Model T. Its charm, its sense of discovery, its respect for the structurally simple yet durable Model T have prompted its inclusion in many anthologies. While the essay reminds older readers of a somewhat less complicated America, it also strongly appeals to young people because it captures the excitement of youth. If the essay generates enough interest in the students, they could also read "Farewell, My Lovely!"—a more detailed tribute to the wondrous Model T written by E. B. White and Richard Lee Strout under the name, Lee Strout White.

B. Setting the Stage

Some possibilities for introducing this unit are:

1. Read to the class a few paragraphs from a student essay (possibly one written in response to a writing Problem in Unit 3) that offends because too much personal opinion is interjected or too obvious an attempt is made to direct the reader's emotional response. Ask the students to comment on the effectiveness of the paragraphs. Does the text support the excess of opinion? Is the opinion or the emotion-laden diction necessary? What is the effect of too much feeling, then?

   Follow this discussion with a similar analysis of a passage that is rigorously "objective" (perhaps a paragraph written for Unit 2 that shows the effects of the writer's trying too hard to "Use Necessary Words Only"). A discussion of these contrasting passages should lead the students to conclude that a combination of the factual and the expressive is preferable to an over-reliance on one mode or the other. Suggest, then, that in this unit they will examine the work of a writer who has achieved an effective combination of the two modes.

2. If student-written examples are not available, you might be able to conduct a lead-in discussion similar to the one suggested above by having the class contrast a passage of hysterical diction from a story in, for example, *True Story* with an especially terse passage from a Hemingway story.

3. Remind the students of the discussion of understatement conducted in conjunction with Unit 2. Ask them what would be the opposite technique? Under what circumstances would exaggeration be appropriate? Read them a passage of description from Mark Twain's *Life on the Mississippi* and have them contrast it with the passage from Hemingway's story used as the unit selection in Unit 2. Suggest that there is a strong tradition of comic exaggeration in American letters and that, toned down a bit, this mode can serve many purposes. The unit selection they are about to read, while striving for the smile rather than the laugh, is in the tradition of Twain.

4. Another way to work into the unit would be to have the students read first "Farewell, My Lovely!" A discussion of this essay would lead to at least a preliminary analysis of White's style which, in turn, would serve as a point of departure for reading "From Sea to Shining Sea" and for examining White's style closely.

TEACHING THE UNIT

A. General Points of Interest and Emphasis

1. You may want to read "From Sea to Shining Sea" aloud, the students following. As you go along, you can prepare the students for the work they will be doing by involving them in the preliminary explication of the

essay. What, for example, does White mean when he says he "planted his flag"? Why does he say, "...America is the sort of place that is discovered only once by any one man"? Questions of this sort along the way will help the students read the essay with perception and will give them some insight into White's unique combination of the factual and the figurative. If you are concerned about the arrested fluency caused by such an analysis, have the students first read the essay silently.

2. There is a certain amount of special pleading in this unit that your students may want to quarrel with. While in certain segments of contemporary society there may be a blind reliance on "facts" and an over-emphasis on objectivity, the reference to lack of religious faith is gratuitous. If the students want to object to this characterization of contemporary society, so much the better; their objections will increase interest in the unit and may even generate some thought. You may want to remind the students that the unit makes a point about language similar to the one that Bertrand Russell makes in his chapter on language in *Human Knowledge: Its Scope and Limits:* Language has two primary functions—expressive and communicative, and seldom are the two not present in an utterance. Passion with information characterizes a forceful style. Ironically, students usually sin on the side of passion, their writing containing more emotion and opinion than verifiable information.

3. At your own risk, relate the unit and its purposes to the students' interest in cars.

4. You may wish to support the analysis conducted in the unit by having the students examine and analyze such other prose models that combine fact and feeling as the excerpts from Saint-Exupéry's *Wind, Sand, and Stars* (Unit 8), Thomas Wolfe's *You Can't Go Home Again* (Unit 17), and Loren Eiseley's *The Immense Journey* (Unit 22).

B. Special Observations for Levels A, B, and C.

1. *Introductory Matter:* It might be wise to remind the students, as a supplement to the paragraphs explaining the purposes of the unit, that different rhetorical styles—or different voices—are suitable for different expository purposes. No one sets out to emulate the style of a telephone book, but the rhetoric of a telephone book is suitable *for* a telephone book. Gradgrind, as the text reminds us, is a caricature, a ludicrous absurdity. The informal, easy manner of White is perfectly suitable for the kind of personal essay he writes.

● 2. *Practice 1. Levels A and B:* To help the students get started, you could have the class analyze orally the combination of fact and feeling in "...my little black roadster was young and new and blithe and gay." What is the exact quality of "little"? Does it just mean small? Or does it also connote an affectionate possessiveness? Are "young," "blithe," "gay" factual? How do they help characterize the roadster? Why use both "blithe" and "gay"?

Level C: First work out on the board with the students one or two sentences for item **a.**—a sentence describing a jaunty hat, another describing a stuffy hat, perhaps another describing an insolent hat. Underline the personal comments in the sentences that characterize the hats. With these examples added to the one in the text, the students should be able to do the Practice without marked difficulty.

- 3. *Practice 2. Levels A and B:* You may want to have a number of the sentences written by the students put on the board for discussion. Ask the students responsible for the sentences not only to identify the personal comments in the sentences but also to explain what these comments add to the objective information. A concomitant to the exercise would be to have the students select and analyze specimen sentences from current periodicals. How much information do they contain? How much personal commentary? Are the two balanced? What is the relationship between the two? Do we learn more about the writer than the subject? See, also, the suggestions for Level C, Practice 1 above.

  Level C: This is likely to be a difficult exercise for C level students. First, review carefully with them the analysis in the text of the last sentence of "From Sea to Shining Sea." Then, help them a bit with some of the words in the sentence to be analyzed. For example, is "blazed" to be taken literally? What is its meaning, and what is White's intention in using it? Why does he use "westering" rather than "western"? What does "to wester" mean? Does "trace" here mean "mark" or "path"? The students should probably have dictionaries at hand for this Practice.

- 4. *Practice 3. (All Levels):* This Practice should appeal to the students, especially to the imaginative. It is good practice to emulate temporarily someone else's style or characteristic way of thinking. The students should enjoy imitating Gradgrind's absurdities. (Some of the characters created by Swift in *Gulliver's Travels* and *A Tale of a Tub* are also suitable material for this type of exercise.) To give the students a fuller understanding of the Gradgrind approach to defining and describing, you could read them the first two chapters of *Hard Times* or the description of Gradgrind in the Additional Writing Topics section. Be sure to have the best imitations of Gradgrind read to the class.

- 5. *Practice 4: (All Levels):* This Practice is a warm-up for writing Problem 1. You might want to have the students write paragraphs for two of the suggested topics; then each student would be able to develop the better or the more promising of the two for Problem 1.

- 6. *Problem 1:* To help prepare the students for this assignment, either have the students criticize one another's paragraphs written for Practice 4, in groups or in pairs, or collect the paragraphs and make suggestions for development on each paper. Use the directions for Practice 4 as the criteria for evaluating the paragraphs; use the unanswered questions raised by the paragraphs as guides for suggesting avenues of development. A helpful practice here would be to duplicate or put on transparencies or on the opaque projector a few of these paragraphs and conduct a class analysis of them, suggesting lines of development for each.

● 7. *Problem 2:* To make this assignment more specific, have the students first frame their topics in controlling sentences and outline their proposed paragraphs briefly. Examining these plans will enable you to help the students eliminate false starts.

IV. EVALUATING THE UNIT

Tell the students that they will be judged on their ability to enliven factual material with personal commentary without sentimentalizing—that is, overemotionalizing—their material. The criteria for judging their compositions will be the principles outlined in the review preceding Problem 1, and ''From Sea to Shining Sea'' will serve as a model. You may prefer to have the students turn in either Problem 1 or Problem 2 as the principal item for evaluation in the unit.

V. ADDITIONAL WRITING TOPICS

A. Get a copy of a recent Sunday edition of *The New York Times*. Select three paragraphs—one from a serious front page news article, a second from an editorial or from a column by someone like James Reston, a third from a book review. Write an analysis of the degree of feeling (as the term is used in this unit) appearing in each paragraph, and explain how the purpose of each paragraph influences the degree of feeling appearing in each.

B. Write an analysis of the use of fact and feeling in the following description of Gradgrind (it is the second paragraph of *Hard Times* and follows immediately the stirring words about facts quoted in the unit). How, especially, does Dickens use indirect commentary to characterize as well as describe Gradgrind?

> The scene was a plain, bare, monotonous vault of a schoolroom, and the speaker's [Gradgrind's] square forefinger emphasized his observations by underscoring every sentence with a line on the schoolmaster's sleeve. The emphasis was helped by the speaker's square wall of a forehead, which had his eyebrows for its base, while his eyes found commodious cellerage in two dark caves, overshadowed by the wall. The emphasis was helped by the speaker's mouth, which was wide, thin, and hard set. The emphasis was helped by the speaker's voice, which was inflexible, dry, and dictatorial. The emphasis was helped by the speaker's hair, which bristled on the skirts of his bald head, a plantation of firs to keep the wind from its shining surface, all covered with knobs, like the crust of a plum pie, as if the head had scarcely warehouse-room for the hard facts stored inside. The speaker's obstinate carriage, square coat, square legs, square shoulders—nay, his very neckcloth, trained to take him by the throat with an unaccommodating grasp, like a stubborn fact, as it was—all helped the emphasis.

[This material may be duplicated for classroom use.]

UNIT 5 — BUILD SENTENCES RICH IN MEANING

Selection from "*The Eighty-Yard Run*"
by Irwin Shaw

(Student Text—A-Level, p. 26; B-Level, p. 27; C-Level, p. 26)

I. PREPARING TO TEACH THE UNIT

A. Purposes of the Unit

1. To help students recognize the relationship between syntactical or structural layers and levels of modification in the sentence.
2. To analyze the relationship between syntactical unit and level of abstraction in the sentence.
3. To illustrate ways of achieving specificity within the sentence.
4. To provide the student with ways of enriching the texture and meaning of his sentences.

B. Skills Students Will Practice

1. Identifying the sentence bases or the highest levels of generality in specimen sentences.
2. Analyzing the levels of generality in specimen sentences.
3. Constructing sentences that have two or more levels of specificity added to the sentence base; creating sentences, that is, that progressively descend the abstraction ladder.
4. Using layers of modification to increase the textural density of descriptive and expository passages.

C. Scheduling the Unit

1. This is the first of a series of units centering on sentence development. It follows naturally the preceding units which emphasize word choice. Because it focuses on the structure-units within the sentence, on the relationship between these structure-units and levels of abstraction, it provides insight into sentence construction not normally provided by the traditional simple-complex-compound type of sentence analysis. At the same time, this unit gives the students specific, concrete ways of increasing the textural density of their sentences.
2. This unit could be used whenever the students' tendency to over-generalize, to follow one generalization with another, becomes an especial problem. Very good students often have trouble being specific. This unit is helpful because it *shows* students how to be specific, how to provide the details that give body to a generalization. Where admonitions fail,

this unit gives concrete help. After working through this material, students should be able to avoid that thinness in their writing which is a bane of the composition instructor.

3. You may wish to use this unit to complement the study of Irwin Shaw's story, "The Eighty-Yard Run." This is a powerful story which challenges some of the adolescent world's facile assumptions and values. Because it is realistic, it poses some instructional problems, but the force and skillful craftsmanship of the story make it worth teaching. As the unit selection is a description of the eighty-yard run itself, the unit offers an excellent opportunity to combine literary analysis with instruction in rhetoric.

II. MOTIVATING THE UNIT

A. Background—Author and Selection

1. AUTHOR: Irwin Shaw (1913-   ) is one of those good, but not great, writers who have produced first-rate work in many forms. A carefully competent journeyman, he has written for radio, the screen, and television. Born in New York and educated in Brooklyn, he first gained recognition as a playwright with *The Gentle People* (1939), and *Sons and Soldiers* (1939) and as a short-story writer with *Sailor Off the Bremen* (1939), *Welcome to the City* (1942), and *Act of Faith and Other Stories* (1946). He later established himself as a novelist who depicted social conflict with power and compassion; his best-known novel is *The Young Lions* (1948), one of the most important novels of World War II. In *The Troubled Air* (1951) he writes of the viciousness of red-baiting and witch-hunting; in *Two Weeks in Another Town* (1959) he uses a man's returning to his town to depict the roots of a generation and the gulf that separates generations; and in his most recent novel, *Voices of a Summer Day* (1965), he shows a man reliving his life through an afternoon of memory.

2. SELECTION: "The Eighty-Yard Run," from the collection *Mixed Company* (published in 1950; many of the stories first appeared in *The New Yorker*), is Shaw's best-known short story. With sympathy and clearheadedness it chronicles the downward trail of a young man who won a shallow and easy early success. The highest point in the protagonist's life was the eighty-yard run, achieved during a college practice session; everything thereafter was anticlimatic. The story is told from the vantage point of fifteen years after the college success, when the emptiness and uselessness of the protagonist are painfully evident. The perennial problem of how to cope with early and easily won success accounts for the continuing popularity of the story. While circumstances change, the problem persists and, indeed, may be even more acute today.

   As suggested above, "The Eighty-Yard Run" would be a challenging story to teach, for it makes young people examine present values from the perspective of time. If you were to teach it, an instructive lesson in taste could be achieved by showing the students, after they had studied the story, the Playhouse 90 television production of the story, a particularly vulgarized and prostituted version.

The unit selection is the first paragraph of the story; it gives detail to the title and provides the point of comparison for the rest of the protagonist's actions. The second paragraph makes it clear to the reader that the run is being recollected fifteen years later. The skill with which the flashback is handled is worth examining itself. If the students do not read the story, you could read the first two paragraphs, summarize the events of the intervening fifteen years, and then read the last few paragraphs of the story—wherein much of the run is repeated—to illustrate the pathos of the main character and to show how the run itself provides a framework for the story (this might prompt some students to read the story on their own).

B. Setting the Stage

1. You could work the class into the unit by having the students examine and criticize some student compositions that suffer from thinness of texture and lack of specific development. Ask the students first to identify the general statements, then the specifying structures, if any, that generate images for the reader or support the generalizations. Ask them to suggest ways to give body to the compositions; then inform them that the unit they are about to work on will delineate ways to add details within the sentence.

2. Another way to start the unit would be to put just the sentence bases on an overhead transparency, then project the transparency and lead a class discussion on what the sentence bases convey and what expectations they leave unsatisfied in the reader's mind. If you wish, reveal one sentence base at a time. Ask the students what is established by "The pass was high and wide and he jumped for it...." Is it a basketball game or a football game or some other game? What is "he"—a back, an end, a forward? Can the students be certain? Does the next sentence base, "The center floated by..." clear up the confusion? These sentence bases advance the action perhaps, satisfy the reader's "and-then, and-then" desire, but they do not supply the specific details that help to make the incident live. How these added details are related to the sentence base and how they can be constructed are what the students will study in the unit.

3. Another way of introducing the unit has been suggested above: studying the story first. The unit selection is the key passage in the story; and if the students studied the story and then the unit, they would get some understanding of literature, composition, and language as integral parts of a complex whole.

4. Still another, and very profitable, way of introducing the unit would be to do some direct teaching of the technique of analyzing sentences by

level of generality. What is a level of generality or abstraction? How do we know the writer has down-shifted to the next level? More specific information on this technique is contained in the next section, "Teaching the Unit" (III,A,1).

III. TEACHING THE UNIT

A. General Points of Interest and Emphasis

1. The originator of the linguistic and instructional principles underlying this unit is Professor Francis Christensen of the University of Southern California. To help us understand the English sentence, Professor Christensen identifies four rhetorical principles operating within the sentence: **addition**—adding modifying structures to the main clause: **direction of modification**—either pointing ahead to the main clause or pointing back to the main clause; **levels of generality or abstraction**—modifying structures after the main clause tending to get progressively more specific; and **texture**—*dense* if much particularity is added to the main clause, *thin* if few or no additions are made. Using these principles, Professor Christensen has developed the technique for analyzing sentences used in the unit. Using the technique profitably depends on one's understanding the relationship between levels of abstraction and structural units of modification. A structural unit of modification is usually signaled by a punctuation mark. Professor Christensen also identifies the grammatical character of the additions, specifying such units as the subordinate clause, the relative clause, the noun cluster, the verb cluster, the absolute, the adjective cluster, and the prepositional phrase. You, too, may want your students to identify the grammatical character of the layers of structure they analyze and compose. The authors of the text and the *Teaching Guide* strongly urge you not only to study Professor Christensen's article ("A Generative Rhetoric of the Sentence," *College Composition and Communication*, Vol. XIV, No. 3, October, 1963), but also to teach the method of sentence analysis outlined in the article and to have the students use the various modifying structures to compose multileveled sentences of their own.

2. You may wish to take the students through the unit selection orally first, conducting a preliminary analysis as you read the passage with them. You could include in this analysis of the relationship between the general and the specific, between structure and meaning, a little detective work: How do the students know that the run described did not occur in a contemporary football game? Here you can draw on the specific knowledge of some of the athletes in the class.

3. While almost any passage of professional prose would serve to supplement the specimens used for analysis in the unit, the following prose models from the text would provide interesting examples of multileveled

generality for analysis: excerpts from Melville's *Typee*, Joyce's "The Dead," and Hayakawa's *Language in Thought and Action* (Unit 12); excerpt from Eiseley's *The Immense Journey* (Unit 22); excerpt from Thomas's "The Crumbs of One Man's Years" (Unit 23); and excerpt from Conrad's "The Lagoon" (Unit 24).

B. Special Observations for Levels A, B, and C.

1. **Introductory Matter:** The idea that the meaning of sentences is enriched by the writer's adding structural units of increasing specificity to the sentence base (or main clause) is generally sound, but some students may object that the abstract expository sentences (those by Huxley and Langer, for example) are "rich in meaning," too. It takes concentration and thought to comprehend them, and their meaning, or reference, is not confined to a single instance. It would be wise to emphasize, therefore, the text's distinction between the ideational and the imagistic. A statement about an idea is rich in meaning if it has wide applicability. A statement about a physical event, static or dynamic, is rich in meaning if it can be imaged, if it is particularized with sensory images. Christensen's concept of textual density may help to clarify the distinction and to illustrate the meaning of "meaning" in the context of the introduction to the unit. A statement about a physical event is impoverished in meaning (that is, thin in texture) until it is fleshed out with specific sensory details. (Please see p. 43 for a special discussion of Shaw's third sentence.)

- 2. *Practice 1. Levels A and B:* Sentence bases from the fourth sentence to the last sentence in the unit selection are as follows:

Sentence 4
    1   He smiled a little to himself as he ran,

Sentence 5
    1   The first halfback came at him and
    1   he fed him his leg, then
            swung at the last moment,
            took the shock of the man's shoulder without breaking stride,
            ran right through him,
(These five verb structures are all part of the sentence base because they are co-ordinate elements, not subordinate structures operating on lower levels of generality.)

Sentence 6
    1   There was only the safety man now,

Sentence 7
    1   Darling tucked the ball in,
            spurted at him,

Sentence 8
    1   He was sure he was going to get past the safety man.

Sentence 9
    1   he headed right for the safety man,
               stiff-armed him,

Sentence 10
    1   He pivoted away,

Level C: Sentences are graphed as follows:

a.   1   He was six years old,
       2   with dark eyes,
       2   quiet and serious.

b.   1   The white tennis ball sizzled over the net,
       2   low and fast,
          3   a perfect serve,
             4   just inside the white line.

c.   1   Wind shook the tree,
       2   swaying the heavy branches,
       2   whispering through the delicate leaves.

d.   2. Pushed off the the diving board,
   1   Tony struggled for balance in mid-air.

- **3. *Practice 2. Level A:*** Sentences are graphed as follows:

a.   1   Aye, many a man ... remembers a day when he ripped down
            a country road in a canary-yellow, bucket-seated Mercer,

       2   master of all he surveyed,
          3   high-riding,
          3   able to see where he was going,
          3   with a wheel in his hands that really steered the car
              instead of slyly suggesting that it change direction.

b.   1   I lowered the tip of mine into, the water,
       2   tentatively,
       2   pensively dislodging the fly,
          3   which darted two feet away,
             poised,
             darted two feet back, and
             came to rest again a little further up the rod.

c.   2   Before the swallow,
       2   before the daffodil, and
       2   not much later than the snowdrop,
   1   the common toad salutes the coming of spring after his
           own fashion, / , and crawls rapidly as possible towards the
                  nearest suitable patch of water.
       2   which is to emerge from a hole in the ground,
          3   where he has lain buried since the previous autumn,

Levels B and C: Sentences are graphed as follows:

a. 1   The poet was a rag of a man,
    2   dark,
    2   little, and
    2   lean,
        3   with hollow cheeks and thin black locks.

b. 1   At a bend of the line the red glare of a foundry flashed into
                                                                     sight,
        2   illuminating a score of workmen stripped to the waist,
            3   their torsos straining,
                4   arms upraised to strike.

c. Same as **a** under Level A.

- **4. *Practice 3 Levels A, B, and C:*** You might want to gradually increase the demands on the students in this exercise by suggesting that they add a second level to the first sentence base, a second and third to the second sentence base, a second, third and fourth to the third sentence base, and so on. Another variation would be to specify the grammatical character of the added layers. You could say: "Add a different grammatical structure to each sentence base. Choose these forms, for example." You could then put on the board examples of subordinate clause, prepositional phrase, verb cluster, noun cluster, and absolute construction. (See Christensen's article.)

- **5. *Problem I:*** You could follow up the work with Practice 3 by suggesting that the students add different kinds of grammatical units to the sentence bases in each sentence: e.g., verb clusters to the main clause of the first sentence, prepositional phrases to the main clause of the second sentence, absolute phrases to the main clause of the third sentence, and so on. Or, if you prefer, you could suggest simply that at least two examples of specified grammatical units appear in the added layers of particularity throughout the paragraph. This is a somewhat mechanical approach, of course, but it will help students gain a sense of the relationship between structural grammatical unit and function. The important point is not the name of the grammatical structure, but the kind of meaning it carries. Once the student creates one structure, the parallelism of successive structures of the same type should carry him along. You could help the students get started by putting one of the suggested sentence bases on the board, say, "The white convertible rounded the corner and picked up speed," and adding with the aid of the class layers of specificity, e.g. "...rushing past the excited spectators, gaining on the car ahead." or "...the driver momentarily losing control, fighting the wheel to regain the road."

- **6. *Problem 2:*** This assignment is, of course, the familiar process essay, given a slightly different twist by the emphasis on providing levels of particularity. To help the students with the orderliness of their presentation, you may want them first to list the steps in the process they intend to describe. Such a list will give them a coherent framework from which to write the essay.

IV. EVALUATING THE UNIT

If you use primarily the process essays to evaluate the students' work in the unit, you may wish to provide them with some such evaluative criteria as the following:

A. Is the process itself, the act the operator is trying to accomplish, clearly defined?

B. Are the steps in the process arranged in a logical order?

C. Is each step in the process adequately particularized (by added layers of meaning)?

D. Could a reader, following the description, perform the process?

V. ADDITIONAL WRITING TOPICS

A. Write an analysis of the degrees of generality and particularity to be found in the following description of Tellson's Bank from Dickens's *A Tale of Two Cities*. Explain how the added layers of meaning contribute to the effectiveness of the description.

> Thus it had come to pass, that Tellson's was the triumphant perfection of inconvenience. After bursting open a door of idiotic obstinacy with a weak rattle in its throat, you fell into Tellson's down two steps, and came to your senses in a miserable little shop, with two little counters, where the oldest of men made your check shake as if the wind rustled it, while they examined the signature by the dingiest of windows, which were always under a shower-bath of mud from Fleet street, and which were made the dingier by their own iron bars proper, and the heavy shadow of Temple Bar. If your business necessitated your seeing "the House," you were put into a species of Condemned Hold at the back, where you meditated on a misspent life, until the House came with its hands in its pockets, and you could hardly blink at it in the dismal twilight. Your money came out of, or went into, wormy old wooden drawers, particles of which flew up your nose and down your throat when they were opened or shut. Your bank-notes had a musty odor, as if they were fast decomposing into rags again. Your plate was stowed away among the neighboring cesspools, and evil communications corrupted its good polish in a day or two. Your deeds got into extemporized strong-rooms made of kitchens and sculleries, and fretted all the fat out of their parchments into the banking-house air. Your lighter boxes of family papers went up stairs into a Barmecide room, that always had a great dining-table in it and never had a dinner, and where, even in the year one thousand seven hundred and eighty, the first letters written to you by your old love, or by your little children, were but newly released from the horror of being ogled through the windows, by the heads exposed on Temple Bar with an insensate brutality and ferocity worthy of Abyssinia or Ashantee.

B. From a short story or novel you have recently read, select a descriptive-narrative passage you regard as especially effective. Write an analysis of the passage in which you attempt to explain its effectiveness. Indicate how added layers of meaning (as defined in this unit) contribute to the success of the passage. Include a copy of the passage with your analysis.

C. You are a witness to a serious traffic accident. Neither driver will accept the blame for having caused the accident. The insurance companies need your testimony to help settle the conflicting claims. Write an objective description of the accident, adding levels of particularity where necessary to make clear the events leading up to the accident. If you wish, consult a police or insurance form for reporting an accident, and include a diagram of the accident.

NOTE: If you compare the "graph" of sentence 3 of Shaw's selection in either Level A or Level B with the graph in Level C, you will note a different treatment of the latter part of the sentence, beginning with "the whole picture..." The reason for this difference in Level C is the struggle in this sentence between the nature of modification, handled on the basis of the specificity of *images*, and the development of meaning, based on the *ideational*. What we have here in the first level 2's is a string of *images* headed by *ing* words; then we are suddenly confronted by words that present an idea, not an image, and comment on it. Our two-dimensional content has become three-dimensional, and the same pattern will not fit. In all three levels, we call attention to this ideational function of "the whole picture...," but in the graph in Level A we let the word group stand; in Level B we place a comment alongside; in Level C we show it as it was analyzed originally in all three levels. We hope the present graph in Level C will be more helpful for slow students than the graph in Levels A and B would have been.

UNIT 6 — VARY SENTENCES TO MATCH IDEAS

Selection From "Such, Such Were the Joys..."
by George Orwell

(Student Text—B-Level, p. 35; B-Level, p. 35; C-Level, p. 34)

PREPARING TO TEACH THE UNIT

A. Purposes of the Unit

1. To illuminate some of the ways the writer's thought and intention influence his choice of sentence structure and length.
2. To help students understand some fundamental uses of sentence variation.
3. To illustrate different categories of sentence variation: level of abstraction, length, and structure.

B. Skills Students Will Practice

1. Analyzing levels of abstraction.
2. Constructing concrete examples to illustrate general statements.
3. Analyzing the relationship between ideational emphasis and sentence length and direction.
4. Using parallel structures for emphasis.

C. Scheduling the Unit

1. This unit follows naturally from the previous unit, which emphasized the relationship between elements of sentence structure and levels of generality. Here, however, Christensen's notion of varying levels of abstraction is seen as one method of varying sentence structure to match ideas; and you can indicate to the students that, while understanding how to add levels of specificity to the sentence base increases their control over the sentences they write, they need to balance this skill with other skills to achieve effective sentence variety—effective because it reflects (mirrors) varying patterns of thought.
2. Often there comes a time during a semester when students' writing seems to dry up or to become uncommonly stilted. This lack of fluency—or unwillingness on the students' part to let their writing flow—usually occurs when the students become overly concerned with avoiding mechanical and structural errors. In an effort to be "correct," they write unimaginative papers burdened with safe sentences constructed in the same monotonous pattern. When, and if, a number of your students seem to be falling into this habit, this unit could serve as an effective antidote.

3. This unit could be used to complement the work the students undertook in Unit 1 because it also emphasizes—although within a different context—the need for concreteness and specificity. Furthermore, because both this unit and Unit 1 use a passage by Orwell, they naturally complement one another. Interest in Orwell as a writer and as a critic of writers can serve as the point of departure for both units.

II. MOTIVATING THE UNIT

A. Background — Author and Selection

1. AUTHOR: See biographical and background information on Orwell in the appropriate section in Unit 1 (p. 7).
2. SELECTION: "Such, Such Were the Joys..." is a long autobiographical essay that was found among Orwell's papers after his death in 1950. It depicts Orwell's life, from age eight to thirteen, as a scholarship student at an exclusive British school. With his characteristic force and insight, Orwell describes and analyzes the inanities, the cruelties, and the snobberies that were practiced in the name of preparing students for the great British public schools. The essay is especially telling because it recaptures the thought and feeling of the child as he is confronted with the inexplicable and contradictory moral injunctions of what appear to be hostile adults. For insight into teaching and learning in general, as well as into the confusions of a child's mind, the essay is a must. It illustrates with utter clarity the great gulf between adult and child. Your students, while they will no doubt object that Orwell's situation was decidedly different from theirs, will acknowledge the psychological truth of his observations.

   The unit selection occurs near the close of the essay and serves to epitomize the values of the school and Orwell's relation to the values (albeit somewhat exaggerated). The values of the students—wealth, social position, strength—were part of the fabric of the school itself, and those who possessed these virtues, as Orwell calls them, were given favored treatment by the school officials. It is in this sense that the strong always won and the weak always lost. The relevance of Orwell's criticisms to the present is worth discussing.

B. Setting the Stage

A few ways of introducing this unit have already been implied:
1. Relate the unit to the previous unit by having a few representative papers written in response to the writing Problems in Unit 5 read to the class. Ask the students what accounts for the differences in the sentences in each of the papers. Having the emphasis of Unit 5 in mind, they will point out the varying levels of generality in the sentences. Indicate that going from the general to the specific is one way of creating sentence variety,

that in this unit they will combine this method with others in order to increase their skill in matching form with content. Or, if you wish, you could use the negative example approach, having the students read and analyze a composition that follows the injunctions of Unit 5 too religiously, every sentence beginning with a sentence base and descending two or three levels of generality. Have the students account for the lack of variety and suggest ways of varying the sentences within the composition so that the sentence forms fit the implied emphasis (naturally, there will be a number of conflicting suggestions here). Then indicate that this unit will deal with three specific ways of creating sentence variety.

2. Another way to introduce the unit would be to confront the students with a paragraph composed entirely of short simple sentences. Ask them to criticize the paragraph, to account for its monotony, and to suggest ways of improving it. Then turn to the unit as a means of studying specific ways of achieving sentence variety.

3. You could, of course, work into the unit through having the students first study "Such, Such Were the Joys..." entire. After the students analyze and discuss the social and psychological content of the essay, they can study the unit selection as an example of the ways Orwell achieved force and intensity in the essay. The unit can, therefore, not only help the students achieve skill in varying the ways they state their ideas, but it can also help them understand the form of the essay.

TEACHING THE UNIT

A. General Points of Interest and Emphasis.

1. It would be wise to teach "Words as Used in the Selection" before the students read the excerpt from "Such, Such Were the Joys...." C-Level students especially will balk at the Briticisms. Their having a clear understanding of such terms as "funk" and "nobbly" is therefore necessary so that they will not allow their distaste for the linguistically unfamiliar to inhibit their receptivity to the passage. If you wish, expand on the definitions given in the text. For instance, put "cricket" on the board and ask the students to define it. Elicit or supply a description of the game that contrasts it with baseball. For "hierarchical," ask the students to supply examples of hierarchical organizations.

2. If the students do not read the complete essay, set the passage from "Such, Such Were the Joys..." into context for them. You may even wish to read them the opening section, depicting the eight-year-old Orwell's problems with bed-wetting at the school, to give them a vivid picture of the kind of educational setting Orwell found himself in. Then read the passage used in the unit aloud, the students following. Conduct a preliminary analysis of the means of emphasis in the passage. Ask the students what feelings and ideas Orwell emphasizes in the passage. How do they know? What, syntactically, signals the emphasis?

3. A major point to stress throughout the teaching of the unit is that sentence form and length should be varied to fit intention, to fit intensity of feeling or force of thought. Sentences should not be varied merely for the sake of variety.

4. Other prose models in the text that might also be analyzed for varying sentence form to match ideas are (a) the excerpt from Hemingway's "Soldier's Home," Unit 2; (b) the excerpt from Shaw's "The Eighty-Yard Run," Unit 5; and (c) the excerpt from Chesterton's "The Ethics of Fairyland," Unit 16.

B. Special Observations for Levels A, B, and C.

1. *Introductory Matter:* To the introductory discussion of the relationship between thought and expression and the necessity for variety, you may wish to add some discussion of emphasis and clarity and some stress on the necessity for revising. Aside from eliminating obvious mechanical lapses, what are we trying to achieve when we revise? How can I make this idea clearer? By adding a concrete illustration? How can I make my conclusion and my principal points more emphatic? What syntactical devices will help? The material in the unit will help students cope with such questions when they revise.

● 2. *Practice 1. Level A:* If you wish, help the students get started by pointing out the use of the colon after "winning." What does a colon usually signal in such a position? What is the relationship of the list of items after the colon to the initial independent clause? How does the last sentence clarify the sentence that precedes it?

Level B: Suggest that an illustrative example be added after the first sentence, that specific examples of rationalizing for failing to meet a deadline be added after the last sentence.

Level C: To make certain that the students understand the example, have the students explain how the second sentence is another way of learning, and the third sentence supplies a specific example of this way; the second sentence is on a lower level of generality than the first, the third still lower than the second.

● 3. *Practice 2. Level A:* For those students who choose item **b.**, ask them what kind of statement will they need if they augment the example by going to the abstract level (a summarizing, characterizing statement); what kind of examples are they obligated to supply if they intend to become more concrete?

Levels B and C: Before the students rewrite the paragraph, have them describe the structural similarities of the sentences. In each instance, where does the sentence base occur? What kind of structure follows the sentence base? Are all these sentence elements necessary? What could be eliminated? What could be reworked and made more emphatic?

● 4. *Practice 3. Level A:* If you wish, analyze with the class the direction of movement in the first sentence. The material before the dash moves to the right; the material within the dashes moves to the left; the forward movement then continues until the "simply by reading. . ." phrase, which qualifies the main clause, therefore moving to the left. The epitaph does have some changes in direction of movement, (the latter parts of lines two and four) but the over-all sweep is forward, and the whole effect is ludicrous because the image is inappropriate to the seriousness of the occasion.

Level B: An example like the following may help the students carry out this assignment:

a. In the fall, my after-school life is always the same: *rushing* to my locker, *unloading* my books, *hurrying* to the gym, *changing* into my uniform, *running* to the field, *practicing* hard, *worrying* about injuries.

b. In the fall, my after-school life is always the same: *rushing* to my locker the moment the bell rings, *unloading* my books helterskelter, *hurrying* to the gym past Sue and that other guy (I'll show 'em both!), *changing* into my uniform, one eye on the clock, *jogging* out to the field, *worrying* about breaking my leg for the fourth time in my vain attempt to be a star in football.

Level C: Help the students by listing the different groupings on the board (e.g., shape: longer, wider, flatter) and suggesting, with the aid of the students, appropriate syntactical structures for each group.

- 5. *Practice 4. Level A only:* Have the students contrast the underlined parallel units in sentence c. with those in sentence b. Why are those in c. punctuated, while those in b. are not?

- 6. *Problem 1. Levels A and B:* To help prepare the students to perform the required analysis, review the sentence elements examined in the unit—levels of abstraction, direction and length of sentence, and parallel structures—and their relationship to thought and emphasis. Suggest, if you wish, that they need not analyze the influence of each element on each sentence. In some sentences, for example, parallel structures may not appear.

Level C: To enliven the assignment, suggest also a contradictory thesis: "The Olympic Games promote rivalry among nations and therefore increase international political tension." You might wish to read them part of Orwell's essay on the subject.

- 7. *Problem 2. Levels A, B, and C:* Have the students make the topic they select more specific by stating their controlling ideas in thesis sentences. Take one of the topics, say, "the qualities of bad or good movies," and with the students work out a list of criteria on the board (see the NCTE publication: *Standards of Photoplay Appreciation*, by William Lewin and Alexander Frazier).

EVALUATING THE UNIT

It would be economical to use the composition written in response to Problem 2 as the chief item for evaluating the students' work in the unit. Indicate that the essays will be judged primarily on the following points;

A. Clarity—achieved through supplying concrete items to illuminate abstractions and through qualifying structures moving to the left.

B. Emphasis—achieved through length of sentence, forward movement, and parallelism.

V.   ADDITIONAL WRITING TOPICS

A. Read the complete text of Orwell's essay, "Such, Such Were the Joys. . . ." Then write a composition in which you illustrate that the passage used as the unit selection does *or* does not epitomize the essay.

B. Using either of the following observations by Henry David Thoreau as your controlling idea, write a composition in which you make the controlling idea clear by supplying specific examples (lower levels of generality) and in which you make it emphatic by using appropriate sentence forms:

1. "Public opinion is a weak tyrant compared with our own private opinion. What a man thinks of himself, that it is which determines, or rather indicates, his fate."—*Walden*, "Economy"

2. "Our life is frittered away by detail."—*Walden*, "Where I lived, and What I Lived For"

UNIT 7 — COMPRESS AND EXPAND YOUR INFORMATION

Selection from *THE STANDARDIZATION OF ERROR*

by Vilhjalmur Stefansson

(Student Text—A-Level, p. 42; B-Level, p. 41; C-Level, p. 40)

PREPARING TO TEACH THE UNIT

A. Purposes of the Unit

1. To help students understand the distinction between compressed and expanded statement, particularly in relation to the conveying of unfamiliar information to the reader.
2. To illustrate the complementary uses of the two types of statement, the interplay, as Hayakawa would put it, between higher and lower levels of abstraction.
3. To relate compression to generalization and expansion to specification.
4. To demonstrate the inherent contradiction in the familiar admonition: "Be brief and to the point!"

B. Skills Students Will Practice

1. Analyzing the relationship between the compressed and expanded expression of an idea.
2. Expanding a general, or compressed, statement with relevant, specific details.
3. Giving focus to an expanded statement by constructing a compressed statement that sums it up or defines its significance.
4. Judging the appropriate interplay of compression and expansion in their own paragraphs.

C. Scheduling the Unit

1. This unit is closely related to the two preceding units, 5 and 6. It is a variation on the principle of varying levels of abstraction introduced in Unit 5 and can therefore be used as an illustration of another application of this principle. Here it is applied to sentences within the paragraph rather than to structures within the sentence.
2. The unit is, of course, concerned with the general problem of support for generalizations and can be used along with Units 8, 10, 18, and 19 as part of the work designed to attack this problem.
3. Aside from its implications for teaching the process of defining (therefore a complement to Unit 18), this unit is rich in paradox and could be

51

used as an introduction or supplement to Unit 16, "Emphasize with Paradox."

II. MOTIVATING THE UNIT

A. Background—Author and Selection

1. AUTHOR: Born in Manitoba, Canada, Vilhjalmur Stefansson (1879-1962) lived a varied and exciting life. He was at times a cowboy, school teacher, insurance agent, organizer of secret society lodges, newspaper reporter, and assistant instructor of anthropology at Harvard University. He was however, known chiefly as an arctic explorer. After an archaeological expedition to Iceland in 1905, he studied the Eskimos of the Mackenzie Delta during 1906-1907. Sponsored by the American Museum of Natural History and the Geological Survey of Canada, he undertook a four-year (1908-1912) scientific expedition to northwest arctic America; he set up his base at Camp Parry, Canada, and lived with and like the Eskimos in order to understand their customs and modes of living and to be able to report his information accurately. He conducted his last arctic expedition between 1913 and 1918, exploring land and seas in Canada and Alaska. He reported his findings and experiences in a series of factually accurate, yet lively books: *My Life with the Eskimos*, (1913), *The Friendly Arctic* (1921), *The Northward Course of Empire* (1922), and others. His books aim to combat popular misconceptions about the far North. They show that the arctic is no more hazardous to live in than other regions, once one learns the proper modes of behavior. This view and Stefansson's distaste for cant and humbug and his delight in exposing misinformation and exploding myths animate and enliven his books.

2. SELECTION: Stefansson pillories man's mishandling of truth in his short book, *The Standardization of Error* (1927), from which the passage about the ostrich comes; the book debunks a number of other popular myths that pass for knowledge. A major satirical thesis of the book is that, although knowledge cannot be absolutely standardized because it changes so quickly and increases so rapidly (what was certain yesterday is revealed a prejudice today), man, because of his insatiable desire for certainty and for codifying what is known, tries to avoid inconsistency and create incontrovertible knowledge by ignoring observation and experiment and agreeing in advance, through definition, on the properties of phenomena. An example Stefansson uses is that a Christian is defined as a good man; if a deacon of the church absconds with the funds collected to build a new chapel, this action does not controvert the certainty of the knowledge: If the deacon was a thief, everyone knows that he was *not* a Christian. In this rather heavyhanded way Stefansson satirizes man's propensity for self-delusion. The ostrich passage, as the unit text implies, is an illustration in the same vein.

B. Setting the Stage

1. One way to begin the unit would be to remind the students of the work they did in connection with Unit 5. Ask them what was the point of Christensen's principle of varying levels of abstraction within a sentence. How could they apply this principle to sentences within a paragraph? What would be its virtue? How do they see the principle operating in a newspaper article? What is the function of the headline? of subheadlines? of the lead paragraph? Bring an appropriate article to class for them to examine.

2. Another way would be to read the section on "Dead-Level Abstracting," pages 177-180 in S. I. Hayakawa's *Language in Thought and Action* (Harcourt, 1949) to the class, and then have the students examine and criticize an example consisting completely of low-level abstractions and another consisting completely of high-level abstractions. This exercise would prepare the students for understanding the interplay between compression and expansion.

3. A third possible approach would be to lead to the content of the ostrich passage: the problem of the certainty of knowledge. Bring to class an old grammar book and a modern structural grammar. Read the different definitions for a noun given by the texts. Illustrate that what was formerly regarded as a special kind of adjective ("the") now seems to be something called a determiner; what was formerly an adverb that modified an adverb or an adjective ("very") is now called an intensifier. Ask the students to contribute examples of changes in knowledge from other fields—from chemistry, from physics, from history (an especially rich field).

TEACHING THE UNIT

A. General Points of Interest and Emphasis

1. It might be wise to go over "Words as Used in the Selection" first, helping the students understand how "purports," "alleged," and "bigoted" (connect "bigoted" with "common sense") can be used sarcastically. (Recall Mark Twain's famous newspaper story in which everything he did not know to be absolutely true he qualified with terms like "allege" and "purport": e.g., "Mrs. Oregano Dillworth, allegedly married to a Mr. Harrison Dillworth of this city, gave what purported to be an afternoon social gathering. . . ." Twain, you will recall, was getting back at his editor.) Note that the satirical vein of the selection is carried over into the "Words as Used in the Selection" only in the Level A text.

2. Set the ostrich passage in context for the students by indicating the tone of the book and the use of the passage as an illustration. The text helps to do this. If you have either *The Standardization of Error* or

Adventures in Error on hand, you might read the introductory paragraphs to help the students understand the ironic thesis.

3. If possible, stress throughout the unit the general application of the compression-expansion principle—its use in concept formation, in classification, and in definition. The single noun, for example, is compression; its qualifiers are an expansion which narrows the meaning of the noun.

4. Other prose models in the text that will serve to illuminate the complementary relationship of compression and expansion are the excerpt from Highet's *Man's Unconquerable Mind* (Unit 11), the excerpt from Wolfe's *You Can't Go Home Again* (Unit 17), and the Mencken selection, "*The Hope of Abolishing War*" (Unit 20).

B. Special Observations for Levels A, B, and C

1. *Introductory Material:* There can be a seeming element of paradox in the introductory explanation of what is meant by compression and expansion. Students customarily regard "expansion" as being synonymous with "enlarging," with "extension" and not, therefore, with "to the point." You will probably have to stress in your review of the introductory section, especially with B—and C—Level students, that in this context to expand the number of words means to particularize the meaning and therefore results in the meaning being precise and pointed. On the other hand, to compress or reduce the number of words ("be brief") means to generalize, or allow the meaning to become large, general, unrestricted. It might be wise to stress many times that the compression-expansion principle applies to information unfamiliar to the reader. It does not refer to poetry, where the poet's goal is often a single word that will create a world of meaning.

● 2. *Practice 1. Levels A and B:* The analysis in the text of how the first paragraph expands the meaning of the title of the selection should serve as a model for this practice. Now we know what the defined ostrich is and how he differs from the observed ostrich: he has only one attribute—sticking his head in the sand. And we find out the uses of the defined bird and how the definition has persisted in spite of observations that contradict it. The meaning of "Defined" in the title is therefore expanded and particularized.

   Level C: The statements have three options here: to expand the introductory clause, the main clause, or both of these clauses in the supplied compressed statement. Ask them what seems to be the principal point of the statement. How do they know? by the structure of the sentence? by its position in the sentence? What expectation does "though" create in the reader? Where, then, will the main point, the force of the sentence come? Questions like these will help prepare them to supply examples of the bird's usefulness to man. Ask selected students to read their responses to the class after they have written their details.

● 3. *Practice 2. Levels A, B, and C:* Collect the papers. Sort out suitable examples to be read to the class; that is, avoid those that might cause undue embarrassment to their authors. Read the papers to the class, and ask the students to try to identify the person described in each. For B— and C—Levels, read the compressed statement first. If the person described cannot be identified, ask the class to suggest what needs to be added to the description.

- 4. *Practices 3 and 4. Level A:* For item a. tell the students to use telegram or newspaper headline style. Ask a journalism student in the class to explain to the rest of the class the customary procedures followed in creating headlines. Have him read some typical headlines to the class.
  All Levels: These exercises require the students to practice the reverse of the process they attempted in Practices 1 and 2. More than that, these exercises compel the student to think, to generalize, to classify the various ideas in the original passages, whereas Practices 1 and 2 require only the cataloguing and adding of information. Here they must condense, must put into a general statement the "point" of a passage. A number of compressed statements that serve this function are in the text of the unit and can serve as examples. Tell the students to think of compressing as a process of summing-up. Have representative samples of the students' work put on the board for criticism by the class. Do the statements adequately sum-up? Do they give a "point" to the expanded passage? Are they accurate, that is, faithful to the content of the expanded passage? Do they omit the details that can be omitted? It would be helpful to have the class compress the statements additionally, working toward the fewest possible words.

- 5. *Problems 1 and 2. Levels A, B, and C:* The directions for the structure of the assigned compositions are explicit and should be most helpful to the students. To help the students get started, you could conduct a class discussion on possible specific topics for both Problems: e.g., academic clubs, social clubs, school government committees, interschool sports, relationship of cliques to membership in various clubs (Problem 1). Follow this exploration of topics with a discussion of possible stances toward the topics, then ask each student to put his focus—what he wants to say about the topic—into a thesis sentence, a guiding compressed statement. If you wish, have the students do either Problem 1 or Problem 2.

EVALUATING THE UNIT

The directions in the Problems give a clear statement of the items to be emphasized in evaluating the students' compositions:

A. Does the title give a summary statement of the content and focus of the composition? Does the composition support the title?

B. Is the first paragraph on a higher level of generality than those that follow? Is it a compressed statement of what is to follow?

C. Do the paragraphs that follow the first supply details that support and particularize the meaning of the first paragraph and of the title?

D. Does each paragraph follow the pattern of compressed statement and expansion? (The compressed statement need not appear at the beginning of the paragraph.)

E. Is there a final compressed statement so that the reader is certain of the point?

V. ADDITIONAL WRITING TOPICS

A. A typical handbook rule says: The pronoun *this* should not be used with vague reference. Get a copy of a magazine like *Harper's Magazine* or *The Atlantic Monthly*. Read all the nonfiction pieces in the issue. Tabulate each instance of pronominal "this"; copy enough of the context of each instance so that the reference of the pronoun will be clear. Write an essay in which you interpret your findings in relation to the handbook rule.
(Reference for instructor: Paul Roberts, "Pronominal *This:* A Quantitative Analysis," *Readings in Applied English Linquistics,* Harold B. Allen, ed.). (New York, Appleton-Century-Crofts, Inc., 1958, pp. 267-275.)

B. Select either of the quotations below. Write an essay in which you explain, support, or oppose the quotation. State your organizing idea in your opening paragraph. Follow the structure of compression-expansion studied in the unit.

1. "All the historical books which contain no lies are extremely tedious."
—Anatole France

2. "If a little knowledge is dangerous, where is the man who has so much as to be out of danger?" —T. H. Huxley

UNIT 8 — REVEAL AN IDEA BY USING EXAMPLES

Selection From *WIND, SAND, AND STARS*
by Antoine de Saint-Exupéry

(Student Text—A-Level, p. 47; B-Level, p. 46; C-Level, p. 45)

The special strength of this unit is its central thesis: Examples test the virtue of most assertions. Much of life in our current culture is a welter of uncatalogued items and unitemized totals. The checker in a modern supermarket, the lawyer, the doctor, and the teacher all know this: The right total consists of the right particulars, and *proof* of the rightness of the total rests in the rightness of each of its specifics. To learn principles, we need examples; to teach principles we must supply examples. The speaker may wait upon a request for examples; the writer cannot. He must anticipate the need, and supply it.

I. PREPARING TO TEACH THE UNIT

A. Purposes of the Unit

1. To bring to conscious control the power of examples in clarifying a general statement.
2. To suggest the application of the relation of part to whole, and so of whole to part.
3. To reveal this relation in such familiar dichotomies as "general" versus "particular," "inductive" versus "deductive," "group" versus "members," and "abstract" versus "concrete."

B. Skills Students Will Practice

1. Identifying the controlling generalization.
2. Selecting typical supporting examples.
3. Arranging selected examples toward a clinching final emphasis.

C. Scheduling the Unit

1. *Position of Unit in Sequence of Skills.* This unit stresses the power and necessity of specificity. It therefore follows naturally and supports the teaching in Unit 5 "Build Sentences Rich in Meaning" and Unit 7 "Compress and Expand Your Information," both of which deal with the relationship of general to specific, of the whole to the part. This unit also supports that section of Unit 6 which deals with varying the abstraction level. Students completing these four units in sequence ought

to have a firm understanding of the important classification relationships of general ←→ specific, abstract ←→ concrete, main ←→ subordinate. This unit might, therefore, be taught in the present printed sequence to help insure that students will be well grounded in skills necessary to much of the normal writing they will do in life.

2. The emphasis on the controlling idea and the careful ordering of examples to develop that idea make this unit a valuable introduction to the writing of the expository composition several paragraphs in length. The nature and the placement of the controlling idea and the careful development by examples, coupled with the rich narrative-descriptive contents, will help students understand that expository composition need not be dull, need not be abstract, and need not conform to the prevailing cultural attitudes (man and machine are *supposed* to be in conflict). Some teachers may therefore want to teach this unit first.

II. MOTIVATING THE UNIT

A. Background—Author and Selection

1. AUTHOR: Antoine de Saint-Exupéry (1900-1944) lived his forty-four years dangerously, rebelliously, and productively. Many stupid men are brave because they lack imagination. He had imagination, talent, skill, and brains, as well as courage. He *knew* the odds against him, and faced them, and died early.

As a youngster he was sent to school to Jesuits, world famous as teachers; they found him ungovernable. He was then sent to school in Switzerland, but World War I forced him home. A summer near an airfield sealed his destiny. His family, worried over his fascination with flying, sent him to naval school, but he successfully failed his naval examinations, went to Strasbourg to study flying, became a cadet, and took further training in North Africa to gain officer's status. He left the service to become a commercial pilot in 1926. In 1931 his memorable novel, *Night Flight*, written during a period of distance flights over Europe and Africa, was published. In 1939 he published his famous *Wind, Sand, and Stars*. And that same year he was awarded the Grand Prize of the French Academy for his books.

At the outbreak of World War II he was appointed to a captaincy in the French Air Corps. In May, 1940 his plane was shot down; he escaped to America. *Flight to Arras*, and *The Little Prince*, (the last a story admirably designed for mature adults and children but for few adolescents) were published in 1942 and 1943. Then he rejoined his old squadron in North Africa as an instructor. Later, in Italy, he was assigned to lone reconnaissance flights over the southern part of his homeland. He completed fifteen successful missions in 1944. From the sixteenth he did not return.

"The pilot who is forever risking his life," says André Gide in his preface to *Night Flight*, "may well smile at the current meaning we give to 'courage.' I trust that Saint-Exupéry will permit me to quote an old letter of his dating from the time when he was flying on the Casablanca-Dakar air-route.

'...I have just pulled off a little exploit; spent two days and nights with eleven Moors and a mechanic, salving a plane. Alarums and excursions, varied and impressive. I heard bullets whizzing over my head for the first time. So now I know how I behave under such conditions; much more calmly than the Moors. But I also came to understand something which had always puzzled me—why Plato (Aristotle?) (sic) places courage in the last degree of virtues. It's a concoction of feelings that is not so very admirable. A touch of anger, a spice of vanity, a lot of obstinacy and a tawdry "sporting" thrill. Above all, a stimulation of one's physical energies, which, however, is oddly out of place. One just folds one's arms, taking deep breaths, across one's opened shirt. Rather a pleasant feeling. When it happens at night another feeling creeps into it—of having done something immensely silly. I shall never again admire a merely brave man.'"

Antoine Marie Reger de Saint-Exupéry was far more than a merely brave man. He wrote of what he loved and knew best, with talent and great care. He sought to do for the air what Conrad did earlier for the sea. His purpose was not merely to recount his personal aviation experiences, but to report the impressions of flight on a sensitive and poetic mind. The literary consequence of such gift and conscience is that as we read him, we fly with him.

2. SELECTION: The unit selection is from the third chapter of *Wind, Sand, and Stars*, an autobiographical account of Saint-Exupéry's career as an airman, from 1926 where he was enrolled as a student airline pilot, to 1936, when he went to Spain during the first months of the Spanish Civil War "because it is man and not flying that concerns me most." (In Spain Saint-Exupéry hoped to "learn what happens to man when the scaffolding of his traditions suddenly collapses" and "How does it happen that men are sometimes willing to die?") The chapters of *Wind, Sand, and Stars* have such titles as "The Craft," "The Men," "The Tool," "The Plane and the Planets." It is a book about flying and brave men and the elements of nature, and it is beautifully told. In the chapter from which our selection is taken, Saint-Exupéry starts telling of the design and construction of an airplane—a series of computations and calculations which ends "in the production of a thing whose sole and guiding principle is the ultimate principle of simplicity...."

Throughout the chapter Saint-Exupéry builds a case for the beauty of the machines man creates and their purpose as the tools of man. But, he says, we are still barbarians "marveling at our new toys"—why else would we race them for prizes? We are still in the period of conquest like colonial soldiers, but the time has come to be colonists and settle down with our machines so that we can "make this house habitable which is still without character." As we do, "Little by little the machine will become part of humanity." Our selection ends the chapter.

B. Setting the Stage

1. "Little by little the machine will become part of humanity." Saint-Exupéry's translated opening statement will strike high school seniors variously. One way to unify their reaction would be to read selections from *Wind, Sand, and Stars*—of the ordeal of being lost, off-course on a flight to Casablanca (Chapter 1); of the courage of Guillaumet, who made himself live for seven days after being forced to land his plane in snow at ten thousand feet in the Andes. These intensely personal, concretely told events will attract readers at first unable to cope with the thesis in the selection. Saint-Exupéry had two potent items in his favor: He had something to say, and what he had to say was backed by direct, unarguable, and extensive experience. Most high school males in need of rhetorical assistance respect experience in the masculine tradition. The author of the selection had much of such experience.

2. Explain the content of Chapter 3 of *Wind, Sand, and Stars* as a lead-in to the unit selection. Point out that Saint-Exupéry's obsession for flying and his love of the airplane probably led him to the position he takes toward the place of the machine in society. Without the airplane, Saint-Exupéry could not have tasted any part of the life he loved—is there any other machine so necessary to an occupation or way of life?

3. The unit stresses revelation by example—the habit of "for instance." The habit—as speaker or interpreter of speech, and especially as writer (since the distant reader cannot ask)—is invaluable. Student papers commonly provide effective illustrations of the "power of example"; unsupported generalizations are mostly outrageous or dull; the theme that "gets specific" has some life even if it lacks direction. Read a few student compositions—discuss the examples used, the specificity. A "Profile" in *The New Yorker* of the college basketball star William Warren Bradley is a treasure of effective exemplification that students can respect.

III. TEACHING THE UNIT

A. General Points of Interest and Emphasis

1. "Words as Used in the Selection" should be introduced before pupils start the unit, preferably orally before being presented visually. Mispronunciations are commonly established in English when we see a word before we hear it. Because of the metaphorical importance of "patina" in the selection, it would be well to establish its correct pronunciation before Saint-Exupéry's use of it is discussed. It is safe to assume that in almost any class there will be several members who

will mispronounce, or not be sure how to pronounce, many or all of the following: "pianist," "duodenal," "rapine," "cerebral," "Cowper," "harass," "Roosevelt," "Eustachian," "Paderewsky," and "machination." These are but random samples of countless words that fall victim to bad guessing about pronunciation upon visual encounter before aural experience provided by an informed speaker. "Patina," for example, presented visually to a youngster familiar with "patrol," "marine," "tiny," "tin," and "Pa" invites the establishment of an ultimately troublesome, because uniformed, pronunciation.

For convenience, here is a pronunciation key:

pĭ·ăn´ĭst (Webster's Second)

dū´ŏ·dē´năl (Webster's Second)

răp´ĭn (Webster's Second)

sĕr´ē·brăl (Webster's Second)

sə 'rēbrəl (Webster's Third)

kōō´pēr (Webster's Second)

hăr´ăs (Webster's Second)

hə 'răs (Webster's Third)

rō´zĕ·vĕlt (Webster's Second)

ŭ·stā´kĭ·ăn (Webster's Second)

yu̇ 'stāshən (Webster's Third)

pä´dĕ·rĕf´skē (Webster's Second)

măk´ĭ·nā´shŭn (Webster's Second)

păt´ĭ·ná (Webster's Second)

The author, of course, used "patina" metaphorically, and in a demanding context. "*Every machine* will gradually take on this patina," he says, "and lose its identify in its function." The students will be ready to acknowledge that few machines are constituted to assume a literal patina—the green film caused by oxidation of the surface of copper or bronze is not suitable to most modern engines, from ice skate to IBM machine; unpolished, they would lose both function *and* identity. But the impossibility of the literal meaning of patina here should make the metaphorical meaning easier to accept. If man is a tool-making and tool-using animal, then the tool must become more and more a part of man. Whether we like it or not, we are blood relatives of the wheel, the boat, and the monkey wrench. Many students may need aid in translating the implications in the selection to an awareness of men everywhere—pilots, surgeons, mechanics, and musicians—mastering themselves and their instruments, blending and veiling both into the background of their accomplishment.

2. A discussion of man as a tool-using animal could well precede a reading of either the selection or the unit, especially for students of lesser ability or of lesser interest in a poetic outlook such as Saint-Exupéry's. What a tool *is*—from screw driver to skyscraper—is probably of more interest to nonbookish students than the power and poetry of the last paragraph of the selection, but a student-led discussion of the nature and use of tools and the reading of a few articles about new inventions for the home or garage could possibly lead more students to a closer reading and a stronger degree of appreciation for Saint-Exupéry's thesis.

3. The passage deserves a good oral reading—that is, it deserves to be heard well rendered, and perhaps twice. (Many high school seniors have not discovered the dramatic and exciting contrast between a second and

first reading of a substantial statement—fact or fiction, verse or prose.) Questions concerning the passage perhaps should not be answered by the instructor on the spot. Most can be dealt with by students in their discussion of the selection. You may want to point out that both "air and water" (the concern of the hydroplane pilot about to take off) are fluids; matter that flows—gases and liquids. Whale and aeronaut swim a translucent sea. Such considerations occasionally help.

4. All of the preceding units should effect, individually and cumulatively, better writing, but it is good to reinforce by memento. Even high school seniors need repeated reminders of such basics as thrift and honesty in writing (Units 2 and 1, respectively), and though the immediately preceding unit—"Compress and Expand Your Information"—may have recency in its favor, even so, its relevance to the present unit may escape one or two of even the more able students.

B. Special Observations for Levels A, B, and C

1. For most Level C, many Level B, and some Level A students the hard thing about revealing an idea is capturing an idea that is, and seems to them, worth revealing. Many may have been taught that independent ideas, if not downright sinful, are certainly risky. The cultivation of an atmosphere of respect for ideas is pertinent at all three levels, and an at least arresting notion is that it is a privilege to view the processes of another mind even through its more bizarre or banal products.

   There is a reciprocal relation between this unit and such an atmosphere. Most entities labeled "ideas" are valuable because they are general: They apply their truth to many situations. They derive from a consistency of a myriad of particulars. (The classic derivation of general from particular is "All Indians walk single-file—at least the one *I* saw did.") Any idea that assumes the status of a generalization can be evaluated in the mind by a review of the examples that gave it origin.

   Saint-Exupéry's idea was deviate. There is substantial literature propounding the enmity of machines to man. Samuel Butler's "Book of the Machines" is notable among many. But Saint-Exupéry sustains and establishes his upstart notion of the gradual humanizing of machines by supplying examples from the present and the past that would be verifiable in almost anyone's experience. He ends with an example from the present that could be verifiable in almost anyone's experience in the future.

   Any youngster can mentally explore the integrity of his "idea" by reviewing a reasonable number of its valid examples *before* verbalizing. He will not, however, always do so without assistance.

2. *Practice 1. Level A:* Every student is expected to pass up **a.** in favor of **b.** or **c.**, which are dangerously identical through their auxiliary verbs and the similarity in the generalizations. The major test is between "take on this patina and lose its identity in its function" and "become

part of humanity," and the latter has brevity in its favor. The fact that the controlling idea is identified in the text at the end of section **B.**, however, elevates this Practice to the level of a thinking exercise. The value of the paragraphs will probably center on the *reasons* why the students reject sentence **b.** in favor of **c.** You may want to have the students exchange papers, make notes on strong and weak arguments, then read the paragraphs aloud and comment.

Level B: The students have been given the central idea—the example given in the Practice should enable almost all students to complete the exercise without further help. Perhaps discussion should follow a reading of several student sentences—many of their sentences may, because of a personal eyewitness quality, be more concrete than the text example.

Level C: You may already have discussed possible examples in III, A, 2. If so, students should have no trouble compiling numerous examples. Otherwise, you may want to follow the suggestions in III, A, 2 now, before the students start to write.

- 3. *Practice 2.* **Level A:** Scholars have differed sharply in their paraphrases of "outworn buried age" and "slave to mortal rage" in Sonnet 64, and differences in their interpretation may be expected from adolescents. "Rich proud cost . . . of age" is surely equated with "patina," though, and brass cannon were familiar enough in Shakespeare's day. Perhaps these points merit mention. The poem mirrors mood as common to youth as to age. "Grass" by Robinson Jeffers ("Winter after winter the sea gnaws at its earth," "stubborn green life, against the cliffeater I cannot comfort you . . .") might stimulate comparison of Stratford and Big Sur. Why did Shakespeare place his examples first? What did he gain by placing the generalization at the end?

Level B: Emerson's controlling idea, like Saint-Exupéry's, is bare and abstract. But the development is achieved through a series of smaller generalizations, not concrete examples. The second and third sentences reduce the generality of the controlling idea in the first sentence; the final sentence offers particulars directly related to the third sentence. The assignment is thus an exercise in analyzing relationships between generalizations and particulars. You might give the students an alternative assignment: "Develop Emerson's controlling idea by supplying concrete examples."

Level C: The assignment is purposely only a slight extension of Practice 1. You might make success even more certain by holding a discussion about the kinds of examples that would be satisfactory, putting the most appealing ones on the board before the students write. Following the writing, read several paragraphs, with the class commenting on the concreteness of the examples.

- 4. *Practice 3.* **Level A:** Because these are largely college-bound students, it is likely they will have little trouble with the organization of the examples in the sonnet—their greater trouble may lie in having to cope with the semantic load. The discussion suggested for Practice 2 will help greatly here.

Level B: This exercise should be recognized as a demanding one. It will be well to discuss the requirements before the students write. Content is purposely separated from form here to simplify the task. Your knowledge of your group will enable you to decide whether to point out that in the best writing, form and content are welded.

Level C: The Practice assumes that the "controlling idea" is clear. You may want to review it before the students write. Because the "best job" will differ for different students depending on their interests and background, the worth of this practice lies in the case each student makes for his choice.

- 5. *Practice 4. Level A:* To questions of Why and How, the answers of bright students may challenge the conclusions of their classmates and the teacher. This Practice calls for a high order of critical ability—time spent in reading these student paragraphs and discussing them thoroughly can produce results far more lasting and important than the immediate goal: preparation for completing the unit Problems.

  Level B: Hopefully, the paragraphs here should reflect the discussion that attended Practice 3—this is an opportunity for the student to apply to his content the same kind of responsibility Saint-Exupéry felt toward his examples.

  Level C: The range of aphorisms from which to choose may wisely be extended for some groups. For other groups, you may want to suggest that everyone work with topic a.

- 6. *Practice 5. Level A:* Some students will want to make written notes summarizing the preceding paragraphs they have supposedly written for this assumed composition. In fact, you may wish to establish a group set of notes which can be placed on the board or duplicated for each student before writing begins. The "clincher paragraphs" can then be more easily evaluated against the content they are supposed to clinch.

  Level B: Practice 3 may have provided sound preparation for this Practice. There, however, the students were comparing details. Here, they are relating Saint-Exupéry's last paragraph to his total argument—the distinction is a fine one, but it is there.

  Level C: Use the same techniques as for Level A.

- 7. *Practice 6. Level B:* Use the same techniques as for Practice 5, levels A and C.

- 8. *Problem 1. Level A:* This topic echoes the thesis in *Wind, Sand, and Stars* that man's integrity, his affirmation of his spirit, is the important thing, the ennobling thing. Students who have read the book will have no trouble with the plain task of coping with the topic. Whether or not most of the class members have read the book, the essays they write will be much better formed and far more concrete if Saint-Exupéry's thesis is discussed along with such familiar concepts as "This is a materialistic civilization"; "Man is becoming a number"; "We are slaves to machines."

  Level B: This is a difficult assignment, of course; its value lies in the fact (a) that the generalization completely lacks exemplification and (*b*) that the exemplification must be chosen by the student *as an individual*. Once FitzGerald's controlling idea is understood (Man's fate is predetermined; there is nothing man can do about it), students will immediately line up to defend or attack the statement (man always has). Students should be encouraged to look for examples supporting or disproving the assertion; they should also be encouraged not to jump to conclusions, for this is a generalization that cannot be proven right or wrong. This becomes, then, an exercise in particularizing, a game to be entered on either side. Questions like these will elicit particulars: Has the invention of the wheel changed men's fate? Without medicine would the average life-span be increasing? The particulars are worth while even though it can be surmised that, for example, the discovery of penicillin is an act of fate.

Level C: This will not be a difficult assignment for C-Level students. The main problem, perhaps, will be to get them to use examples that are concrete and relevant and arranged in an effective order.

- **9. Problem 2. Level A:** This controlling idea is typical of the kind that needs the delimiting that comes about through defining. *Instinct, reason, and 'intelligence'* (with its separate quotes) must all be defined before the essay can be developed significantly.

  Level B: See Problem 1, Level A.

  Level C: The value of this essay will depend on the preciseness of the controlling idea. This should be a character sketch, not merely a description of a person's appearance. Discussion of Krebs in Unit 2 and of the way E. B. White reveals his personality in "From Sea to Shining Sea," Unit 4, will help set the direction of this paper. So also will a reading of a "Profile" from *The New Yorker*. Once the subject and the controlling idea are in mind, the student should start setting down concrete examples. Students should be aware that as they develop examples, their controlling idea may need to be revised.

V. EVALUATING THE UNIT

In this unit the target is developing among pupils a sense of appreciation and control of an instrument: the principle of exemplification. Every evidence of such appreciation and control, oral or written, deserves credit. The student should be expected to keep a central focus on revelation by example while paying peripheral attention to the disciplines stressed in previous units. It may be well to review the salient points of prior units before pupils settle down to the central task of the Problems.

V. ADDITIONAL WRITING TOPICS:

Some students require a subject area as close and congenial to their experiences as flying was to Saint-Exupéry. The following generalizations may more fully satisfy their topical requirements or even suggest others that do:
1. I, like one or two other people I know, don't always do as well as I might. For instance, . . .

2. The ideal driver keeps a number of important disciplines under control. He throttles his temper, for example, as he applies his brakes. He...

3. The game I enjoy most demands several special skills.

UNIT 9 — SHARPEN MEANING BY COMPARISON

Selection from
"On the Difference Between Wit and Humor"
by Charles Brooks

(Student Text—A-Level, p. 52; B-Level, p. 51; C-Level, p. 50)

PREPARING TO TEACH THE UNIT

A. Purposes of the Unit

1. To show how ideas are developed by comparison and contrast.
2. To offer practice in using the techniques of comparison and contrast to sharpen meaning.

B. Skills Students Will Practice

1. Examining a subject by comparing or contrasting it with a similar subject.
2. Writing papers of comparison and contrast using three different patterns of organization.
3. Using metaphor as a means of implied comparison.

C. Scheduling the Unit

There are several ways to schedule this unit:

1. This unit can stand on its own—as a writing exercise that employs a way of thinking and writing as natural as breathing. Because it is fundamental to our thought processes to explain one idea in terms of another (we say that book A is in certain respects like book B, or that student A is different from student B in several ways), this unit could be taught first, as an introduction to our *thinking* approach to writing.
2. This unit is one of a series of units that concern the paragraph. Unit 7 follows the principle of expanding the main idea by the general-specific relationship. Unit 8 gives practice in developing paragraphs by examples; Unit 9, by comparison and contrast; Unit 12 by time, space, and logic. Units 10 and 11 consider relationships within and between paragraphs—matters of transition and sequence. These six units, 7 through 12, should work well as a block in sequence, whether they are taught in their regular position or earlier in the school year.
3. Explaining the uses of language in comparison leads inevitably to the use of metaphor. This unit, which has a section devoted to metaphor, would effectively supplement Unit 23, "Create Images Through Metaphor."
4. Unit 13, "Emphasize Through Parallelism," is also closely related to

this unit. In Unit 13 students practice using balanced structure in sentences—to give emphasis to the items they are comparing or contrasting.

II. MOTIVATING THE UNIT

A. Background—Author and Selection

1. AUTHOR: Charles S. Brooks (1879-1934) was born in Cleveland, Ohio. Upon graduation from Yale University, he returned there and worked for fifteen years for his family's printing firm, Brooks and Company; then he retired and spent full time in theater work and writing. He eventually became one of the founders and president of the famous Cleveland Playhouse. The most well known of his essay collections are *There's Pippins and Cheese to Come* (1917), *Chimney-Pot Papers* (1919), and *Hints to Pilgrims* (1921). He also wrote several travel books—*Journeys to Bagdad* (1915) and *Roundabout to Canterbury* (1926)—and collections of little theater plays—*Frightful Plays!* (1922) and *A Window at the Inn* (1934).

2. SELECTION: The model selection from "On the Difference Between Wit and Humor" is not typical of the entire essay, which is informal, written in the first person, and replete with anecdotes. But the rest of the essay does develop the point made by Brooks in the model selection: Humor has more comfortable qualities than wit; it is also more enduring because it relates to man's essential humanity rather than to the circumstances of a particular place or time. "Humor," the essay concludes, "must be founded on humanity and on truth."

   One of Brooks's illustrations of the difference between a humorous and a witty man is particularly hard to forget: "A humorous man—and here lies the heart of the matter—a humorous man has the high gift of regarding an annoyance in the very stroke of it as another man shall regard it when the annoyance is long past. If a humorous person falls out of a canoe he knows the exquisite jest while his head is still bobbing in the cold water. A witty man, on the contrary, is sour until he is changed and dry: but in a week's time when company is about, he will make a comic story of it."

B. Setting the Stage

1. Since Brooks's essay is short and frequently anthologized, you may want to begin this unit by reading the entire essay. Students will see even more clearly from the total essay than from the model passage that defining wit and humor separately would be an almost impossible task. One has to see these related words as a pair in order to see either of them clearly.

2. Level C students who do not read well and who may not respond to

Brooks's essay may be more stimulated to explore comparison and contrast if they discover how they use this method in everyday conversations. Have a pair of students talk in front of the class: One of them has the task of describing to the other an unusual movie he has seen, a new gadget he wants to buy, a distant city he has visited, the feelings he had the first time he skied or surfed, a new television performer. Listening to this conversation, the class can make notes on all the comparisons that are made ("Honolulu reminded me of San Francisco in a way...." Part of the movie was like the old Frankenstein bit....""Your sense of balance in snow skiing is not at all what it is in water skiing....").

II. TEACHING THE UNIT

A. General Points of Interest and Emphasis

1. Since a close examination of the passage will be necessary when the students study Brooks's use of metaphor, it will probably be sufficient at the beginning of the unit to give the passage one reading and discuss the main distinctions between wit and humor that Brooks describes.

2. Although the skill of the unit and the kind of thinking involved can be taught without reference materials, students may be interested in checking various dictionaries to see how much distinction is made between wit and humor. Most students are sufficiently awed by dictionaries; perhaps it is time some of them discovered how much there is about words that dictionaries do not have the space to say.

3. If dictionary work seems profitable, you might pursue this kind of activity with *Roget's Thesaurus*. Have each student compile a list of synonyms for one word; ask him to find as many differences as he can between the words. The list could provide the material for an essay like Brooks's.

4. Somewhere during this unit you might want to consider the problem of *false analogy*. You might ask the students, if they do not ask you first: What are some of the dangers in making comparisons? What is wrong with statements like these: (a) "If strict discipline is good in the army, it is also good in schools." (b) "A presidential campaign is little more than a popularity contest." You will find very useful Richard Altick's discussion of false analogy in *Preface to Critical Reading* (Holt, 1960).

B. Special Observations for Levels A, B, and C

• 1. *Practice 1.* **Level A:** As the example illustrates, students may find it best to begin by stating the similarities and then look for the points of contrast. You may want to compile a list of distinctions between one of the pairs, drawing from everyone in the class.

Level B: Students will be using this chart again when they work Practice 5. Since they will be examining the metaphors closely then, it is not necessary that they do so here.

Level C: If these students are slow to get started on a new unit, you may want to work Practice 1 orally. As in Level A, the best beginning is with similarities. A cheerful man and a happy man, for example, both smile frequently and generally have pleasant expressions on their faces. Once this and other similarities are established, the differences will follow.

- 2. *Practice 2. Level A:* In the paragraphs they develop in Practice 2, **b.,** students should attempt to write balanced sentences. You may want to refer here to Unit 13. If they can achieve a good final sentence like Macaulay's, so much the better.

   Level B: Students will profit from comparing notes and discussing possible ways to develop an essay from their observations.

   Level C: Since they are reversing what they did in Practice 1, students should begin by finding the important points of difference before they seek the similarities.

- 3. *Practice 3. Level A:* When they have finished their paragraphs it may be interesting to discuss which kind of development they prefer, the point-by-point modeled after Macaulay, or the separate development of Schopenhauer's. Some may observe that the Macaulay method seems to place a heavier burden on the writer: He has to balance his ideas and yet avoid the monotony of too much repetition. Yet they may find that their essay of Practice 2 is the superior one, even though it was more difficult to execute.

   Level B: See Practice 2, Level A.

   Level C: If the passage from Macaulay seems to puzzle them, the students will profit from your going over it with them until they understand it. Read the passage aloud; stress the balance in the sentences. Note the repetition of *aim.* They will undoubtedly need to know that *vulgar* in this passage means "usual," "commonplace," or "everyday." Once they understand the passage, they will more easily see how Macaulay has developed his paragraph by moving back and forth from Plato to Bacon: Plato lived in Greece, 427?-347 B.C.; Bacon lived in England, 1561-1626. These facts, developed briefly, will help the students understand why the two philosophers differed in their outlooks.

- 4. *Practice 4. Level A:* Students will discover, if they do not already know it, how difficult it is to explain a metaphor. If this happens to be the right time to work on metaphor, you may want to use part of Unit 23 here.

   Levels B and C: See Practice 3, Level A, substituting Brandeis for Schopenhauer.

- 5. *Practice 5. Level A:* Even for the best writers in the class, defining by metaphor will prove to be difficult. Rather than spend considerable time—and it may require that—debating the aptness of their metaphors, you might suggest that they file these papers and evaluate and revise them later in the light of what they learn about metaphor in Unit 23.

   Level B: See Practice 4. Level A.

   Level B: The best way to work this Practice is, perhaps, by class discussion. Many students experience difficulty with metaphor because they do not understand that the implied comparison refers to some, not *all*, of the attributes of the figurative term. With "Wit wears silk...," for example, Brooks is implying that wit prefers a more sophisticated setting than does humor: wit needs to be "dressed up," but humor can exist comfortably anywhere, even in the wind. It is also suggested that wit is less durable (silk as opposed to homespun). But the metaphor does not imply *all* of the attributes of silk.

- **6. Practice 6. Level B:** See Practice 5. Level A.
- **7. Problems 1 and 2. Level A:** Before they do Problem **2b.** you may need to discuss Thoreau's use of the word *fabulous*.

  Level C: Better writing will result in Problem 2 if there is careful planning in Problem 1. The students should decide before they begin to write whether their development will be back-and-forth (mentioning, for example, city A and then city B) or separate (describing city A completely and then city B). For all levels, it may be helpful to discuss the points in "The Act of Writing."

IV. EVALUATING THE UNIT

A. Students should understand that the writing Problems will be graded on the basis of how well they handle the skills emphasized in this unit. Their sentences should be balanced to match their ideas, and their paragraphs should have a clear, balanced, orderly development. If the students attempt figurative language, they should be applauded for their efforts; it would hardly be fair to penalize them if their metaphors are not good ones.

B. Many teachers of writing believe that students should be encouraged to attempt difficult things and be permitted to risk doing rather badly in these attempts. Otherwise, they will keep doing over and over those things they can already do well.

   Problem 1, Level A and B, is a difficult writing assignment. Perhaps for the students in Level B classes, the exacting demands should hold only for Problem 2, which they should be able to handle well; Problem 1, because of its difficulty, need not be graded. This, of course, depends on the make-up and morale of the class.

V. ADDITIONAL WRITING TOPICS

A. Find another model selection in this text where the development is by comparison or contrast. Write a paragraph analyzing the author's method. The selections in Units 7, 8, 13, and 20 are good examples.

B. Find a "false analogy," and comparison that lacks basis, and explain the fallacy in the writer's reasoning. (See Teaching the Unit, III,A,3.) Unit 20 may be of help here.

UNIT 10 — CONTROL YOUR PARAGRAPHS

Selection From

"Touch and Sight : The Earth and Heavens" in THE ABC OF RELATIVITY by Bertrand Russell

(Student Text—A-Level, p. 58; B-Level, p. 57; C-Level, p. 56)

I. PREPARING TO TEACH THE UNIT

A. Purposes of the Unit

1. To illustrate that the paragraph is a tool of thought and that therefore there is no one "ideal" paragraph form; the thought controls the shape of the paragraph, not vice versa.
2. To help students understand that the length and structure of paragraphs are influenced by the content, the audience, and the conventions of the day.
3. To show how paragraphs within a larger unit are related to one another; a paragraph should be clearly related to those preceding and following it and should have a clearly defined function within the whole of which it is a part.
4. To show that the modern paragraph is fluid in structure—advancing the thought of the whole, qualifying, illustrating, and summarizing—therefore, it fits many purposes.

B. Skills Students Will Practice

1. Analyzing the influence of the intended audience and of the part-to-whole relationship on the length of paragraphs.
2. Analyzing the various relationships between paragraphs.
3. Analyzing the structure—the internal relationships—of selected paragraphs.
4. Writing paragraphs to fit model structures.
5. Writing a paragraph and then defining the relational function of each sentence within the paragraph.

C. Scheduling the Unit

1. This unit is part of a number of units (Units 7 through 12) emphasizing paragraph construction and the relationship between the purpose of a paragraph and its form. It serves not only to sum up explicit and implicit observations about the paragraph contained in preceding units, but also

to provide a perspective toward the forms and purposes of paragraphs that will prepare the student for the units to follow. The unit therefore may be viewed as a transition unit. Inasmuch as the unit does, however, view the paragraph as part of a whole and therefore places it in a larger context than do the other units, you may wish to teach it after Unit 12, using it as a summary unit for the entire sequence.

2. The unit could, of course, be used at any appropriate juncture during the semester. It would be an appropriate lesson whenever a significant number of students exhibit too hazy or, conversely, too strict a notion of paragraphing. While the unit explodes a number of copybook myths about the paragraph, it does provide the students with an understanding of the internal consistency of a paragraph and of the relationships between paragraphs.

3. Another possibility is that the unit could serve to complement the class's studying of the scientific essay or the essay that popularizes scientific knowledge (see, for example, the work of Stefansson, Laird, and Eiseley). Russell's four paragraphs can serve as a capsule version of the popularizing essay at its best. The familiar diction, the use of analogies for clarity, the influence of the intended audience—these and other elements of the form are readily apparent in the unit selection.

II.   MOTIVATING THE UNIT

A. Background—Author and Selection

1. AUTHOR: In 1950 Bertrand Russell (1872-   ), on hearing that he had been awarded the Nobel Prize for literature, said that he felt like a grandmother being crowned Miss America. Certainly, the award does seem a bit out of the ordinary once we realize that Russell did not make his debut as a writer of fiction until the publication of a group of short stories entitled *Satan in the Suburbs* in 1953, when he was eighty-one. Yet the aptness of the Nobel prize becomes apparent once we understand that it was awarded in recognition of Russell's many-sided authorship (he has written over forty books on subjects ranging from philosophy of the mind and theoretical mathematics to marriage customs and primary education), and in honor of his consistent defense of humanity and freedom of thought.

    Russell first gained recognition as a theoretical mathematician when he published with Alfred North Whitehead perhaps the most important work of the 20th century in this field, *Principia Mathematica*, a book twenty years in the making. Caught up in the controversies engendered by World War I, he then turned his attention to social and political questions, writing a number of books on political systems, social institutions, and ethical problems. While this interest has continued throughout his life, his most lasting work after his initial recognition has been accomplished in philosophy in modern empiricism and the philosophy of logical analysis. Some fifteen volumes comprise his philosophical writings, this work culminating in 1948 with the publication of his comprehensive *Human Knowledge: Its Scope and Limits*.

Unquestionably one of the great minds of the century, Bertrand Russell has remained responsive to the social and ethical problems of our time, not hesitating to become embroiled in public controversy over such problems as the use of the Bomb and the duplicity of international politics.

2. SELECTION: First published in 1925 and revised in 1959, *The A B C of Relativity* lucidly explains for the educated layman Einstein's theory of relativity; the title is apt. Russell shows how Einstein's theory differs from previous theories, how it has drastically altered our conception of the physical world, and how it has influenced the course of science. All this is rendered in a lively, familiar diction that helps the reader clearly understand the theoretical and pragmatic implications of Einstein's work. The unit selection occurs at the very beginning of the book, being the first four paragraphs of the opening chapter, "Touch and Sight: The Earth and the Heavens." They introduce the topic of the book, help to provide a framework for what is to follow (without underrating the difficulty of the material), and serve to illustrate the clarity of the style. The remainder of the chapter continues to explain the distinction between astronomy and terrestrial physics, defines briefly the special meaning of "relative," explains how Einstein's theory has altered the notion of force, and indicates the steps needed to understand the concept of space-time. It would be interesting to have one of your students who is taking physics read the chapter and give a critical explanation of it to the class.

B. Setting the Stage

1. You could work the class into the unit by duplicating a number of expository paragraphs written by students and leading a class discussion of what makes them paragraphs—how they are similar and how they differ. What generalizations can we make about paragraphing? Should paragraphs have a common structure? What accounts for the differences in paragraph shapes? You may want to use paragraphs similar in structure (say, some written for Unit 8) for this exercise so that the unit-lesson will gain force through contradicting too readily assumed conclusions.

2. Another way to start the unit would be to ask the students to write a definition of a paragraph and of the structure of a paragraph. Then through class discussion point out the varying conceptions of paragraphing held by members of the class, perhaps listing the major variations on the board. Then get the class to try to account for the differing conceptions, gradually eliciting such points as purpose, mode, and audience, and thereby preparing them for the teachings in the unit.

3. As suggested above, you could make the unit part of the study of the scientific essay. The students could first read a number of essays from anthologies and such journals as *Scientific American*, and by studying

and discussing these essays, they could try to determine the characteristic form of a scientific essay. The unit selection would then serve as an epitome of such an essay, and the unit-lesson as a close examination of the form.

III. TEACHING THE UNIT

A. General Points of Interest and Emphasis

1. Teach "Words as Used in the Selection" before the students read the excerpt from *The A B C of Relativity*. Use the text or, if you wish, list the key words on the board and ask for informal definitions from the students. "Metaphysics" is likely to cause some trouble; you may want to go beyond the definition supplied in the text. First, what do the parts of the word tell us? *Physics* suggests the physical; *meta* means "after or beyond." Thus, beyond the physical. Where does this lead? You might want to give the students an idea of how ontology, cosmology, and epistemology are related to metaphysical inquiry, of how Plato's theory of perception influenced his conception of the Real, and of the predominance of empiricism and the distrust of metaphysical speculation in modern philosophy.

2. Read the four paragraphs by Russell aloud, the students following. Conduct a preliminary analysis after the reading. For example: What is the principal idea of the selection? How is it expressed in the first paragraph? How is the fourth paragraph related to the first? How do we know what the relationship is? Set the unit selection in context for the students. Indicate that the paragraphs are the first four in Russell's book. What purposes do they serve, therefore? If you have the book on hand, you might want to read the rest of the chapter to the students. Of equal interest would be the last chapter, wherein Russell discusses the philosophical implications of modern physics. This chapter would likely provoke discussion and might prompt the students to examine the entire book. The chapter also indicates the range of Russell's interests and illustrates his ability to bridge the "two cultures"—Arts and Science—about which C. P. Snow has written.

3. Other prose models in the text that can serve as supplementary examples for the kind of paragraph analysis carried on in the unit are the excerpt from Laird's *The Miracle of Language* (Unit 19), Hicks's review of Golding's *The Spire* (Unit 21), and the excerpt from Eiseley's *The Immense Journey* (Unit 22).

B. Special Observations for Levels A, B, and C

1. *Introductory Matter:* You can reinforce the introductory discussion on paragraph length and fashion by having the students bring to class examples of paragraphs from different sources: newspapers, news magazines, scholarly journals, serious works of nonfiction. These examples

will graphically illustrate the points made in the beginning of the unit and should lead to a better understanding of how purpose influences paragraph form.

- **2.** *Practice 1.* **Level A:** What would be Russell's intended audience? We have said he is writing for the educated layman. Why "educated"? How does this observation relate to item **c.**? For **b.** and **d.**, notice that the four paragraphs are part of the book's introduction. How does this purpose influence the length and tone of the paragraphs, especially of the first paragraph? These are some questions you can ask your students to help them do Practice 1.

   Levels B and C: You might wish to qualify the direction that the paragraphs should be as short as possible and say that they should be about the length of newspaper paragraphs but should not unnecessarily chop up the review. The passage would usually be divided as follows:
   first paragraph—(1) to (3)
   second paragraph—(4) to (9)
   third paragraph—(10) to (13)
   fourth paragraph—(14) to (17)
   fifth paragraph—(18) to (22)
   sixth paragraph—(23)
   Other divisions are of course defensible—that is one of the points of the exercise. The major importance is to get the students to defend their choices with reasons that are related to audience, purpose, and internal consistency.

- **3.** *Practice 2.* **Level A:** The controlling idea of the second paragraph is that *our conception of the earth, even of "reality," is based primarily on the sense of touch.* The second paragraph explains how we form our conception of the world, what our pre-Einsteinian imaginative picture of the world is. This is the imaginative picture, mentioned in the first paragraph, that must be changed. Three sentences such as the preceding would suffice for the kind of analysis of each paragraph that the exercise requires. You might want to use this analysis of the second paragraph as an example and have the students construct similar analyses for the remaining two paragraphs.

   Levels B and C: Stress that the controlling idea is not necessarily stated in a single sentence in the paragraph (notice how the text states the controlling ideas of the first two paragraphs); it is the idea that shapes the paragraph and therefore may be more comprehensive than any one sentence in the paragraph. To get at the controlling idea, the student needs to view the paragraph from outside, not inside. The relationship of the third paragraph to the preceding one is evident: It indicates what is wrong with the pre-Einsteinian imaginative picture of the world, the picture based on the sense of touch. And the first sentence of the last paragraph tells us how it is related to the preceding paragraphs.

- **4.** *Practice 3.* **Levels A, B, and C:** This will be a difficult exercise, especially for C-Level students. For them, you may wish to make it a class exercise, working it out on the board. For Levels A and B, you will probably want to work out at least the first two sentences with them to get started. Of the first sentence, you could say that it is introductory, rather general but more specific than the first sentence of the first paragraph—it does mention the surface of the earth, and it does single out two of the senses: touch and sight. The second sentence begins to particularize how we use touch and sight, giving illustrations of how past generations used visual and tactile sensations to measure space.

- 5. *Practice 4. Levels A, B, and C:* Have a number of these paragraphs read to the class and conduct a class analysis of the relationship between general and specific statements in each paragraph. Ask the authors of the paragraphs to describe the structure of their paragraphs (here, too, they'll need to stand back, to view their paragraphs from outside). Notice that this exercise complements the work done in Units 5 and 6.

- 6. *Problem 1. Levels A, B, and C:* So that the students can have a model from which to work, you might suggest that they bring to class a science article from a newspaper or a popular magazine. The class could discuss and analyze the paragraphing of two or three of these before they begin the assignment. In their rewriting of Russell's paragraphs, they could also use another journalistic technique designed to aid the reader—supplying headings at appropriate junctures. Note that in Levels B and C the students are asked to reparagraph only the first paragraph of Russell's selection, whereas Level A students are asked to work with the entire essay. Suggest that Level A students do only one or two paragraphs and devote most of their energy to Problem 2.

- 7. *Problem 2. Levels A, B, and C:* Propose that the students may use the statements of the suggested controlling ideas as topic sentences for their paragraphs but that, if they wish, they may regard these statements as general ideas behind the paragraphs and may, therefore, construct topic or organizing sentences to fit their particular paragraphs. They may balk somewhat at the format of the required analysis, feeling that it creates an artificial sense of lack of continuity. The format is suggested for the convenience of the reader (the sample in Section C makes this obvious).

    The students may turn in, along with the analysis, a copy of their paragraph in conventional form.

IV.   EVALUATING THE UNIT

Use both writing Problems in the formal evaluation of the students' work in the unit. The introduction to the Problems clearly indicates the criteria for judging the students' work:

A. For Problem 1:
   1. length of paragraphs—influence of intended audience? necessary emphasis?
   2. relationship of one paragraph to another and to the whole
   3. cogency of reasons for divisions

B. For Problem 2:

1. coherence, internal consistency—is one sentence clearly related to the preceding and the following sentences? how?
2. cogency of analysis—is the sequence clearly defined? is it defensible? is the general-specific relationship part of the analysis of each sentence?

ADDITIONAL WRITING TOPICS

A. If you have read H. G. Wells's *Tono Bungay,* write a brief analysis of the plot function of "quap" in the novel. What seems to be the scientific significance of this substance?

Or, if you have read Aldous Huxley's *Brave New World,* write a brief explanation of the population control method practiced in the society depicted in the novel. What is the Controller's defense of this method?

Or, describe briefly the application or projection of a scientific principle or discovery in a story you have read. What appears to be the writer's intention in using science in his fictional work? In your description or analysis, practice the paragraphing skills studied in this unit.

B. In 1927 Bertrand Russell wrote: "...It has at last become technically possible, through the progress of machinery and the consequent increased productivity of labor, to create a society in which every man and woman has economic security and sufficient leisure—for complete leisure is neither necessary nor desirable. But although the technical possibility exists, there are formidable political and psychological obstacles." ("Introduction," *Selected Papers of Bertrand Russell,* New York, Random House, Inc., 1927, p. xv.) Write an essay in which you describe and evaluate those political and psychological obstacles mentioned by Russell.

C. The following passage is from "A Voyage to Laputa...," in *Gulliver's Travels,* by Jonathan Swift; in it Swift describes Gulliver's first encounter with the Laputians. Break the one paragraph into a number of shorter paragraphs. Write an explanation of your division (to suit the fashion of the time? to suit a particular kind of reader?). If you wish, put the passage into modern, contemporary diction.

> At my alighting, I was surrounded with a crowd of people, but those who stood nearest seemed to be of better quality. They beheld me with all the marks and circumstances of wonder, neither indeed was I much in their debt; having never till then seen a race of mortals so singular in their shapes, habits, and countenances. Their heads were all reclined, either to the right, or to the left; one of their eyes turned inward, and the other directly up to the zenith. Their outward garments were adorned with the figures of suns, moons, and stars; interwoven with those of fiddles, flutes, harps, trumpets, guitars, harpsichords, and many other instruments of music unknown to us in Europe. I observed, here and there many in the habit of servants, with a blown bladder fastened like a flail to the end of a

stick, which they carried in their hands. In each bladder was a small quantity of dried peas, or little pebbles, as I was afterward informed. With these bladders they now and then flapped the mouths and ears of those who stood near them, of which practice I could not then conceive the meaning. It seems the minds of these people are so taken up with intense speculations, that they neither can speak, nor attend to the discourses of others, without being roused by some external taction upon the organs of speech and hearing; for which reason, those persons who are able to afford it always keep a flapper (the original is *climenole*) in their family, as one of their domestics; nor ever walk abroad, or make visits without him. And the business of this officer is, when two, three, or more persons are in company, gently to strike with his bladder the mouth of him who is to speak, and the right ear of him or them to whom the speaker addresses himself. This flapper is likewise employed diligently to attend his master in his walks, and upon occasion to give him a soft flap on his eyes; because he is always so wrapped up in cogitation, that he is in manifest danger of falling down every precipice, and bouncing his head against every post; and in the streets, of justling others, or being justled himself into the kennel.

UNIT 11 — LINK MEANING THROUGH TRANSITIONS

Selection from *MAN'S UNCONQURABLE MIND*
by Gilbert Highet

(Student Text—A-Level, p. 66; B-Level, p. 66; C-Level, p. 65)

I. PREPARING TO TEACH THE UNIT

A. Purposes of the Unit

1. To help students understand that coherence is achieved not in a mechanical way but through a matrix of natural transitional and linking elements that bind sentence part to sentence part, sentence to sentence, and paragraph to paragraph and to controlling idea.
2. To illustrate how conjunctive words and phrases, pronouns, and repetition and echo words not only tie a passage together but also carry the reader smoothly from point to point.
3. To help the student consciously use these transitional elements in his own writing.

B. Skills Students Will Practice

1. Identifying conjunctive words and phrases and defining the relationships—addition, concession, condition, chronology, etc.—they establish.
2. Identifying and explaining the uses of pronouns in the unit selection.
3. Analyzing the function of repetitions, synonyms, and echo words in the unit selection; consciously using these linking elements in paragraphs of their own.
4. Writing compositions in which the transitional elements studied in the unit are consciously used.

C. Scheduling the Unit

1. This unit is a natural extension of some of the topics introduced in Unit 10. There, the relationships between paragraphs and between paragraph and controlling idea were explored. The students studied how paragraphs were linked to one another. Here, the focus narrows to the specific elements within the paragraph and the sentence which relate part to part and part to whole. There is, moreover, a quite formal structure to the unit selection that is explicitly marked at the beginning of each of the paragraphs following the first. The students can compare the transitional markers within this structure with those used by Russell in the preceding unit selection.
2. The material in the unit will not necessarily be new to the students, especially if they have used Books 1 and 2. However, the transitional

material is not examined in isolation but as it functions within the context of an inherently interesting passage of connected discourse. The unit can therefore be used to review transitional and connecting elements at any appropriate point in the semester—after the students have written their first few compositions, for example, and problems of internal reference and cohesiveness begin to manifest themselves. You might assign the unit for review purposes to individual students or to the entire class.

3. The unit is, of course, an indirect way of approaching the subject of the purpose of education. The subject is certainly topical, and students have a natural interest in pursuing it. ("Do we *have* to do this? Why?") Highet presents the classical view and somewhat exaggerates the "errors" he finds. One may even question if the errors exist to the pervasive degree that he implies. The unit may therefore be used within the context of an examination of the purposes of education.

II. MOTIVATING THE UNIT

A. Background—Author and Selection

1. AUTHOR: Born in Glasgow, Scotland, Gilbert Highet (1906-   ) received a master's degree from the University of Glasgow in 1929, and went on to win scholastic honors at Oxford University and to teach there. He was invited to Columbia University for one year in 1937 and then, in 1938, he joined the permanent staff of Columbia as professor of Greek and Latin.

     Known for his Scottish wit and for his comprehensive knowledge of the past and its uses in the present, he gave a series of very successful weekly radio talks which were collected in *People, Places, and Books* (1953). These talks are good illustrations of the combination of erudition and urbanity that have gained him a wide following beyond the University.

     His book on teaching, *The Art of Teaching* (1950), is a minor classic of its kind. Free from the stultifying jargon that pervades many discussions of pedagogy, it lucidly defines the responsibilities, professional and ethical, of the teacher and gently insists on recognizing teaching as an art—an art based on a solid mastery of craft. Highet's most recent publications—*Talents and Geniuses* (1958), *The Powers of Poetry* (1960), *The Anatomy of Satire* (1962)—illustrate his continuing interest in the topical and the scholarly.

2. SELECTION: *Man's Unconquerable Mind* (1954) is a brief exposition of the powers and limits of the mind, of what makes us human, and of the influence of knowledge on civilization. It is Highet's dedicatory statement to the life of the mind. The first section of the book sketches the achievements of the mind; the second section outlines the external and internal forces that limit the desire for knowledge. Throughout the book,

Highet illustrates how the past informs and illuminates the present. The four paragraphs that comprise the unit selection occur in that section of Highet's book devoted to analyzing the external hindrances on the acquisition of knowledge. Miseducation is obviously one such hindrance. Other hindrances Highet analyzes are sloth, poverty, and authoritarian restrictions. The class might discuss how these forces hinder the advancement of knowledge. Are there others?

B. Setting the Stage

1. One way to prepare the students for the unit would be to rewrite a passage the students have already worked with, for example, a paragraph from the Russell selection, eliminating most of the conjunctions, transitional words and phrases, pronouns, and synonyms from the passage. Ask the students to contrast this version of the passage with the original. What, specifically, are the differences? Can they identify the elements that have been omitted? What did these elements accomplish? Have the students revise the rewritten version without looking at the original. A similar approach would be to use examples of jerkiness, thinness, and ambiguity in student papers for class analysis. All of these materials can, of course, be dittoed or shown on an opaque projector.

2. Another approach would be to put the second paragraph of the unit selection on an overhead transparency and block out all the connectors and transitions. Ask for student reaction to the gaping paragraph. With a grease pencil, insert into each blocked-out space appropriate words and phrases suggested by the students. Then compare with the original. This exercise will help to illustrate not only the importance of transitions but also the naturalness with which some fall into place.

3. Other ways of beginning the unit are suggested under Scheduling the Unit: relate to the previous unit's emphasis on paragraph transition, review previous semesters' work on transition, and discuss (in conjunction with appropriate readings) the purposes of education.

II. TEACHING THE UNIT

A. General Points of Interest and Emphasis

1. Read the excerpt from *Man's Unconquerable Mind* aloud, the students following. Ask them what specific words and phrases signal the progression of the thought in the excerpt. What words in the first paragraph control the over-all structure of the passage? Point out that just as paragraphs need to be related to one another and to some larger framework, so do sentences and parts of sentences need to be clearly related to each other and to the controlling idea. If you have the book on hand, read the paragraph preceding the unit selection to show that it, too, is part of a larger context and that it serves as an illustration of a more

general idea. Further set the passage in context by outlining how it fits into the second section of the book, "The Limits of Knowledge." The relationships among sections, subsections, and sub-subsections are all clearly marked with transitional words, phrases, sentences, paragraphs, and even chapters.

2. At the outset of the unit, have each student select one of his compositions that he would like to improve. As the class works through the sections of the unit, have the students revise their papers in accordance with the emphasis in each section. Thus, students will be using the teachings in the unit to improve their own work.

3. Students can confirm the lessons of the unit by examining the extent of transitional material in such passages as the excerpt from Melville's *Typee* (Unit 12), the excerpt from Benét's letter submitted to the Guggenheim Memorial Foundation (Unit 15), and Mencken's "The Hope of Abolishing War" (Unit 20).

B. Special Observations for Levels A, B, and C

1. *Introductory Material:* The relationship between thought and fluency or thought and development is difficult to define. But we may help our students gain an understanding of this relationship by pointing out that there are a few basic ways of developing a controlling idea: conjunctive ("and-and-and," "then-then-then"), disjunctive ("either-or"), concessive ("though-yet"), and conditional ("if-then"). These ways of developing an idea follow naturally from the predication we make about the idea and should, therefore, control the kinds of transitions we use from point to point. (See Josephine Miles's, "Essay in Reason," *Educational Leadership*, February, 1962, pp. 311-314.) Ask the students what kind of development Highet uses. Is it just a mechanical one, two, three? Or is there another kind of development, perhaps more basic, undergirding this overt organization?

● 2. *Practice 1. Levels A and B:* The "yet" and the "but" signal contrasts with what has immediately gone before. Both emphasize the importance of what is to follow. What follows the "yet," however, is subordinate to what precedes it; while what precedes the "but" is subordinate to what *follows* it. Into which development category outlined above do both signals fall?

   Level C: The distinction between connectives and transitional expressions may be a bit difficult for these students to grasp. The text seems to say that co-ordinate and subordinate conjunctions and conjunctive adverbs are connectives, while linking phrases are transitional expressions. The distinction may be wasted on these students, and you could advise them to ignore it, telling them simply to record words and phrases like those listed in the text. To help them get started, work out the list for the first two paragraphs on the board; make it a class exercise.

● 3. *Practice 2. Levels A and B:* Some students may object that "this" has a vague reference. If they do, they have missed the central meaning of the entire last paragraph. This practice provides an opportunity for reviewing some of the pronoun-referent problems: reference which is valuable because it is purposely broad or ambiguous, as well as pronoun-referent relationships which are valuable because the interdependence is unmistakable.

Level C: Help the students identify the connecting words; it will not matter if they have more than five to choose from. "Yet" they will have from the example; "and" is no problem. Some others: "also," "but," "for," "then."

- 4. *Practice 3. Level A:* Perhaps you should warn your students that the uses of repetition and variation are not always as clear-cut as the use described in the example. "Such feats," "prodigious achievements," and "performances" are obvious enough; but "practical use" is a little more difficult to pin down, and the instances of "powers" are not simple repetitions. What about "wonder"? What does that echo? The Practice looks easy, but it will tax the students.

  Level B: In addition to its stated intent, this exercise will help students clear up pronoun usage problems as well as help them understand syntactical relationships. Have some of the paragraphs put on the board for analysis and criticism.

  Level C: You may want to supplement this exercise with some direct teaching of the kinds of pronouns and pronoun usage problems. If possible, avoid the workbook approach. Work inductively from the knowledge the students have, e.g; "Give me a sentence with 'me' in it. 'Me' is another form of what word? When do you use 'I'? Give me an example. How is 'us' like 'me'? Give me a sentence with 'who' in the middle; with 'which' in the middle; with 'that' in the middle. When (in writing, not speech) do you use 'whom'?" (Use board throughout.)

- 5. *Practice 4. Level A:* This Practice offers an opportunity to discuss the content of the Highet passage. The students will probably want to criticize his explanation of the first two "errors." His discussion shows the shortcomings of time and limited perspective. But since students usually lack a sense of time or topicality, remind them that the passage was written in 1954, not 1965 or later. What changes have occurred in those intervening years to weaken the force of Highet's criticisms?

  Levels B and C; A number of synonymous expressions for "to be sociable" are listed in the first sentence; but from there on, the repetition is not as marked or as frequent. Stress the notion of variation. What phrase in the last sentence brings us back, pejoratively, to the idea of social living?

- 6. *Problem 1. Level A:* To help the students get started, discuss the implications of the suggested theses. How has machinery severed man from his sense of responsibility? How could fear cause racial prejudice? Fear of what? What is the idea of the hero? How could it be dead? What caused it to die? If the paragraphs are to be developed by reasons and examples, what kinds of connecting expressions are the students likely to use? Refer them to the list in the text. Review the introductory discussion.

Levels B and C: To give the assignment more specific focus, have each student construct a thesis sentence before he writes his paragraph. What kind of connectives will this thesis sentence have to have to meet the requirements of the assignment? (Applies to Level B primarily.) Have some of these put on the board for discussion and criticism.

- 7. *Problem 2. Level A:* Make the direction "Discuss" more specific by suggesting possible lines of approach: definition, application, analysis, interpretation, support, refutation. Again, the point of view taken will influence the choice of transitions.

   Level B: Point out that the contrasting points made in the paragraph written for Problem 1 can each be developed into paragraphs for this Problem.

   Level C: Suggest that, in addition to establishing a spatial reference, the students indicate an attitude toward the object in their first sentence. Work out a few beginning sentences on the board.

IV. EVALUATING THE UNIT

In evaluating the students' work for the unit, you may want to give most weight to the composition written in response to Problem 2. The over-all structure and progression of the composition should be clearly marked. A test: Is it clear to the reader why the third paragraph follows the second and precedes the fourth and how the third paragraph relates to the first? Indicate that major emphasis will be given to judging the use of transitional devices to achieve unity and coherence within paragraphs.

V. ADDITIONAL WRITING TOPICS

A. Write an analysis and evaluation of the passage by Highet. What are the three "errors"? Why are they errors? What evidence does he give in support of his criticism? Do you agree or disagree? Why? Support your evaluative statements with evidence and reasons.

B. Select a topic from your study of literature, say, "The Influence of the Heath on Eustacia's Decisions in Hardy's *The Return of the Native*." Write four different thesis sentences that will serve as controlling ideas for the development of this topic: the first requiring conjunctive development, the second requiring disjunctive development, the third requiring concessive, and the fourth requiring conditional. Put the four thesis sentences at the top of your paper. Write a composition developing the one most appealing to you.

C. Write a composition developing either of the quotations listed below. Illustrate, apply, interpret, support, or attack. State your controlling idea in your opening paragraph. Begin each paragraph with a transitional word, phrase, or sentence that clearly indicates the paragraph's place in the over-all structure of the composition.

1. "Soap and education are not as sudden as a massacre, but they are more deadly in the long run." —Mark Twain

2. "We do not know what education could do for us, because we have never tried it."—Robert Hutchins

UNIT 12 — ORGANIZE COHERENT PARAGRAPHS

Selections from *TYPEE* by Herman Melville,

"The Dead" by James Joyce, and

LANGUAGE IN THOUGHT AND ACTION

by S. I. Hayakawa

(Student Text—A-Level, p. 74; B-Level, p. 73; C-Level, p. 73)

I. PREPARING TO TEACH THE UNIT

A. Purposes of the Unit

1. To help students understand that coherence within a paragraph—that is, a consistent integration of parts—depends on a clear ordering of chronological, spatial, or logical relationships.
2. To illustrate techniques used in creating consistent chronological order.
3. To illustrate techniques used in creating consistent spatial order.
4. To illustrate techniques used in creating consistent logical order.

B. Skills Students Will Practice

1. Identifying time markers in a chronological sequence.
2. Writing a description of a process.
3. Analyzing the effectiveness of spatial markers in the description of a scene.
4. Writing a description of a static scene.
5. Using comparison/contrast and logical order to structure a written analysis of the relationships between two concepts.

C. Scheduling the Unit

1. This unit follows naturally from Unit 11, which emphasizes the cohesive function of transitional and linking expressions. It is also closely related to Unit 10, which views the paragraph as part of a larger whole and emphasizes the unique function of each paragraph. Unit 12 is therefore part of a sequence of units on paragraph function and organization; it emphasizes those controlling relationships—time, space, comparison/contrast, etc.—that help us plan the step-by-step development of paragraphs.
2. Because of its omnibus quality, the unit can be taken out of sequence and used as part of a general review of paragraph organization and development. Such a review is often customary during the beginning weeks of a course, and this unit would be a good starting point for going over various ways of developing paragraphs.

II. MOTIVATING THE UNIT

A. Background—Authors and Selections

1. AUTHORS: Herman Melville (1819-1891) came from a genteel but financially unstable family. His father, a New York merchant, died when Melville was thirteen. He tried to help out by working, first as a bank clerk and then, on the basis of less than four years of formal education, as an elementary schoolteacher, but the family fortunes did not improve. He shipped out as a seaman in 1839 and spent some five years as a seafaring man. Many of the adventures and experiences he had during this time served later as the raw material for his books, most notably in *Typee: A Peep at Polynesian Life* (1846). Although *Moby Dick* (1851) is his best-known and greatest work, he wrote ten novels, a number of short stories, and three or four volumes of poetry. Among his other works are *Omoo* (1847), *White Jacket* (1850), *Pierre* (1852), *The Confidence Man: His Masquerade* (1857), and *Billy Budd* (1924). After *Pierre*, Melville lost the attention of the reading public. The deep symbolism in his latter books baffled and disturbed his readers. He refused to write the adventure stories the public wanted, and they refused to read what he did write; therefore he spent the latter part of his life in relative obscurity. At present, Melville scholarship is almost an industry in itself. Newton Arvin's *Herman Melville: A Critical Biography* (Sloane, 1950) presents a careful synthesis and a sound estimation of Melville's artistic accomplishment.

James Joyce (1882-1941), generally regarded as the major English-language novelist of the 20th century, was born and educated in Dublin, but spent most of his adult life in exile from Ireland. After rejecting academic life, he pursued his career as a literary artist with unique single-mindedness. His major works are a book of short stories, *Dubliners* (1914), and three novels: *A Portrait of the Artist as a Young Man* (1916), *Ulysses* (1922), and *Finnigans Wake* (1939). His works, especially the latter two, are difficult, combining as they do startling innovations in technique with linguistic virtuosity and out-of-the-way learning. Because his works challenged, in the frankest terms, accepted values and hypocrisies, he had much trouble getting them published. Their publication forms a chapter in the history of 20th-century censorship. A lucid critical introduction to Joyce is Harry Levin's *James Joyce* (New Directions, 1941).

S. I. Hayakawa (1906-   ) is a professor at San Francisco State College. As a student of linguistics, he early became interested in the work of Alfred Korzybski, the founder of the general semantics movement. He has written several lively and penetrating books on language and general semantics, *Language in Action* (1939), *Language in Thought and Action* (1949) and *Symbol, Status, and Personality* (1963); he also edited

Language, Meaning and Maturity (1954), *Our Language and Our World* (1959), and *The Use and Misuse of Language* (1962), collections of essays on semantics. He has been the editor of *ETC.: A Review of General Semantics* since 1943.

2. SELECTIONS: *Typee*, loosely based on Melville's experiences in the South Seas when he jumped ship, was his first published book. Part travelogue and part fictional romance, it caught the fancy of a public eager for information about the curious and the exotic. Melville used the travel-account framework to contrast the idyllic, free, innocent life of the Polynesians with the mechanistic, brutal, hypocritical ways of civilized man. The book, therefore, is part of the body of literature about the "noble savage." The tappa-making explanation occurs about midway in the book, and its context admirably illustrates the dual nature of the book. While the explanation itself is typical travelogue information, it is immediately preceded by an account of the narrator's trying to arrange his escape from the Typees and of the savages' determination to keep him in their village.

"The Dead" is the last story in *Dubliners*. It chronicles the emotional sterility of Gabriel Conroy, a fortyish university instructor, and those with whom he should be intimate. With the possible exception of one character, all the major characters are either dedicated to the past or inhibited by a fussy vanity from any purposeful commitment. The appropriate setting for such a dissection is, of course, a party. The superficial liveliness and the richness of the refreshments contrast with the emotional barrenness of the characters. The function of the sumptuously appointed table should, therefore, be obvious.

Language in Thought and Action is an explanation, within the framework of general semantics, of human symbolic behavior and human interaction through symbolic mechanisms. It analyzes the social function of language and the dependence of thought on language. The excerpt about scientific truth occurs in the chapter explaining the mechanism of classification. The chapter cautions against closed classifications and against not recognizing that each member of a class has unique features not included in the classification. It illustrates, among other things, that "truth" in the loose sense is not an inherent property of the symbol to which it is applied but a socially agreed upon attribute. Strictly speaking, truth and falsehood are properties that should be applied to propositions or declarative statements that can be perceptually verified. The truth of the statement "John is six feet two inches tall" is ultimately verified by perceptual observations. Classifications, on the other hand, are definitions and can be true only in the sense of being "true to" actual usage.

B. Setting the Stage

1. Review the work done in Units 10 and 11. Two of the emphases in Unit 10 reveal the ways one paragraph is related to another and how the

function of a paragraph within a larger unit helps control the ordering of elements within the paragraph—both influences on the organization of a paragraph. Unit 11 illustrates how transitional devices help to hold a paragraph together.

This unit continues the emphasis on paragraph organization by illustrating how the studied use of different kinds of relationships—chronological, spatial, and logical—helps to create coherent paragraphs.

2. Duplicate three or four of the papers written in response to the writing Problems of Unit 4; make certain they vary in quality. Distribute them for class analysis and criticism. Raise questions about chronological and spatial order (the two previous units have emphasized logical order). Can the reader follow the happenings in the order they occurred? If the order is interrupted, is the break justified? Is the scene or object described from a consistent point of view? Are you certain about right-left, up-down, north-south, etc.? What makes one paper superior to another? Work out a series of questions with the class that will serve as a transition to the unit: What writing situations call for chronological order? Do we use just "and's" and "then's"? How do we indicate spatial relations clearly? How does logical order differ from chronological and spatial? Do the three orders occur in isolation?

3. Jumble the order of the sentences in some paragraphs; put the paragraphs in their jumbled state on ditto sheets, or on transparencies and project them for the class. Ask the students to put the sentences in their correct order. Number the sentences. As you go, ask questions like: "How do you know this sentence is first?" "What tells you this sentence is the fourth one?" "What extra information would we need to decide the order of these two sentences?" "Why is the first paragraph easier to correct than the third one?" Lead from this exercise to the unit.

III. TEACHING THE UNIT

A. General Points of Interest and Emphasis

1. Teach "Words as Used in the Selection" before having the students read the unit selections (especially C-Level students). Put on the board the sentences in which the words appear, and ask the students to suggest meanings to fit the context. "Demonic" should be easy; anyone with a mild interest in science should be able to help with "bacillus." Students in the A-Level, at least, should be able to supply the Latin derivatives for "incipient" and "prostrate." If some words cannot be defined from context, ask the students what other information they would need to define them.

2. Read the unit selections aloud, the students following. Conduct, if you wish, a preliminary analysis. Ask the students what kind of information is given to the reader in the excerpt from *Typee*. (A process.)

What must the reader follow, then? (The steps.) What syntactical devices signal the movement from step to step? What kind of rhetorical statement is made in the excerpt from "The Dead"? (A description.) Is it static or dynamic? How does the Joyce selection differ from the *Typee* passage? How does the Hayakawa passage differ from the other two? What kind of statement is it? And so on.

3. To generate some interest in the unit selections themselves, set them in context for the students. Interest in Melville should be high, for instance; a good many students will be familiar with *Moby Dick*, but they will have little knowledge of Melville's prosaic beginnings. To show how the principle enunciated by Hayakawa might be applied, put the single word *tappa* on the board and ask the students, assuming they had no prior knowledge, what they would guess its meaning to be. Most will say that it is probably some kind of food. This simple exercise will illustrate how concept meaning is dependent upon social agreement. (The relationship between word form and meaning is, of course, another topic here. What associations caused the students to guess that tappa is a food?)

4. For insight into the relational thought patterns that help to control, and in some instances dictate, paragraph development and organization, you might wish to consult two articles by Josephine Miles: "Essay in Reason," *Educational Leadership*, February, 1962, pp. 311-314 and "What We Compose," *College Composition and Communication*, October, 1963, pp. 146-154.

5. Other prose models in the text that could be used as supplementary examples of the kinds of organization studied in this unit are the excerpt from Hemingway's "Soldier's Home," Unit 2 (chronological); the excerpt from Russell's *The A B C of Relativity*, Unit 10 (logical); and the excerpt from Conrad's "The Lagoon" and Crane's "The Open Boat," Units 24 and 25 (spatial).

B. Special Observations for Levels A, B, and C

1. *Introductory Material:* The students may want a fuller explanation than the text provides outlining what constitutes logical development. This you will be working on throughout the semester, of course, but here you could briefly explain, or review, such reasoning processes as cause and effect, comparison, analogy, concession, definition, and evaluation. (See Richard Altick's *Preface to Critical Reading*, Holt, 1960.)

2. *Practice 1. Level A:* Ask the students to identify the functions of the time words. How does Melville avoid monotonous repetition of time signals? What is the function of the verbs in helping to signal a change? *Levels B and C:* Ask the students also to make a list of the words that signal the movement from step to step and then to identify the ways they indicate passing of time. Hopefully, the B-Level students will point out that the description of the mallet interrupts the time sequence. How many times is each word used? Does the repetition cause monotony? Why or why not?

- 3. *Practice 2. Levels A and B:* You could have the students make a list of the steps before they write the paragraph. Have them suggest some topics: selecting a book in the library, analyzing a short story or poem, preparing for an examination, getting a pass to leave school, choosing a motion picture to see.

  Level C: Help the students get started by developing a model list on the board. Be prepared for some wry contributions from the students.

- 4. *Practice 3. Level A:* The students may want a clearer picture of Joyce's "parallel lines." Ask them to indicate how they would make the description more precise. What would this do to the effect created by the paragraph? Have some of the criticisms read to the class for discussion. Emphasize supplying evidence and reasons for criticisms.

  Levels B and C: Put one or more of the symbols on the board and have the students suggest topography or structures appropriate to the symbols (e.g., an office building or a school building, a mountain or foothills, the course of a stream or a highway cutting through the countryside). With a rough drawing show how one of the symbols can stand for a structure; for example, two strings of classrooms connected by a corridor may resemble the letter *H*.

- 5. *Practice 4. Level A:* Suggest other possible structuring symbols, e.g., an inverted teacup for a hill or a mountain, a kidney bean for a pond, or a Burmese carving knife for a seashore.

  Levels B and C: Have the students suggest some possibilities, e.g., a modernistic painting, the bulletin-board wall of the journalism room, a teacher's cluttered desk top, or the inside of a dishwasher.

- 6. *Practice 5. Level A:* Some theses that may help the students get started: "Both science and religion depend on acts of faith." "All art is propaganda, but not all propaganda is art." (Orwell)

  Level B: Some possible starters for the students: "A right without an accompanying duty is an undemocratic special privilege." "Fear is an indispensable part of courage."

  Level C; The students will need help with this exercise, indeed, with all of section three (depending on the abilities of your students, you may want to make this section optional). Start them out with the first sentence: "strictly practical" points to the concluding statement. In the second sentence, "produce predictable results" or, if you wish, all of the second main clause, point to the conclusion. And so on.

- 7. *Practice 6. Level C:* See suggestions for Levels A and B of Practice 5 above.

- 8. *Problem 1. Levels A, B, and C:* Review the first section of the unit. Have the students make a list of the steps first. Will some steps or the key features of some steps require extended explanation (like the mallet in the tappa-making model)? How will these explanations be worked in without losing continuity? What words or phrases will be used to signal the movement from step to step?

- 9. *Problem 2. Levels A, B, and C:* Have each student work out a thesis sentence (controlling idea) for his topic, then have him decide what order—conjunctive, disjunctive, concessive, or conditional—his thesis sentence suggests. Is this the development he wants? If not, should he rewrite the thesis sentence? Does he know enough to support his thesis? What will he have to find out?

This problem may be too difficult for all C-Level students in a given class; make it optional for this group.

V. EVALUATING THE UNIT

A. For Problem 1: The review of the first section of the unit conducted before the students do Problem 1 should provide the standards for evaluating the compositions. Some guiding questions:

Are the steps recorded in the order in which they would be performed?

Is each step clearly marked with a chronological or spatial signal?

Are the signal words varied?

Are special terms or instruments adequately explained?

Could the reader perform the process after having read the composition? (This is the key question.)

B. For Problem 2: Again, the review preceding the writing should help to set the standards for evaluation. Some guiding questions:

Is the controlling idea clearly stated in the opening paragraph?

Is the implied structural development—conjunctive, disjunctive, etc.—followed?

Is the conceptual scheme—comparison/contrast, definition, cause and effect, or analogy—appropriate and consistently followed?

Are the steps in the reasoning clearly marked?

Is each paragraph a coherent part of the whole?

Is the thesis adequately supported?

V. ADDITIONAL WRITING TOPICS

A. Defining truth with a capital *T*—What is Truth?—has been a central problem of philosophy for centuries. One theory of truth, the pragmatic, maintains that an idea is true if it has good effects. That is, if we are confronted with two conflicting ideas, we are to choose the one that has the more worth-while effects; that is the true one. A truth of an idea is defined by its consequences, by how well it works in action. Write an essay in which you defend or attack this theory. Explain the theory in your own words; illustrate how it would work; apply it to specific situations; then evaluate.

B. In *Language in Thought and Action*, S. I. Hayakawa says that if we call both "All men are created equal" and "Water is composed of hydrogen and oxygen" true statements, we are using "true" in two different senses.

Write an essay in which you explain what the two senses are and what is a responsible attitude to take toward each sense. As applying the same term, *true*, to two different categories of statement is likely to cause confusion, what linguistic changes would you recommend to eliminate the confusion?

C. The following paragraph is from an autobiographical sketch by Thomas Henry Huxley. Write an analysis of the time and space words used in the paragraph. Identify the time words and explain their functions. What is the chronological sequence in the paragraph? Is it clearly marked? Identify the space words and explain their functions. What picture do they help to create?

THOMAS HENRY HUXLEY

My regular school training was of the briefest, perhaps fortunately, for though my way of life has made me acquainted with all sorts and conditions of men, from the highest to the lowest, I deliberately affirm that the society I fell into at school was the worst I have ever known. We boys were average lads, with much the same inherent capacity for good and evil as any others; but the people who were set over us cared about as much for our intellectual and moral welfare as if they were baby-farmers. We were left to the operation of the struggle for existence among ourselves, and bullying was the least of the ill practices current among us. Almost the only cheerful reminiscence in connection with the place which arises in my mind is that of a battle I had with one of my classmates, who had bullied me until I could stand it no longer. I was a very slight lad, but there was a wildcat element in me which when roused, made up for lack of weight, and I licked my adversary effectually. However, one of my first experiences of the extremely rough-and-ready nature of justice, as exhibited by the course of things in general, arose out of the fact that I—the victor—had a black eye, while he—the vanquished—had none, so that I got into disgrace and he did not. We made it up, and thereafter I was unmolested. One of the greatest shocks I ever received in my life was to be told a dozen years afterwards by the groom who brought me my horse in a stable-yard in Sydney that he was my quondam antagonist. He had a long story of family misfortune to account for his position, but at that time it was necessary to deal very cautiously with mysterious strangers in New South Wales, and on inquiry I found that the unfortunate young man had not only been "sent out," but had undergone more than one colonial conviction.

—Joseph J. Reilly, *Masters of Nineteenth Century Prose*

UNIT 13 — EMPHASIZE THROUGH PARALLELISM

Selections from *MAN AND SUPERMAN*
    by George Bernard Shaw
    and *Preface to the DICTIONARY*
    by Samuel Johnson

(Student Text—A-Level, p. 82; B-Level, p. 81; C-Level, p. 81)

I. PREPARING TO TEACH THE UNIT

A. Purposes of the Unit

1. To help students recognize the various forms of parallel structure.
2. To help students see the relationship between parallel structures and co-ordinate ideas.
3. To illustrate the effective use of parallelism for emphasis.
4. To illustrate the effective use of antithesis.
5. To emphasize the importance of varying parallel structures.

B. Skills Students Will Practice

1. Analyzing the structure of parallel sentences and of parallel units within the sentence.
2. Putting synonymous or co-ordinate ideas in parallel structures for emphasis.
3. Using antithesis for emphasis.
4. Using parallel or antithetical ideas as the controlling or organizing ideas of compositions.

C. Scheduling the Unit

1. This unit is the first of a series of units—13 through 17—on emphasis. It analyzes the familiar rhetorical device of parallelism and prepares the student for the examination of less familiar devices that create emphasis. It follows a series of units on unity and coherence and is therefore part of the classical triad of rhetorical skills: unity, coherence, and emphasis. The students have been examining, closely, some syntactical and stylistic elements that help make a paragraph a coherent whole. Here they turn to an analysis of a syntactical device that gives force and balance to thought.
2. If the study of effective speaking techniques is also carried on in your class, this unit could certainly form part of that study. Parallelism, including antithesis, is a technique frequently used in formal speeches, and this unit would help students understand why it is used and what

97

accounts for its effectiveness. The unit could complement the class's examination of some well-known speeches, e.g., Lincoln's Gettysburg Address, John F. Kennedy's Inaugural Address, and William Faulkner's Nobel Prize Acceptance Speech.

3. This unit provides the student with a way of understanding comparison and contrast and is therefore closely related to Unit 9, "Sharpen Meaning by Comparison." The two units could be taught in conjunction.

II. MOTIVATING THE UNIT

A. Background—Authors and Selections

1. AUTHORS: George Bernard Shaw (1856-1950), unquestionably the greatest English-language dramatist of the 20th century, started his writing career as a novelist, producing five rejected novels in as many years. He then (in his thirties) turned to journalism and politics, and became a successful music and drama critic. During this period he became interested in socialism, and in 1884 he helped to found the Fabian Society; throughout his career, Shaw remained an advocate of public ownership of resources and of a more equitable division of social wealth. He developed an interest in the new drama of Ibsen and, soon, began writing his own plays. Success as a dramatist came slowly for Shaw; he was well in his forties before the public began to take him seriously. But by 1910 he was the acknowledged master of English drama, and in 1925 he won the Nobel Prize for Literature. His ceaseless production, his sharp ridiculing of conventional values, his showmanship, and his ability to make his audiences laugh at their own foibles combined to force his work on the public and to gain for him an unprecedented popularity. He wrote over thirty plays during a career as a dramatist that lasted more than half a century. Among his more enduring works are *The Devil's Disciple* (1897), *Caesar and Cleopatra* (1898-1907), *Man and Superman* (1903), *Pygmalion* (1912), and *Saint Joan* (1923).

Shaw wrote so much about himself and his plays that the best sources for a better understanding of his work are his autobiographical sketches and the prefaces to his plays. A critical biography to which Shaw gave his consent is Hesketh Pearson's *G. B. S.: A Full-Length Portrait* (Harper, 1942).

Samuel Johnson (1709-1784), subject of the first great biography in English literature—Boswell's *Life of Samuel Johnson*—was the foremost British man of letters in the latter half of the 18th century. In his time, he gained his preeminent position as an essayist, a critic, and a lexicographer. Today, owing to Boswell's biography, he is known primarily for his conversational powers. His prose was ornate and mannered—not in the vein of the idiomatic but learned prose established by Dryden. But his criticism was sound to the extent that it consistently judged English poets according to classical standards. His *Lives of the Poets* (1779-1781) is a landmark in literary criticism. Joseph Wood Krutch's *Samuel Johnson* (Holt, 1944) is a modern biography, and Bertrand H. Bronson's *Johnson and Boswell* (University of California Press, 1944) examines the relationship that proved so productive for both men.

2. SELECTIONS: *Man and Superman* combines Ibsen's notion of the genius—the "superman" who is ten years ahead of his time—with Shaw's conception of the Life Force, the force that drives woman to pursue man to ensure the continuation of the species. John Tanner is the genius who wants to establish the new social order; in arguing for his conception of social freedom, he comically insults the Establishment of the time. Ann Whitefield is the pursuing woman who loves to hear John talk but pays no attention to what he says; her mind is on making the catch. The excerpt from the play used in the unit occurs in the "Don Juan in Hell" interlude, the dream sequence in the third act. Tanner and his party have been captured by the philosophical bandit, Mendoza, on their way to Nice. Tanner falls asleep listening to Mendoza's doggerel, and the dream sequence begins. It is a long philosophical discussion between the Devil, Don Juan (John Tanner transmogrified), Doña Ana, and her father. Hell represents all earthly, all bodily pleasures. The Devil argues that Heaven is cant, is self-denying hypocrisy. Don Juan argues that pleasure-seeking and happiness are self-defeating because they are stultifying. Because there is no striving to bring into being a better existence, Hell has all the repressive vices of conventional morality, as the unit selection illustrates. Don Juan says that because the inhabitants of Hell are doing the Devil's will—seeking pleasure, rather than tracing out their own destiny they are "false, restless, artificial, petulant, wretched creatures." This remark prompts the Devil's mortified response, which in turn leads to Don Juan's peroration.

Johnson's *Dictionary of the English Language* (1775) was the first work of its kind that undertook to explain all the words in common use. Seven years in the making, it gained Johnson a reputation as a scholar and, through the use of illustrations, established the principle of historical lexicography. The *Preface* explains the scholarly bases of the dictionary and is in itself a succinct exposition of the principles of a language. The excerpt used in the unit is the first paragraph of the *Preface* and indicates well the attitude Johnson had toward his work.

B. Setting the Stage

1. To introduce the idea that balance is a basic feature of language, you could ask the students to identify the two basic parts of any common English sentence: subject and predicate, one set off against the other. In any system of sentence analysis the primary division is between these two parts. This is a basic kind of balance in the English language. Then expand the idea to metrical balance in poetry. Take some lines written in Anglo-Saxon verse form, from *Piers the Plowman*, or a modernized

version of *Beowulf*, for example, and illustrate how the second half of the line is metrically balanced against the first half. Get some examples of the heroic couplet, e.g., from Pope, to illustrate how one line is balanced against another. Then mention how a similar principle operates in music, starting with the basic two-beat, or heartbeat, balance. For contrast, turn to Emerson and his notion of compensation, and use some antitheses from Pope for illustration.

2. Another approach to introducing the unit would be through the spoken word—after all, the Don Juan passage is meant to be spoken. Here you might ask the students why Hamlet's soliloquy, beginning; "To be or not to be," is so easy to remember. Read them part of one of Edmund Burke's speeches, another of John Tanner's, and one of Professor Higgins's and ask the class to explain what makes these passages emphatic and memorable. The students will probably name repetition first, but ask them to clarify that—what kind of repetition? They will come to identify balanced structures as one of the emphatic devices. From this point it is an easy transition to the unit.

3. Other approaches to the unit (relationship to other units, etc.) have been suggested under Scheduling the Unit (I,C).

III. TEACHING THE UNIT

A. General Points of Interest and Emphasis

1. The excerpt from *Man and Superman* should be read aloud, and it should be read with force and dramatic emphasis. If it is not read with timing, variations in force, and a conscious building to the climactic summing up of "liars every one of them, to the very backbone of their souls," there is a danger of the passage's seeming monotonous and unduly long and repetitious. The students will not be able to supply the proper emphasis to their silent reading and will therefore miss the dramatic impact of the speech. It would be wise to read also Don Juan's speech preceding the Devil's mortified response. This speech will not only help set the excerpt used in the unit in context but will also give the class an understanding of Don Juan's (and Shaw's) positive theory of dynamic evolution. Although audio-visual devices are sometimes more trouble than they are worth, in this instance it might be helpful to play the appropriate sections of a recording of "Don Juan in Hell." (Some years ago Charles Boyer, Charles Laughton, Agnes Moorehead, and Cedric Hardwicke recorded an excellent version.)

2. Graphic devices—board work, overhead projections—will help students analyze the parallel structures in the unit selections. A number of ways to make the balanced structures graphic are suggested in the unit: underlining, graphing, spacing. The method need not be elaborate——the simpler, the better, in fact. The point of breaking the sentence up is to help the students see the balance. For example, the following sentence

from Johnson's famous letter to Chesterfield does not need a complex analytical scheme to illustrate its balanced elaboration:

The notice which you have been pleased to take of my labors,
      had it been early,   had been kind;
but it has been delayed
      till I am indifferent,   and cannot enjoy it;
      till I am solitary,   and cannot impart it;
      till I am known,   and do not want it.

The important question to ask after the students have identified the structures in balance or contrast is: *Why* did the author organize his material in this fashion?

3. Other models in the text that may be used to illustrate balance and antithesis are the excerpt from Ecclesiastes, Unit 1; the song from *Love's Labour's Lost,* Unit 3; the excerpt from Brooks's "On the Difference Between Wit and Humor," Unit 9; and the excerpt from 1 Corinthians, Unit 14.

B. Special Observations for Levels A, B, and C

1. *Introductory Matter:* You may want to supplement the introductory discussion of parallelism and co-ordination with a review of the difference between co-ordination and subordination and of the word classes or markers that help us indicate co-ordinate and subordinate relationships. How do "and" and "but" differ from "if" and "when"? What different relationships do "and" and "but" signify? Need we always have a word or phrase to signal co-ordination? What is the function of punctuation? What are correlative conjunctions? How do they illuminate the relationship between syntax and sense?

2. *Practice 1. Level A:* To add another level to this exercise, ask the students to explicate the four parallelisms they select. For example, what does Shaw mean when he says, "They are not clean; they are only shaved and starched"? What could be the meaning(s) of "clean" here? Explain in your own words. Illustrate with specific examples. This will help the students focus on the content as well as the form. If students are to understand the distinctions Shaw makes in the Don Juan passage, they will need to add specific illustrations and concrete details to the Shavian generalizations.

Level B:

And therefore,
      if a man write little,   he had need have a great memory;
      if he confer little,   he had need have a present wit; and
      if he read little,   he had need have much cunning,
                       to seem to know that he
                         doth not.

Ask the students to put this sentence in modern idiom and then to explain its meaning in their own words. Do they think the advice sound?

Why or why not? To what kind of an audience was Bacon writing?

Level C: To help the students get started, put the first pair on the board and, with the aid of the students, work out some sample sentences: e.g., "To be foolish in action is to be ignorant of consequences"; "Foolish in heart often marries ignorant in head."

- 3. *Practice 2. Level A:*

to be   exposed to censure without hope of praise,

to be   disgraced by miscarriage

or

punished for neglect

where   success would have been without applause

and

diligence without reward.

Ask the students to write an explanation of the meaning of Johnson's sentence.

Level B: To break out of the Shavian mold of parallelism, start the students off. Work out some samples for the first pair on the board: e.g., "The rich get richer and the poor get children." Have samples of the students' work read to the class.

Level C: This exercise should help the students who are prone to faulty parallelism. Try to get some examples from the students' own papers to augment the exercise.

- 4. *Practice 3. Level A:* Suggest that the students *not* follow the pattern Shaw uses in the Don Juan passage. The students will not have reference for a "they," and they will not be building to a climactic statement with their sentences. Have them make a statement about each of the paired terms: e.g., "To the materialist, the difference between the real and the artificial is the difference between sensation and abstraction."

Level B: This will be a rather difficult exercise for most of the students. If you wish, help them work out an abstract syntactical pattern for the sentence; perhaps three possible patterns would be helpful. While this may seem artificial, it will help the students get started. They can polish the sense once they get into the assignment. Have samples of the students' work read to the class.

Level C: Again, help the students get started: e.g., "Always to desire the new is to undervalue the old."

- 5. *Practice 4. Level A:* Have some of the sentences written for Practice 3 read to the class and discussed for possibilities of development. Have some put on the board; indicate how they might be developed: by examples, by details, by enumeration, etc.

Level B: Ask the students to include in their analysis an explanation of the contrast between hearing the Shavian passage and merely reading it. For item **b.** first ask the students to put Johnson's sentence in their own words. Discussion of their versions will help clear up any uncertainty about the meaning of the sentence.

Level C: Indicate some of the grammatical patterns used in the examples, e.g., infinitive + be + adjective / infinitive + adjective. Then list words that could fit the slots in the pattern.

- 6. *Practice 5. Level A:* Have the students analyze the syntactical structure of the sentence (e.g., "that" clauses used as appositives). How would the sentence likely be punctuated today?

  Level B: Take one of the thesis sentences, say, "There are decided advantages in being a nonconformist," and have students suggest possibilities for balanced or contrasting statements that could be used in developing the thesis. List these on the board. Suggest that students may support or attack the thesis sentences.

  Level C: Most students will choose **b.** Have students suggest specific examples that could be used to precede the quoted sentences. Indicate that the students should have at least three examples or particulars in their paragraphs.

- 7. *Practice 6. Level A only:* Have the students first construct a thesis sentence for their paragraphs. Parallelism, whether in balance or in contrast, should be in the thesis sentence. As this practice is preparation for the writing Problems, have samples of the students' work discussed and criticized by the class.

- 8. *Problem 1. Level A:* Suggest that the kind of piling up of parallelism used by Shaw would be appropriate for the first paragraph. Then the second paragraph could be developed in a less rigid manner and serve as a contrast to the first, not only in matter but also in manner.

  Level B: Students who choose **b.** should make the general statement more specific; i.e., "There are three (or four) important differences between high school and college."

  Level C: Some communities do not change, at least in the physical sense indicated in the problem. Suggest other possible topics, e.g., the student before and after he read a certain book, story, or article; saw a certain film or play; met a certain person; acquired a certain possession.

- 9. *Problem 2. Levels A and B:* If the students select their own topics, have them first frame a thesis sentence which contains parallel structures. Remind students of the conjunctive and disjunctive patterns of organization studied in other units.

  Level C: A discussion of several of the paragraphs written for Problem 1 will not only clarify the contrasts in the content of the two paragraphs each student has written, but will also help students solve the organizational problem this assignment poses. The suggestion for the content of the final paragraph will lead to the conclusion that an opening paragraph might introduce the two-sided nature of the composition idea. Also, establishing at the outset a controlling idea which comments on the advantages or disadvantages of the "change" may be suggested by the discussion.

IV. EVALUATING THE UNIT

Use the composition written in response to writing Problem 2 as the principal means for evaluating the students' work in the unit. Suggested criteria for judging the compositions are:

A. Are the controlling co-ordinate or antithetical ideas clearly stated in the opening paragraph?

B. Are these ideas grammatically, as well as conceptually, balanced?

C. Do the paragraphs evolve in co-ordinate fashion, one balanced off against another? Or do they evolve in subordinate fashion, one illustrative of another? Is the development from paragraph to paragraph consistent?

D. Are parallelisms used for emphasis? Are they placed effectively?

E. Are parallelisms varied or used sparingly for maximum effectiveness?

F. Are all parallelisms syntactically balanced?

V. ADDITIONAL WRITING TOPICS

A. To *Man and Superman* Shaw appended "The Revolutionist's Handbook," supposedly written by John Tanner. It was designed to provoke the complacent and to irritate those who defended the social and intellectual *status quo*. The following are observations from the Handbook. Write an essay attacking or defending any *one* of the observations:

1. "Every man is a revolutionist concerning the thing he understands. For example, every person who has mastered a profession is a sceptic concerning it, and consequently a revolutionist."

2. "Every genuine religious person is a heretic and therefore a revolutionist."

3. "The golden rule is that there are no golden rules."

4. "The populace cannot understand bureaucracy: it can only worship the national idols."

5. "He who confuses political liberty with freedom and political equality with similarity has never thought for five minutes about either."

6. "Nothing can be unconditional: consequently nothing can be free."

7. "Liberty means responsibility. That is why most men dread it."

8. *Mens sana in corpore sano* is a foolish saying. The sound body is a product of the sound mind."

B. Alexander Pope, the 18th-century poet, was a master of the heroic couplet and the memorable saying. Select one of the quotations below, and write a composition of moderate length developing the thought of the quotation through explanation and specific illustration:

1. "Words are like leaves; and where they most abound,
   Much fruit of sense beneath is rarely found:"—*Essay on Criticism*
2. "In words, as fashions, the same rule will hold;
   Alike fantastic, if too new or old:"   —*Essay on Criticism*
3. "True ease in writing comes from art, not chance,
   As those move easiest who have learned to dance." —*Essay on Criticism*
4. "Some judge of authors' names, not works, and then
   Nor praise nor blame the writings, but the men."—*Essay on Criticism*
5. "Charms strike the sight, but merit wins the soul."—*The Rape of the Lock*

6. "Not always Actions shew the man: we find
   Who does a kindness, is not therefore kind;"   —*Moral Essays*

UNIT 14 — COMBINE BASIC SKILLS FOR EMPHASIS

Selection from *THE HOLY BIBLE*, King James version, 1 Corinthians, Chapter 13

(Student Text—A-Level, p. 88; B-Level, p. 86; C-Level, p. 87)

I. PREPARING TO TEACH THE UNIT

A. Purposes of the Unit

1. To help students achieve a clear, forceful prose style.
2. To advance students' understanding of the concept of emphasis, i.e., to make sure the reader will answer correctly in the fewest possible words the question, "What is it about?"
3. To help students learn to emphasize their central ideas by practicing these language skills: brevity, repetition and balance, and the use of concrete devices.

B. Skills Students Will Practice

1. Eliminating wordiness.
2. Using repetition and balance for emphasis.
3. Using concrete examples, analogies, and figures of speech to emphasize ideas.
4. Rewriting to gain emphasis—through brevity, simplicity, repetition, balance, direct statement, and concrete imagery.

C. Scheduling the Unit

1. This unit is one of five units on emphasis (Units 13-17) and should achieve its purpose most strongly if it is taught as part of this series.
2. Because, however, this unit gives students practice in many of the skills that are basic to good writing, it would make a good remedial, or general purpose, unit. When there is an epidemic of fuzzy, wordy, rambling prose—when it seems that improvement will come only if certain language devices are studied simultaneously or in close sequence—this may well be the best unit to use. For this purpose, the unit may be taught much earlier in the year.
3. This unit encourages purposeful rewriting. It can lead students to a sense of style, the magic that results when, from all the language resources he has at his bidding, the writer makes the wisest choice. You may want to use this unit, therefore, when the class is writing a long paper and needs to do intelligent rewriting.

II. MOTIVATING THE UNIT

A. Background—Author and Selection

1. AUTHOR: Saint Paul, the "Apostle of the Gentiles," was the first great Christian missionary and theologian. He made a clear distinction between Judaism and the Gospel of Christ and presented Christianity as the universal religion for man, not merely as a sect of Judaism.

   Paul, born a Roman citizen in Tarsus, was sent to Jerusalem to be educated by a rabbi. He was schooled in the strict Jewish faith, and he was actively engaged in suppressing Christians when, on the road to Damascus, he had a vision and was converted to Christianity. From this moment his life was entirely changed. He began at once to preach the gospel of Christ and spent the rest of his life founding churches, making speeches, and writing. His life was always in danger, and he was executed about A.D. 64 by the command of Nero.

2. SELECTION: Epistles to the Corinthians, the seventh and eighth books of the New Testament, are letters written by Saint Paul to the Christian church in Corinth.

   The first Epistle, written in Ephesus in A.D. 55 or 56, is in answer to a letter from Corinth, where Christians were disputing over various practical and legal problems. It offers a detailed picture of the experience of a Christian church in a center of Greek life. In his letter Paul discusses marriage, law suits between Christians before heathen judges, participation in feasts at heathen temples, and the rights of women. Chapter 13, the famous sermon on charity, concludes Paul's discussion of "gifts of the Spirit," the unusual gifts or powers possessed by Christians. In this sermon Paul explains that gifts are valuable in proportion to their usefulness to others, and that charity surpasses all else in its value.

B. Setting the Stage

1. Review the unit on parallelism (Unit 13); this unit will be an excellent sequel.

2. Read aloud the selection from 1 Corinthians. Before you begin to read, ask the students to be prepared to write a single statement summarizing Paul's message. They will undoubtedly agree that his message is emphatic and clear. Then, as a contrast, read the passage from Altick (Level B, Practice 2) or the passage from Taylor's oration (Level A, Practice 1). There will be confusion about the meanings.

   In other words, raise the question that this unit attempts to answer: How does a writer achieve clarity and emphasis?

I. TEACHING THE UNIT

A. General Points of Interest and Emphasis

1. Parts of Unit 2, "Use Necessary Words Only," offer additional material on brevity.
2. The question of ambiguity may arise. Someone will ask: "How can you say that writers must always be clear? Some of our greatest literature is ambiguous, even obscure." The problem is worth looking into, and perhaps there is no easy answer, but many answers have been attempted. In his article, "Shock Reaction to Poetry," (*Saturday Review* Vol. 40, July 20, 1957, pp. 9-11+) John Ciardi made a distinction between unintelligibility and obscurity: "Obscurity is what happens when a writer undertakes a theme and method for which the reader is not sufficiently prepared. Unintelligibility is what happens when the writer undertakes a theme and method for which he himself is not sufficiently prepared."
3. Sometimes particular classes benefit greatly from making a survey of *style*. Style (see I,C,2 above) has something to do with the writer's choices, his own personal way of suiting language to his purpose; and because this unit offers many suggestions on ways to achieve emphasis, it may stimulate students to investigate style. As a starter, you can suggest that they collect excerpts from *The New Yorker* (casual style) and *Time* (clever inversions, series of hyphenated adjectives), from legal documents, political speeches (prosaic style) and from writers like Hemingway, Faulkner, Thurber, Dickens, Melville. Some students may be interested in the styles of particular eras (18th century: Neoclassicism; Victorian Age: Romanticism.)

   A discussion of the various currents of language and thought that resulted in the style of the King James Bible of 1611 may be found in Emilé Legouis and Louis Cazamian's *A History of English Literature*, New York, The Macmillan Company, 1927, pp. 376-381. Students will be interested in the fact that King James I of England commanded the preparation of this version and that it represents the work of a group of forty-seven scholars.

B. Special Observations for Levels A, B, and C

- 1. *Practice 1.* **Level A:** A preliminary discussion of the selection may be helpful here. What *is* Taylor's subject? Whom is he addressing? If the eye is an appropriate figure, and it may well be, then where has the writer failed?

  Level B: These sentences may prompt lively dispute. There may even be a few students who admire this inflated style. Sentence **c.** is so fuzzy that one can hardly determine its meaning, and the arguments over the meaning will help make your point: With all his words, the writer failed to make his central meaning clear; he did not emphasize what he wanted most to say.

Level C: Students will be surprised at how difficult it is to say something in a few words. You may wish to limit them to eight or ten words per sentence. After they have written their first sentences, you may want to have several examples put on the board so that you and the class can conduct group revisions. You may want to include examples of each of the five topic words, or restrict the revisions to one or two of the five.

- 2. *Practice 2. Level A:* Students will be interested in comparing their papers after they have struggled with Taylor's passage. Clarity alone is not sufficient—they must decide what quality they want to emphasize, and then communicate that emphasis to the reader.

  Level B: The passage *does* seem to have a message, but it is certainly a rather trite message that hardly needs saying. (Perhaps this is why the writer felt obliged to dress his plain idea in such fancy finery. *Is* this the reason for ornate language: The writer feels obligated to hide his prosaic or fuzzy thoughts under verbal decorations?) One possible restatement of the passage: "Often when a marriage is unhappy the reason is that (*a*) the partners come from very different backgrounds, (*b*) the wife works and makes more money than her husband, or (c) there is a marked difference in the partners' educational levels. Any of these conditions may cause arguments and eventually even lead to divorce."

  Level C: One possible "translation": "People have long regarded language as philosophical and deep when it is merely vague and wordy. They have similarly respected language which was unnecessarily difficult and meaningless. Consequently it will not be easy to convince them that such language is merely the cover for ignorance, and, is therefore, a hindrance to true knowledge."

- 3. *Practice 3. Levels A, B, C:* Sentence 4, outlined to show its balance, might look like this:

  > Charity suffereth long,
  >> and is kind;
  >
  > charity envieth not;
  > charity vaunteth not itself,
  >> is not puffed up,

  Notice how much the sentence loses, when it is read aloud, if *and* is inserted before "is not puffed up." This and other variations (like the inverted placement of "not") serve to highlight the unvaried repetitions of those words on which the writer wants to place his emphasis—on the word *charity* primarily.

- 4. *Practice 4. Levels A, B, C:* Students may find that writing their first draft in verse form (one statement to a line) will help them achieve the balance and tight structure they are aiming for here. Once they have their verse sentences, they can rewrite them in prose form.

- 5. *Practice 5. Level A:* It may be a good idea to ask students to list as many as ten concrete details for their topic and then select only those which best contribute to the organizing idea of their paragraph. The writer always has more material than he can use; wise selection is an important part of writing.

Level B: Remind the students that each example of a figure of speech should relate clearly to their topic sentence.

Level C: There is no Practice 5 in the Level C text. If you or the students feel the need of one, you may want to duplicate or put on the board the Level B version of Practice 5, using the example only at first for reading and discussion. The class could then work out a group topic and furnish group figures of speech as examples.

- 6. *Problems 1 and 2. Levels A, B, and C:* These assignments offer an excellent opportunity for careful rewriting. The first draft should be considered only as a beginning. As he revises, the student should strive always to improve his control of the *emphasis* he intends. He should never lose sight of the fact that he is practicing the basic skills of the unit in order to achieve unmistakable emphasis. He strives for clarity and brevity, not only to be clear and brief, but also to gain emphasis that results from clear, brief expressions.

  With this broad goal in mind, students, while revising, should examine each sentence, asking: "Is this clear? Can it be said more simply? more briefly? Where can I use repetition most effectively in this paragraph? Are my sentences *too* balanced—should I introduce some variations? Will a very short sentence serve my purpose in this particular spot? Have I illustrated my idea with enough examples? Does the figurative language serve my purpose?

  To encourage careful rewriting, have them submit their first drafts along with their final copies.

  In Problem 2, Level A students could write an analysis of their own or each other's themes, enumerating the devices of emphasis used and analyzing (even outlining) several sentences as they analyzed those in the selection from Corinthians. For Level B and C students, this kind of analysis could perhaps best be conducted orally.

EVALUATING THE UNIT

Students should understand that their themes will be graded primarily on the quality of emphasis they have achieved. They should realize that every language device they employ must serve this purpose. Frequently language that achieves emphasis through brevity, repetition and balance, and the use of concrete examples will attain emotional quality that readers will characterize variously as dignity, universality, power, beauty. Saint Paul's language, as interpreted by the writers of the King James version of the Bible, probably has this quality for many adult readers of the Bible. It may also have this quality for many students. Class discussion of these qualities in 1 Corinthians may lead to their emergence in some student writing. If so, to avoid forcing any semblance of ornate prose or overwriting in student papers, we might regard the qualities of beauty and power as a consummation devoutly to be wished, but not taught.

V. ADDITIONAL WRITING TOPICS

A. Look over other reading selections in this text and select from one a paragraph to analyze for its brevity, simplicity, balanced sentences, uses of repetition, and concrete imagery. Write a short analysis of the paragraph, pointing out the techniques the writer used to gain emphasis.

B. Rewrite one of your old themes, using some of the techniques you have reviewed in this unit.

C. Select a paragraph from one of your favorite authors. Subject it to the kind of analysis suggested in A. Decide what makes you admire this writer's style.

D. Find a paragraph unnecessarily ornate and wordy (like Taylor's or the passage from Altick). Such passages should not be difficult to find, unfortunately. Rewrite the passage, making the prose clear and forceful.

UNIT 15 — EMPHASIZE BY POSITION AND PROPORTION

Selection from a letter submitted to the John Simon Guggenheim Memorial Foundation
SELECTED POETRY AND PROSE
by Stephen Vincent Benét

(Student Text—A-Level, p. 94; B-Level, p. 93; C-Level, p. 93)

PREPARING TO TEACH THE UNIT

A. Purposes of the Unit:

1. To indicate the key positions for emphasis in sentences and paragraphs.
2. To encourage students to experiment with their placement of ideas in sentences and paragraphs as a way of achieving the emphasis they want.
3. To illustrate the placement and use of direct statement as a means of emphasis.
4. To show the relationship of proportion to emphasis.

B. Skills Students Will Practice

1. Using direct statement to give a particular emphasis to a paragraph.
2. Arranging the elements in a sentence in various ways to achieve a desired emphasis.
3. Writing sentences and paragraphs that build to a climax.
4. Analyzing the relationship of proportion to emphasis.
5. Writing compositions giving particular attention to successful emphasis.

C. Scheduling the Unit

1. This unit is third in a series of five units on emphasis. What the students learn in this unit will naturally relate to the skills in the two preceding units—13 and 14—and help prepare the students for the special and less logically based kinds of emphasis taught in the two following units, 16 and 17.
2. For students who are ready for more work with sentence structure following Units 5 and 6, this unit would be a worth-while follow-up, particularly in sections **A.**, **B.**, and **C.**

MOTIVATING THE UNIT

A. Background—Author and Selection

1. AUTHOR: Stephen Vincent Benét (1898-1943) (younger brother of William Rose Benét, an important American poet) was born in Bethlehem, Pennsylvania, and began writing even as a young child. He published his first book at the age of seventeen. His education at Yale University was interrupted by civilian government service during World War I; when he got his M.A. degree after the war, he submitted a third volume of poetry instead of a thesis.

After he published the *Ballad of William Sycamore* (1923), three novels, and several short stories, he and his wife went to France on a Guggenheim Fellowship. While he was there, he wrote his most famous work, *John Brown's Body* (1928), a long narrative poem that records much of the history of the Civil War. For this poem he received the Pulitzer Prize for Poetry in 1929. In 1944 he was awarded a second Pulitzer Poetry Prize posthumously for *Western Star* (1943), the first section of a planned epic poem based on western migration. He also wrote short stories; the two most often read are "The Devil and Daniel Webster" (1937) and "Johnny Pye and the Fool-Killer" (1938).

2. SELECTION: This excerpt from Benét's letter comprises about half of the original, which was dated December 11, 1925. In a very short paragraph he introduces his subject, explaining that he cannot be as definite about "unaccomplished creative work" as he would like to be. Then follows the quoted selection, two long paragraphs. The rest of the letter gives fuller detail about his plans and his wife's academic background. His wife, Rosemary, has written an interesting introductory note to this letter in which she expresses their gratitude to the Guggenheim Fellowship. Her note and Benét's letter are printed in the Rinehart edition of *Selected Poetry and Prose* (1959) by Stephen Vincent Benét, edited and with an introduction by Basil Davenport.

B. Setting the Stage

1. Reading Benét's letter may stimulate interest in the work that resulted from this grant—*John Brown's Body*. Reading passages from the book and relating them to the statements Benét makes in the selection covering his development of his craft will give students an interesting double view of the act of creating a literary work. Knowing the stringent financial condition Benét was in when he wrote *John Brown's Body* may give added meaning to the constructions Benét used as he composed his letter.

2. There is a more direct route to this unit, one that may prove very interesting: the exploration of famous letters—those, for example, of Héloïse and Abélard, Leonardo da Vinci, Samuel Johnson, Thomas Jefferson, John Keats, Abraham Lincoln, Robert and Elizabeth Barrett Browning. Such an activity will encourage students to explore libraries; it will also introduce them to some fine prose and whet their appetites for biography. A few of these letters could be duplicated and given close analysis during the unit.

One letter in particular will stimulate lively discussion when it is contrasted with Benét's—the letter Richard Wagner wrote to Baron Robert von Hornstein on December 12, 1861, demanding an immediate loan of ten thousand francs. *A Treasury of the World's Great Letters*, M. Lincoln Schuster, ed. New York, Simon and Schuster, 1940, pp. 350-351. The letter is blunt, even insulting, and Wagner did not get his loan.

III. TEACHING THE UNIT

A. General Points of Interest and Emphasis

1. Level C students may profit from a practical approach to this unit. You might ask them what kinds of letters have given them the most difficulty. Why is it usually harder to ask a favor in a letter than it is in person? A discussion of Benét's letter may be much more satisfactory if these students have first discussed their own experiences in letter writing.

2. An important question may arise during discussion: Shouldn't a writer be honestly direct? If money is what a man wants, shouldn't he say so in the most direct way he can? A discussion of these questions may lead to some helpful conclusions: Of course a writer should, like anyone else, be honest. And if he writes well and if he achieves exactly the emphasis he wants, then he will reveal himself truly and honestly. An unskillful writer, however, no matter how honest his intentions, can create a wrong impression or fail to communicate his real purpose. Benét, as revealed in this letter, was a skillful writer; later events proved him also honest and sincere in his statements. Benét needed money, but he needed money only because his work demanded it; his letter gave a true picture of his need. He was not underplaying money or overplaying his work; he was giving an exact and direct account of his predicament. Because he was a good writer, he was able to control his tone and emphasis; he was able, in short, to communicate his intentions honestly.

B. Special Observations for Levels A, B, and C

- 1. *Practice 1, Levels A and C:* Level A students should not experience difficulty writing this paragraph, especially if they describe a scene about which they have strong feelings. Have students read each other's papers and decide where direct statement has been used with special effectiveness. Level C students may find difficulty in writing the three long sentences to precede the direct statement. It will be wise to discuss thoroughly the example suggested—Benét's first four sentences. A model paragraph on the board would be helpful.
  Level B: "This is not a complaint—it is merely a statement of fact," underlines what Benét wants his reader to understand: He is currently forced to give most of his time and energy to work other than his poetry.

115

- **2.** *Practice 2.* **Level** **A:** Allow students to add all the words they need to avoid a contrived, artificial effect.

   Level **B:** See Practice 1, Levels A and C. Discuss both the example in the Practice and the first four sentences of Benét's selection.

   Level **C:** You may want to work one problem at the board with the class contributing suggestions. For example, they might compare the effects of these two arrangements of **b**:

   a. During the Battle of Chancellorsville, the Confederacy lost one of its greatest generals, Stonewall Jackson, who was fatally wounded when he was returning from a night inspection of his lines. He was shot by one of his own sentries.

   b. During the Battle of Chancellorsville, Stonewall Jackson, returning from a night inspection of his lines, was fatally wounded by one of his own sentries. His death was a blow to the South.

   The first arrangement suggests the irony in Jackson's death; the second emphasizes the loss to the South.

- **3.** *Practice 3.* **Level** **A:** Some students may need to be cautioned that overuse of the periodic sentence makes prose sound contrived and affected. There is a right moment, a right spot in a paragraph or a theme for the periodic sentence, and the good writer learns to sense just where this is.

   Level **B:** Students will probably agree that Fleming's rustic environment receives minor attention and that the reader is led to concentrate on his terror and his flight into the woods. Allow time to discuss the sentences developed in response to exercise **c.**; this is the profitable part of the Practice.

   Level **C:** Again, students should compare the effects of different arrangements in these sentences. For example, in **b.** there is a difference in the effects of the following:

   a. While he waited for the train, he nervously crumpled bits of paper and threw them down the embankment.

   b. As he nervously crumpled bits of paper and threw them down the embankment, he waited for the train.

   If the analysis of isolated sentences seems to lead nowhere, it may be that students are discovering that sentences out of context are rather meaningless. Point out that this Practice will have most value in the sentences the students construct in paragraphs where the varying emphasis in sentences is controlled by paragraph development of an idea.

- **4.** *Practice 4.* **Level** **A:** Students may prefer writing about someone they know personally. The only requirement they must meet here is the "periodic development" in their paragraph.

   Level **B:** These sentences should be easy for most students. Perhaps you will want to work them orally and allow more time for the writing assignments that follow.

   Level **C:** *Time* seems to be the chief emphasis in the first paragraph; in the second paragraph Benét describes his projected work in both his first and last sentence. The last sentence in this paragraph makes reference to his need for both time *and* money.

- 5. *Practice 5. Level A:* If time allows, discussion may prove more valuable here than writing.
  Level B: See Practice 4, Level A.
  Level C: Ask the students to list the ideas they plan to discuss in their paragraphs and to make a tentative decision about which idea they plan to stress; tentative, because, as every writer knows, the best laid plans often change when actual writing begins.
- 6. *Practice 6. Levels A and B:* As with Practice 5, Level A, oral analysis may be more beneficial, but only after everyone has examined the second paragraph carefully and made notes on how he believes Benét has achieved emphasis by proportion.
  Level C: Students should enjoy rewriting this terrible review, heartened perhaps by the realization that someone is a worse writer than they. If, despite the example, they are not sure how to begin, you might ask them to identify and correct in a preliminary discussion some of the "crimes" committed in the review.
- 7. *Problem 1. Level A:* Students will realize that they are faced with Benét's problem, and they will begin to appreciate the difficulty in achieving just the right tone and emphasis in such a letter. The writer does not dare be overmodest about his achievements in scholarship or his aspirations about college. Yet he dreads sounding egocentric. This assignment will be challenging.
  Levels B and C: Writing applications for jobs will have personal relevance for many of these students, and they should take this assignment seriously and write well. You might divide them into employer-employee groups and have the employers read the applications and comment on them.
- 8. *Problem 2. Levels A and B:* In this Problem the topic (advertising or films or subjects of conversation) is one in which they have no personal stake; they are not requesting funds or jobs. They do, however, have a cultural stake in these topics. You might discuss whether this difference affects the importance of emphasis in any way.
  Level C: Because they will be writing about an organization familiar to them, students may raise the question: How does the writer decide which things are important when he has so much to say? This is a crucial problem for writers—the problem of selection. They may need to discuss this thoroughly before they plan their compositions.

EVALUATING THE UNIT

You may not want to grade the Practices; in fact, you may find it wise to encourage students to experiment with tone and emphasis without concerning themselves about grades. Your grading policy for the Problems can be definitely stated: Papers will be evaluated on how well the writer has employed position, direct statement, and proportion to achieve emphasis.

Students would profit by reading each other's Problem 1 papers and commenting specifically on the success or failure in emphasis. Their evaluation could be made very meaningful if the writers attached to their compositions carefully planned statements in which they reveal their intentions. Then the evaluation would constitute the reader's reply to one question: How well did the writer achieve his stated intention?

V. ADDITIONAL WRITING TOPICS

A. Collect letters-to-the-editor from your local newspaper or from a periodical like *Saturday Review* or *Time*. Write an analysis of one letter in which you discuss (1) the total impact of the letter and (2) the means the writer has used to achieve this impact (and note especially his use of direct statement, position, and proportion).

B. Re-examine your old compositions. Consider the effect in relation to your intention and write an analysis similar to the one in **A**.

C. Select a local issue that interests you and write a letter to the editor. In your letter give careful attention to your emphasis. Write a statement describing your intentions and attach it to the letter to help your teacher and your fellow students evaluate your success in achieving your intentions.

UNIT 16 — EMPHASIZE WITH PARADOX

Selection from "*The Ethics of Fairyland*" by G. K. Chesterton

(Student Text—A-Level, p. 101; B-Level, p. 98; C-Level, p. 99)

I. PREPARING TO TEACH THE UNIT

A. Purposes of the Unit

1. To define paradox, so that students can recognize it in literature and in their own thinking.
2. To enable students to handle paradox effectively in their writing.
3. To encourage students to examine their ideas in depth.

B. Skills Students Will Practice

1. Identifying paradox.
2. Learning how to state and resolve a paradox.
3. Learning the compact, balanced sentence structure essential to well-stated paradox.

C. Scheduling the Unit

1. Paradox is related to analogy. To put it paradoxically: The fact that two things are different implies that they are similar. This unit could, then, be studied in conjunction with Unit 9, "Sharpen Meaning by Comparison."
2. Since paradox frequently seeks expression in metaphor, this unit could accompany Unit 23, "Create Images through Metaphor."
3. This unit will serve very well as an adjunct to the study of poetry, since paradox is so often the atmosphere of a poem.

II. MOTIVATING THE UNIT

A. Background—Author and Selection

1. AUTHOR: Gilbert Keith Chesterton (1874-1936), an astonishingly versatile British writer, began his literary career as a journalist. He functioned as a kind of Victorian Addison, directing his sharp wit against all that was prosaic in the thinking of the late Victorians. In addition to his polemic writing in religion, sociology, and politics, he wrote biography (Dickens, Shaw, and Browning are among his subjects), fiction (the delightful and romantically drawn Father Brown detective stories are the

most often read), literary criticism, and some good poetry. His gay, brilliant style is a delight to read.

For essays similar to that from which the model selection is taken see "All Things Considered," "Tremendous Trifles," "The Uses of Diversity," and "Avowals and Denials"; the very titles suggest the paradox one finds everywhere in his work. For an analysis of his work as paradox see Hugh Kenner's *Paradox in Chesterton* (Sheed and Ward, 1948).

SELECTION: "The Ethics of Fairyland" is a short essay that was originally published in *The World*, a British newspaper, on September 27, 1904. It is one of many of the previously uncollected writings of G. K. Chesterton to be found in *The Man Who Was Orthodox* (1963), arranged and introduced by A. L. Maycock.

The selection is typical of Chesterton's brand of paradox. He presents his arresting statement immediately and then gently, step by step, leads his reader to understanding and acceptance. Maycock's collection will provide innumerable similar passages that would offer excellent opportunity for analysis.

Giving this selection a close analysis is perhaps the best way to lead students to an understanding of what paradox is and how a writer can handle it effectively. A discussion of the selection follows in Practice 1, Level A.

B. Setting the Stage

1. Read several paradoxical statements to the students (from Thurber's *Fables for Our Times*, 1940, or Lewis Carroll's *Alice in Wonderland*, 1865), or use some of the statements from this unit. The following verse contains examples of paradox:

>   A mountain's a plain
>   (To a person a-wing)
>   A king is a waif
>   (When freedom must ring)
>   A wall is a gateway
>   (To one who seeks peace)
>   A word is a world
>   (Yet a word's not a thing).

   Ask the students to come to a tentative definition of paradox.

2. Try this unit "cold"; that is, have students read the Chesterton selection and ask them if they find anything intriguing about his first sentence. The class should move then quite naturally into questions about paradox.

III. TEACHING THE UNIT

A. General Points of Interest and Emphasis

1. Throughout this unit it may be necessary to stress that paradox is *not* some sort of rhetorical trick, an ace up the sleeve that a writer can flash at his reader to shock him into attention. This unit should involve philosophical discussion; otherwise, some students may never see what is essential here: Paradox is concerned with the contradiction that exists in the nature of things, and the philosopher who seeks truth often encounters something that resembles a riddle.

2. The distinction between paradox and irony will probably require some clarification. Both paradox and irony involve the unexpected and both involve the idea of opposites. Irony implies that there is a discrepancy between what is and what should be or between what is said and what is meant. Paradox marvels at the same kind of strangeness in the make-up of the universe, but it places the strangeness not in the discrepancy but in the "bothness." Irony: "The innocent man was rewarded with a year in jail." Paradox: "This man was rewarded in being punished."

B. Special Observations for Levels A, B, and C

1. You may want to change the order of the first few Practices, depending on what turns the class discussion takes. If students are puzzled by the meaning of Chesterton's passage, and this may well be the case with B- and C-Levels, then perhaps Practice 2 at those levels should come first, before the students encounter poems or write about their own experiences. You may want to read all three levels before you begin to teach the unit so that you will be ready to move in any direction. And you may want to use both Ciardi's and Wordsworth's poems with all three levels.

● 2. *Practice 1. Level A:* Answering a. and b. in anything but a perfunctory manner will require a close examination of the passage. Following are some observations that may be helpful:

   a. The first sentence presents the paradox: Fairy tales give a truer picture of life than does any other form of literature.

   b. Sentences 2 and 3 reassure the reader. Chesterton admits "errors in details," the giants and beanstalks that he names in sentence 3. Of course, he implies, these phenomena are not literally true. But already he hints at how he will resolve the paradox: He says such objects are not too *strange* to be true.

   c. Sentence 4 begins resolving the paradox. The atmosphere of fairy tales, we are told, is very true.

   d. The concluding sentence of the first paragraph describes the atmosphere of fairy tales, the magic in common things like stones; the paragraph concludes by saying that the magic is indeed there.

   e. The next paragraph develops examples that clarify the paradox and its resolution. The first four sentences describe life as a chain of talismans, in the fairytale sense of magic trees, flowers, and numbers. The "poetic sense" of the next sentence refers to this fairytale world of talismans. Chesterton says, in this important sentence, that the poetic description of life as a series of strange, magical objects and moments is more true and more practical than any scientific explanation of life.

     f. We never know, says Chesterton, when we have done something that will affect the whole course of our lives. The object that determines our destiny may be as "innocent" as a tree, a bus, an advertisement. Why, then, are trees or buses or advertisements not truly as magic as beanstalks and giants? Chesterton has brought his resolution around full circle.

Level B: Read the poem aloud. Students will see its paradoxical assertion about decency and humility. In the particular sense of this poem, that which is "decent" is *not* decent. The student paragraphs should be as brief as possible but should contain specific references to the poem.

Level C: These essays, written from personal experience, may be interesting to read aloud. If they are painfully personal, students may prefer to use pseudonyms.

- 3. *Practice 2. Level A:* Students will find, as Chesterton did, that the best way to "explain" a paradox is to illustrate it.

  Level B: See Practice 1, Level A above. Students should make a sentence-by-sentence analysis of the selection before they answer **a.** Similarly, before they answer **b.**, they should explicate Ciardi's poem.

  Level C: See Practice 1, Level A above for an analysis of the selection.

- 4. *Practice 3. Level A:* Students are working here for concise, balanced sentences that will give their paradoxes emphasis. Suggestions follow, but the students can do better: (*a*) "Only he who fears can be brave." (*b*) "The man who knows nothing knows most." (c) "Only the hermit can know the world."

  Level B: See Practice 1, Level C above.

  Level C: The line, "The child is father of the man" will seem to some students as if it must be a misprint. Perhaps **a.**, **b.**, and **c.**, will best be achieved in discussion: Does a child have a kind of knowledge that a man may not have? What, that he values so highly, has Wordsworth the man learned from Wordsworth the child? In what special ways is a child the father of the adult he is to become?

- 5. *Practice 4. Levels A and B:* The emphasis here is on citing concrete illustrations. The writer will not convince his reader unless he is concrete and clear.

  Level C: Encourage students to look beyond clichés. It may be best to discuss the six pairs extensively before they try to construct their sentences. Emphasize the need for conciseness and balance.

- 6. *Problem 1. Level A:* Thurber's *Fables for Our Times* could be used to advantage here. Some students may want to challenge a cliché with Thurber's medium, the fable.

  Level B: Insist that the paragraphs contain concrete illustrations.

Level C: Lead the students to understand that their task is to find *one particular sense* in which the quotation seems to be quite true. It might be helpful to review all of the paradoxes they have met in this unit, asking, for example: In what sense are fairy tales true to life? In what sense is the child the father of the man? Their task here is to explain *in what sense* something that seems contradictory can be very sensible and true.

- **7** *Problem 2. Level A:* Any of the four paradoxes from Chesterton (quoted just before Practice 3) would make interesting development.

  Levels B and C: A rereading of the Chesterton selection may be helpful here. Students will feel more secure if they follow his method of development: (*a*) State the paradox in a bold sentence; (*b*) Reassure the reader that you *do* have something sensible to say; (*c*) Move gradually into resolution; (*d*) Illustrate with many concrete examples.

V. EVALUATING THE UNIT

Because an understanding of paradox requires considerable imagination as well as a decided philosophic bent, grades for C-Level students should be based primarily on rather clearly defined and achievable objectives: how completely and accurately the student has fulfilled the assignments and how actively he has participated in class discussions. With Level A students you might be able to expect insight and depth in their explorations of paradox. Certainly in Problems 1 and 2, Level A, you can demand a well-stated paradox as well as clear development through concrete example.

ADDITIONAL WRITING TOPICS

A. Explore the relationship of humor and paradox. Is it true that all humor must in some way involve paradox?

B. Find a poem that contains a paradox. Explicate the poem.

C. Examine a current issue in politics, economics, or ethics. Find a paradox; present it and resolve it in a Chestertonian essay.

UNIT 17 — EMPHASIZE THROUGH RHYTHM AND CADENCE

Selection from YOU CAN'T GO HOME AGAIN by Thomas Wolfe

(Student Text—A-Level, p. 106; B-Level, p. 103; C-Level, p. 104)

I. PREPARING TO TEACH THE UNIT

A. Purposes of the Unit

1. To increase students' awareness of the rhythms in prose writing.
2. To help students recognize the value of rhythm in achieving emphasis in prose writing.
3. To illustrate various means of establishing rhythmical emphasis in prose writing: placement, repetition, punctuation.

B. Skills Students Will Practice

1. Making use of repetition of sounds and sentence elements to achieve rhythmical emphasis.
2. Organizing a paragraph as a rhythmical unit, with attention to the part played by punctuation in the unit.
3. Placing words and patterns for rhythmical emphasis.

C. Scheduling the Unit

1. Unit 17 is the last in a sequence of five units concerned with emphasis; the skill it teaches is, of course, the subtlest one to examine and to attain. Its following four other units treating emphasis gives *it* a kind of emphasis as a skill and as a refinement in writing. By the time the student comes to this particular unit, the concept of emphasis in prose writing should be clear to him, and he should be ready to examine and attempt to employ the subtler devices used by skillful writers in stressing their ideas.
2. This unit is useful in preparing students for a study of literature, especially fiction, in which the author communicates ideas and mood indirectly; careless readers (including many rapid, "get-the-point" readers) often miss a good deal of what is important to a full understanding of a work. The rhythms of a Melville, a Crane, a Faulkner, a Knowles have to be caught if the reader is to appreciate the writing and understand fully what is happening. The unit might be especially useful as a transition between studies of poetry and prose, thereby stressing that both are on the same continuum and that where they come together, no one can properly distinguish between them. (William Faulkner, for one, used the words *poet* and *novelist* synonymously.)

II. MOTIVATING THE UNIT

A. Background—Author and Selection

1. AUTHOR: Born and reared in Asheville, North Carolina, Thomas Wolfe (1900-1938) is one of very few Southern writers not distinctly identified with the South, even though his first novel (*Look Homeward, Angel*, 1929) is set in a fictional community closely resembling Asheville, and his later novels make further use of Wolfe's native region. After his undergraduate years at the University of North Carolina (he entered at fifteen), he worked for two years, then entered Harvard, where he studied dramaturgy in George Pierce Baker's famed "Workshop 47"; his earliest ambition was to become a playwright (his second, to become a poet). He began writing his first novel between two stints of teaching English at New York University; he completed it in two and a half years. Most critics point out that in effect Wolfe wrote but one long novel, which closely parallels the threads of his own experience, even though the hero of the first two works (*Look Homeward, Angel* and *Of Time and the River*, 1935) is nominally abandoned in the last two (*The Web and the Rock*, 1939, and *You Can't Go Home Again*, 1940—both published posthumously). Indeed, many sequences appearing in one work had originally been planned for another work.

   It may be that the parallel between the life of Wolfe and that of his heroes has been responsible for generalizing the author as an *American* novelist. Wolfe traveled widely and spent a good portion of his writing life away from his native region, and his abiding interest was to comprehend the American experience. Like Walt Whitman, Wolfe seemed to think of himself as a kind of chronicler of America, and he possessed the powers to evoke the hugeness, the newness, the strangeness of it.

   The place of Thomas Wolfe in American literature has not, of course, been fully determined; his reputation waned during the late 1940's and the 1950's but has been rising in recent years. There can be no question, however, that *Look Homeward, Angel*, like Hemingway's *A Farewell to Arms* and Faulkner's *The Sound and the Fury*, both of which also appeared in 1929, will keep its place as a staple in our literature.

   One of the best critical and interpretative studies of Thomas Wolfe's work is *The Art of Thomas Wolfe* by Pamela Hansford Johnson (Scribner, 1963—formerly entitled *Hungry Gulliver*).

2. SELECTION: *You Can't Go Home Again* is generally considered the loosest of the four novels; at the same time, however, it offers quite effective pictures of the period it deals with—the late 1920's through the middle 1930's—including some striking shots of the Depression (especially the "crash" period) and the first years of Hitler's regime. Too, the novel shows close up the excitement of a novelist's success (the hero, of course, is also a writer) and the extreme pain the writer suffers when the people in his hometown, thinking he has held them up to ridicule, turn against him. And in *You Can't Go Home Again* are some of the

most effective poetic passages found in the body of Wolfe's work, which has been praised as perhaps the richest in rhetoric in modern American literature.

The selection for Unit 17 is characteristic of the many passages in Wolfe's work in which he tries to communicate some of the truths of the human experience which are difficult to express, paradoxically, because they are so simple and commonplace and obvious. This passage expresses permanency of life as life; one hears echoes of Ecclesiastes— "One generation passeth away, and another generation cometh: but the earth abideth for ever." The great paradox of life is its unchanging change; what lives, dies and becomes a part of the earth, which in turn produces that which lives, dies ....Coming as it does in the last of Wolfe's work and expressing as it does a kind of communion of life, the passage stands as an interesting contrast to a passage introducing the author's first novel, where we find the question, "Which of us is not forever a stranger and alone?" It would be gross to suggest that the selection for the present unit answers that question, but not unreasonable to say that the examination of the truths of the human experience has widened the possibility.

B. Setting the Stage

1. It would seem profitable, before beginning this unit, to review through a question-and-answer session the means of emphasis studied in the preceding units (if, of course, the class has followed the progression this book offers): parallelism, combining basic skills, position and proportion, and paradox. (Generally speaking, the progression beginning with Unit 13 and ending with Unit 17 moves from the more obvious means of achieving emphasis to the subtler ones.) Once the review has been completed, the following question might be posed: Through what means are ideas in popular songs emphasized? For illustration, you might ditto copies of an "old standard," say, a Cole Porter lyric or one by Lorenz Hart. The music of "conventional" poetry and prose, to be sure, is much less pronounced; but some of the ideas and techniques treated in this unit are certain to be touched on in the preliminary class discussion, and contact will be made between the student's immediate experience and the unit-lesson.

2. Another means of introducing this unit would be to offer two examples in which essentially the same idea is expressed and then to test the two for effective communication. There is a certain risk in this kind of device because some students, perhaps many, may prefer the less effective example. Yet, this possibility offers advantages, too, since the unhappy preference will help the teacher to anticipate individual and group difficulties during the unit. The value of this device, however, is chiefly in the focusing of attention on the points treated in Unit 17. Sample: a. "Which of us has known his brother? Which of us has looked into his father's heart? Which of us has not remained forever

prison-pent? Which of us is not forever a stranger and alone?''

—Thomas Wolfe, *Look Homeward, Angel*

b. For all our devices for communication, we cannot know one another deeply.

III. TEACHING THE UNIT

A. General Points of Interest and Emphasis

1. You might first read the selection aloud, at a normal reading pace, with the class following their copies. Then, it might be pointed out that the "normal reading pace" is essentially controlled by what the author has written. For the sake of demonstration of this observation, you might exaggerate the speed, first by a rapid reading of the third paragraph, then by a very slow reading of the same passage. A question of value for discussion: What is lost when the reading speed is exaggerated? Or, what tells the reader that his reading rate is suitable—is it only his ability to catch the meaning of the words?

2. It might be quite profitable for the class to read the passage as a group, for individual students may have difficulty in "hearing" the passage as they read it silently, as they are asked to do in working some of the Practices. Reading in unison may help them catch the rhythm and cadence. Too, it is important that students recognize that much prose is meant to be heard, and tends to stem from the "bardic tradition" as much as poetry does. We have de-emphasized the significance of oral reading in the last few decades (because it leads to slower reading rates?) and, in doing so, have left undeveloped not only the skill of reading aloud, but also the ability to hear what is read silently. One who does not hear the brilliant passages in *Moby Dick*, for example, may very well conclude that here is an author who takes a long while to say little. In any case, what Unit 17 teaches will be more readily learned as the student comes to hear with his mind's ear.

3. Other prose models which may be of use as illustrations for the skills treated in Unit 17:

   a. Unit 1—excerpt from Ecclesiastes (placement of words)

   b. Unit 9—excerpt from "On the Difference Between Wit and Humor" (repetition; punctuation)

   c. Unit 14—excerpt from 1 Corinthians (repetition; punctuation)

   d. Unit 24—excerpt from "The Lagoon" (rhythmic patterns)

   e. Unit 25—excerpt from "The Open Boat" (rhythmic patterns; punctuation)

B. Special Observations for Levels A, B, and C

● 1. *Practice 1. Levels A and B:* It will probably be best to work at least part of this Practice as a class. For example, you might ask the class

127

to arrange the words in the first sentence according to stress, follow with placement of the arrangement (according to general agreement) on the board, and discuss the results, attempting to account for whatever variation was suggested by individuals. Then, the students may work the remaining sentences individually with more confidence. (Likely arrangement for first sentence: A-tarantula, adder, asp, never, change; B-will, also; C-The, the, the, and.)

You may find it better to work the entire Practice in this manner—that is, one sentence at a time, each followed by a general check and discussion. Or you may wish to have the class work the entire paragraph before comparing results.

The important point of the Practice is to establish an understanding between stressed and unstressed words in passages which rely on rhythm in good part for emphasis of ideas. Therefore, a rather full discussion, in one form or another, should accompany the Practice.
Level C: Here, too, it might be best to begin with a group effort. You might select one of the items in the Practice and ask for suggestions, put the sentence on the board, making whatever improvements individuals offer. Or you might have the class work the first exercise individually and then place a few samples on the board for comparison (which may lead to combining the results of various efforts). Before asking the students to go on to Practice 2, you may want to read several samples of the best work done during this Practice. Exercise **a.** might produce sentences like these: "The waves roll in, long dark-green swells, leaden folds, rumbling heavily, wave on wave." or "Choppy, white-topped, foamy, the short thin waves dart ceaselessly against the rocky beach, churning bits of seaweed in quick eddies."

● 2. *Practice 2.* **Level A:** This Practice might begin with a brief discussion of the example offered; the class should note the repetition of sounds (represented by the *s*'s, *d*'s, *t*'s, *w*'s) as well as of words. How do these contribute to the rhythm and meaning of the sentence? Too, in keeping with the instructions, some attention should be given to the words which contribute to the motion, not only by denotation, but also by sound. How do the words *drifting* and *silently* suggest (connote) slow movement? The words must be spoken with relative slowness if they are to be spoken distinctly, and this requirement adds to the meaning of the words. (A good side illustration is a comparison of the words *speed* and *slow:* It does not require an especially sensitive ear to recognize that the first is normally spoken more rapidly than the last. For what reason?)
Level B: The comments for Practice 1, Level C, above will also apply to this Practice.
Level C: This Practice is difficult; it should begin with careful preparation. It might be worth while to go over each of the topics with the whole class, listing the effects a writer might include in his paragraph. It should be pointed out that each topic should suggest a dominant rhythm (i.e., a back-and-forth motion for the swing), and the writer must attempt to catch that rhythm in his paragraph. Once the preliminary discussion

has been completed, the students might work on their topics individually, producing work drafts, which may be either submitted to the teacher for comment or read in small groups for suggestions. The small-group method is helpful in two ways: It offers a variety of suggestions, and it affords the individual student the opportunity to see strengths and weaknesses in other people's work that he might not see in his own. After receiving your comments or those of his group, the student can rewrite his paragraph, incorporating the suggested improvements. The paragraphs need not be long. Here is an example:

The swing would barely move at first. Then, gaining momentum, I started an arch ahead and back, ahead then back, longer and stronger, strongly forward, strongly back. I made a breeze brush my face. I made a breeze curl past my ears. I made the earth tilt up, tilt down.

● 3. *Practice 3. Level A:* You may wish to remind the class that each of the situations suggests speed or motion; thus the writers should concentrate on establishing pace or changing pace in their sentences. It might be best to work these items one at a time, first working individually on the item, then following with a discussion and comparison. The emphasis of the Practice should be on the oral, rather than the written.

Level B: The same kind of approach as that suggested for Level A can be used for this Practice, although the teacher may wish to offer an example for general discussion first. An example for this kind of discussion—immediately before the student is asked to practice the skill discussed—might be purposely flawed or weak, so that the student may improve it and move a step closer to achieving the skill. The following example is only partially successful:

The jackhammer chattered eccentrically in the street, chipping the pavement and spitting seeds of concrete into the air, choking and stammering when its single tooth caught in the earth beneath, and screaming angrily on its release.

Level C: Possibly the most effective approach to this Practice is to offer an example for the first item in each section, directing the discussion to the reasons for the pace. Examples:

a. At noon the city streets swarm with crowds of people, jostling clusters of men and women, a man here weaving in and out, a woman there being swept forward by a group pressing from behind, a tangle of noisy girls stringing along like a bright thread in a billowing cloth, a child disappearing into a flowing grove of giants and appearing briefly in a clearing before losing himself again in another grove, another cluster in the crowd swarming the city streets.
b. In the softening light of late afternoon, the fisherman lay alongside the stream which murmured and mumbled under the contrasting buzz and hum of summer insects, lay quietly asleep, as still as the line that hung like wire from his unmoving pole.

● 4. *Practice 4. Level A:* There will, of course, be some variation in the responses to these questions, since there are no absolute answers to any of them. The important aspect of the Practice is the review of the techniques the questions require. This assignment can be as effective without written responses; in fact, oral discussion is probably the best preparation for Practice 5.

Level B: A brief review of the rhythmic devices studied in this unit should precede the working of this Practice. You might make use of the questions presented in Practice 4, Level A, as the basis for the review; or, of course, the class could turn to the beginning of the unit and briefly discuss each section.

Group work might be practical here, with each member of the group reading his work draft to the rest for comment and suggestions before revision and the final draft. In preparation for the Problems given in "The Act of Writing," the teacher might read a few of the most successful efforts to the entire class.

Level C: A variation on the group method suggested above can be effectively employed in this Practice. Each group could select a single topic, each member writing a work draft and presenting it to the others; the group then could write a single paragraph with the best efforts of all included. Even though it is likely that one or two members will contribute most of the material for the final draft, all will have had the opportunity to consider the skills employed.

- 5. *Practice 5. Level A:* This Practice should follow Practice 4 as soon as possible, and it would likely be profitable for the class to work in groups of four or five, in which case the comments for Practice 4, Level B, would apply.

- 6. *Problem 1. Levels A, B, and C:* For this writing there should be some preliminary discussion of what the directions call for. The discussion might begin with the general question: What are the chief differences between busy and deserted streets? The teacher might list the suggested features for each scene on the board. (This listing will be especially useful for the Level C.) Following the listing, there should be discussion of the part rhythm will play in reinforcing the descriptions.

    Examples of the paragraphs might be dittoed and distributed for analysis before Problem 2 is undertaken.

- 7. *Problem 2. Levels A, B, and C:* Before this final writing is assigned, there should be a full review of all skills studied in this unit. Too, there might be value in relating these skills to the topics suggested in this Problem. You might suggest some of the features specifically relating to the topics, with the purpose of emphasizing the importance of the writer's seeing and hearing what it is he means to describe (the kind of tree, the location of the window, the kind of animal).

IV. EVALUATING THE UNIT

Since the skills treated in the lesson are refinements developed over a long period of time, the success of the students' efforts will be rather difficult to judge by high standards. If the students demonstrate an understanding of the techniques, they have made some advancement, even though they may not be able to apply the techniques very effectively. This is to say, you might expect a passage or two in which emphasis through rhythm and cadence is achieved, but you might also not be alarmed to find other passages weak or flawed. The unit skill is a delicate one, and it should perhaps be measured mainly by the ear. You may want to include oral reading of the students' work in any evaluating of this unit.

V. ADDITIONAL WRITING TOPICS

A. Ask the class to write about a solemn occasion which they have observed or taken part in (a graduation ceremony, a religious observance). Remind the students to emphasize the solemnity through rhythm and cadence as well as through selection of details.

B. Variation on the preceding topic, of course, is possible: a humorous occasion, a dangerous situation, a monotonous experience.

C. Ask students to write a brief essay in which two or more seasons are contrasted by rhythm and cadence as well as by visual imagery.

UNIT 18 — DEFINE AN ABSTRACT TERM

Selection from *ASPECTS OF THE NOVEL* by E. M. Forster

(Student Text—A-Level, p. 112; B-Level, p. 110; C-Level, p. 110)

I. PREPARING TO TEACH THE UNIT

A. Purposes of the Unit

1. To help students understand that highly abstract words are often ambiguous or vague in meaning and that the sense in which they are used should therefore be made clear to the reader.
2. To illustrate defining by genus and difference.
3. To illustrate defining by example.
4. To illustrate defining by function.
5. To demonstrate how an extended definition is constructed.

B. Skills Students Will Practice

1. Constructing genus-difference definitions (classifying), and differentiating one subclass from other subclasses.
2. Constructing examples to illustrate a concept.
3. Explaining the function(s) of the abstract entity to which the word refers.
4. Using the various defining techniques to write extended definitions of abstractions.

C. Scheduling the Unit

1. In Units 13 through 17 the students studied various ways of achieving emphasis; they focused on a rhetorical skill: how to make the form reflect the relative weight of the material. In this unit they turn to one of the purposes of exposition: defining. You might make this bridge for the students: "The rhetorical skills function within larger purposes. The purposes of exposition are few—to explain, to reason toward a conclusion, to support or refute a position, to define, to illustrate. We have met these purposes throughout the text; but now, in the next few units, we are going to concentrate on some of them, using the rhetorical skills we have studied, as well as some skills especially germane to the purposes under examination. Definition is the first of these expository purposes we are going to examine rather closely."
2. Defining is a form of classifying and is, therefore, essential to concept formation. To articulate, to make explicit the thought processes of concept formation, is helpful to the student at any point; to be conscious of how we form concepts and abstractions is a first step in critical thinking. The unit does, therefore, serve as an apt introduction to the

next three units, which emphasize various patterns of critical thinking. But the unit, because of its emphasis on a basic thinking process, could also be used at any appropriate juncture in the semester.

3. Because of the content of the unit selection, the unit could also be used as part of the critical study of the short story or the novel. The unit selection does define a basic critical term and understanding how to use the terms of criticism is an essential part of critical analysis.

I. MOTIVATING THE UNIT

A. Background—Author and Selection

1. AUTHOR: At the turn of the century, E. M. Forster (1879-   ) was a member of the famous "Bloomsbury Group," a loosely defined group of intellectual leaders of England, among whom were Bertrand Russell, Virginia Woolf, Lytton Strachey, and Maynard Keynes. The spiritual and intellectual leader of this group was G. E. Moore, the British ethical philosopher. His influence can be seen in the liberal-humanitarian cast of Forster's works, in Forster's interest in art as a way of life, and in Forster's insistence on the primacy of personal relations. Forster believes that the most basic human impulse is the desire of individuals to understand one another; he believes as well that it is the duty of each person to seek out his true nature and then pursue it fearlessly in spite of social censure, and he thinks the individual rather than the group must be our ultimate measuring-stick.

   Forster has had a rather curious career as a writer. Almost from the first regarded by critics as a serious writer of major importance, he received the highest critical acclaim with the publication of his fifth novel, *A Passage to India* (1924). This turned out to be his last novel, although he has published some essays, biographies, and travel pieces since. It is almost as if Forster is saying that he accomplished all he could with the novel form in *A Passage to India* and that there is therefore no justification for his writing any more novels. Possessing a mind of firm independence, distrustful of doctrines and abstractions, giving his first loyalties to individuals, Forster has gone his own way, indifferent to fame. Sensitive studies of his life and his work are Lionel Trilling's *E. M. Forster: A Critical Guidebook* (New Directions, 1943) and K. W. Gransden's *E. M. Forster* (Grove, 1962).

2. SELECTION: *Aspects of the Novel* (1927) is a title which aptly indicates the nature of the book: a series of penetrating observations on such "aspects" of the novel as story, people, plot, fantasy, prophecy, and pattern and rhythm. First given as a series of lectures, the book presents the novel from the point of view of the practicing novelist who is impatient with a systematic, exhaustive approach to the criticism of the form. Yet his brief book is an important critical text for any serious study of the novel. Although written in 1927, his definitions of critical

terms, as evidenced by the unit selection, are so lucid and so grounded in specifics that they are still viable. The definition of plot used as the unit selection occurs in the fifth chapter of the book. In an early chapter of the book Forster discusses the story-telling aspect of the novel, characters, and characterization. In the fifth chapter he turns to the difference between the novel and the drama (why Aristotle's dicta do not necessarily fit the novel) and to those elements that give the novel its art. Here the element of the plot becomes paramount; hence the definition which serves as a beginning point for a discussion of the imaginative constructing that taxes the intelligence and memory of the reader.

B. Setting the Stage

1. Definitions are all around us, and it might be interesting to introduce the unit by pointing out the constant need for definitions in a highly literate culture strongly influenced by mass media. The interpretive newscaster attempts to define the meaning of the policy of containment; a national news magazine attempts to explain the latest dance craze and in so doing defines the dances. A new play is produced on Broadway that does not quite fit the established genre; the reviewer attempts to define what kind of play it is (this may take up the major part of the review). Leonard Bernstein devotes a telecast to explaining what makes opera "grand"; he is fashioning a definition of grand opera. Certain events used to be known as "hip"; a different group of events were regarded as "beat"; then a whole new group of events were designated as "camp." "Camp" must be defined; it's an "in" term. Definitions appeared in *Partisan Review* (Fall, 1964) and *The New York Times Magazine* (March 21, 1965). Soon the topic will trickle down to *Life;* then the term will lose its "in" value. This process illustrates not only the intense demand for definitions but also the snobbishness inherent in vogue terms. Bring these or similar examples of definition to class; have the students supply examples of their own; indicate the necessity for knowing how to define.

2. Another way to approach the unit would be to confront the students with two different uses of the same word and then ask them what communication problems arise if the two uses are taken to have the same meaning. Example: "All men are created *equal.*" "X *equals* Y." What does "equal" mean in each instance? What problems arise if the two meanings are confused?

3. A third way to introduce the unit would be to put a high-level abstraction on the board, such as "democracy," "socialism," or "alienation," and have each student write a definition of the term. Then read enough definitions to illustrate the many different meanings given to the term and the necessity for establishing some ground rules for the process of defining.

III. TEACHING THE UNIT

A. General Points of Interest and Emphasis

1. It is important for the students to understand that this unit does not attempt to treat the processes of definition exhaustively. It familiarizes the student with the more common ways of developing an extended definition, ways that will serve him in most of the expository situations he encounters. The A-Level student in particular should, however, realize that definition as a subject is broader and more technical than the unit treatment; that the subject contains distinctions between real and nominal definitions, lexical and historical definitions, denotative and connotative definitions; that there are stipulative definitions and ostensive definitions, among others, and that there are such technical terms as *definiendum* and *definiens*. Texts that will serve as references for discussion of these items are Harold C. Martin's *The Logic and Rhetoric of Exposition* (rev. ed., Holt, 1963), Irving M. Copi's *Introduction to Logic* (2d ed., Macmillan, 1961), and R. T. Harris and J. L. Jarrett's *Language and Informal Logic* (McKay, 1956).

2. After the students have read Forster's definition of plot, ask them to identify the various ways he defines the term. Does he use just one method? two? three? How would you characterize them? This would be a preliminary discussion. Then have them discuss the aptness of his definition. Can they apply it to novels they have read: *Great Expectations, The Return of the Native, The Red Badge of Courage, The Catcher in the Rye, Lord of the Flies?* Here the students might profit from your reading to them the paragraphs on Aristotle and the difference between the novel and the drama that precede the definition in Forster's book. book.

3. An activity that the class could carry on concomitantly with their studying of the unit would be to collect definitions that they find in their current reading—in newspapers, magazines, or books. These could be put on the bulletin board, or the class could identify the techniques of definition used in each. Some could be used for criticism.

4. Some of the other prose models in the text that contain definitions or elements of definition are the excerpt from Orwell's "Such, Such Were the Joys..." (Unit 6), the excerpt from Chesterton's "The Ethics of Fairyland" (Unit 16), the excerpt from Laird's *The Miracle of Language* (Unit 19), and Mencken's "The Hope of Abolishing War" (Unit 20).

B. Special Observations for Levels A, B, and C

1. *Introductory Matter:* Ask the students to supply examples of their own that would fit the three occasions for definition. List these on the board for further reference. For a humorous example of another kind of occasion for definition—the stipulative definition—read the class the famous exchange from *Alice in Wonderland* between Alice and Humpty Dumpty about Humpty's making a word mean whatever he chooses it to mean.

- 2 *Practice 1. Levels A and C:* It is important that this Practice be done within the period so that students will have to rely on their own resources and will not resort to the dictionary. One of the purposes of the Practice is to have students experience difficulty in constructing genus-difference definitions. Are all the words usually defined in this fashion? "Courage" or "bravery," for example? How else might they be defined? By synonym? What are the limitations of this method? For the Level A students, you might want to introduce the terms *definiendum* and *definiens* here and use them as column headings on the board to identify the major terms of the definitions:

Definiendum	*Definiens*	
	(Genus)	(Difference)
a. a monarchy	*a.*	*a.*
b. a short story	*b.*	*b.*

Level B: This Practice lends itself to oral treatment. In any event, discuss the answers with the class; make certain they understand the difference between plot and story.

- 3. *Practice 2. Level A:* This Practice should enable the students to sharpen the definitions they created for Practice 1. If you have used the columnar scheme suggested above, you can add the new terms to the *definiendum* column and, with the help of the students, illustrate that only the difference need be added to the *definiens* column; each genus should fit two of the terms under *definiendum.*
  Level B: See suggestions for Levels A and C under Practice 1.
  Level C: Stress that the students use examples they are familiar with, examples they have experienced or observed, e.g., a specific kindness they have rendered or received, a story climax they remember vividly.

- 4. *Practice 3. Level A:* Discuss with the class possible specific examples that will help clarify the distinctions between the words of the same genus. For example, will just any monarchy do? What about the monarchy will have to be stressed? The point to be made in item **b.** is that the more abstract the term, the more difficult it is to pin down. You might review the abstraction ladder at this point.
  Level B: See suggestions for Level A under Practice 2.
  Level C: After the students complete this Practice, have each select the one complete definition he regards as his best work and revise it for evaluation. Read some of the best definitions to the class. This will be good preparation for the writing Problems.

- 5. *Practice 4. Level A:* After the students have finished this exercise, they will have complete but fragmented definitions for six terms. Have each student select his most promising definition and attempt to make it a coherent whole by adding appropriate transitions (refer them to Units 11 and 12). Then have some of the definitions read and discussed by the class.
  Level B: For item **a.**, suggest that the structures of the one-sentence sample plots reflect their different intentions. In the first, the king

comes at the beginning of the sentence; in the second, the queen comes at the beginning, and the king is not introduced until the very end. The first is syntactically simple: two brief declarative statements connected by a co-ordinate conjunction. The second is syntactically complex: a brief introductory declarative statement, followed by an interruptive but not exactly parenthetical clause (because the subordinate element following is tied to it, not to the opening declarative statement), in turn followed by a subordinate clause that contains a noun clause that is semantically probably the most important element in the sentence—all governed by complex time relationships. Here is a compact example of how form or structure reflects meaning.

You might ask the students if Forster is recommending the mystery or detective story. How would a work like *Lord Jim* fit into his scheme?

As for item **b.** suggest that the students use examples they are familiar with, examples they have experienced or observed.

- **6.** *Practice 5. Level A:* This Practice is intended to help the students bring together the techniques of definition they have been practicing separately in the preceding Practices. It is also a preparation for the writing Problems. Point out that the example contains more than just the three kinds of definition tied together with transition words; it contains a restatement, summary statements, and generalizations that lead to the next point. This discursiveness illustrates that an extended definition is not a mere mechanical putting together of different kinds of definition, but is governed by inherent demands of its own. The point for the students is: Do not just do the assignment; write a definition that will stand on its own.

  Level B: Use this as preparation for the writing Problems. After the students have completed the Practice, have each select the definition he believes contains the sharpest distinction and attempt to make it into a coherent whole by adding appropriate transitional elements (refer them to Units 11 and 12). Have the class discuss and criticize some of these revisions.

- **7.** *Problems 1 and 2. Levels A, B, and C:* Before the students do these Problems, have them review the processes studied. Need they confine themselves to the three techniques examined? Synonym may be useful also, and restatement may be appropriate. Have them compare the definitions they constructed throughout the Practices with dictionary definitions of the same words. Dictionaries of varying quality should be on hand. This exercise will help students understand the limitations of even good dictionaries as well as sharpen the genus-difference distinctions they made for their own definitions.

  C-level students will need help with these Problems. For Problem 1, work out through class discussion possible appropriate examples. This will help the students understand the definition supplied in the text. For Problem 2, through class discussion help the students understand "smugness," "indifference," and "perseverance."

IV. EVALUATING THE UNIT

Some rules for defining may help the students avoid the more obvious pitfalls:

A. Definitions should not be circular; genus and difference should not repeat any part of the term being defined, and genus-difference should be substitutable for the term being defined.

B. Examples should be concrete and specific and should help the reader distinguish the term being defined from closely related terms.

C. If possible, definitions should be affirmative rather than negative.

D. A definition should be suitable for the purpose it is to serve; an explanation of function, for example, should be directed to the intended audience and should not contain unnecessarily technical terms or terms that are on a higher level of abstraction than the term being defined.

These rules and the guidelines in the unit should give the students an adequate understanding of the standards by which their work will be judged. Probably one of the compositions written in response to the writing Problems would be sufficient for evaluating the students' work in the unit.

V. ADDITIONAL WRITING TOPICS

A. Today we hear increasing use of the phrase "to bear witness." While this is an ancient use of the word "witness," it is not the most common use today. Usually we think of someone witnessing something, of being a witness *to:* but more and more people are using the word in the sense of being a witness *for.* Write a composition in which you explain these two uses of "witness." Supply specific examples that help the reader understand the distinction between the two meanings. Explain clearly the purpose of being a witness *for.*

B. Here are a number of class words used to describe types of musical drama or entertainment: Musical Comedy, Operetta, Grand Opera, Revue, Comic Opera. Using these categories to help make distinctions, write a definition of Musical Comedy.

(*Note for Teacher:* See Leonard Bernstein's television script, "American Musical Comedy," in his *The Joy of Music,* Simon and Schuster, 1959.)

C. Write an essay in which you define the literary practice of foreshadowing. Include examples of foreshadowing from works you have read. Explain the artistic function of foreshadowing. Distinguish between effective and ineffective foreshadowing.

UNIT 19 — STATE AN ISSUE — MEET OBJECTIONS

Selection from *THE MIRACLE OF LANGUAGE*
by Charlton Laird

(Student Text—A-Level, p. 118; B-Level, p. 116; C-Level, p. 115)

I. PREPARING TO TEACH THE UNIT

A. Purposes of the Unit

1. To give students an understanding of some of the principles of sound and fair argument.
2. To illustrate how to define an issue.
3. To illustrate that considering opposing arguments is a necessary part of developing a thesis.
4. To examine the common types of evidence and the standards for judging evidence.

B. Skills Students Will Practice

1. Analyzing the assumptions of an argument.
2. Clarifying a general thesis by stating it more specifically, defining key terms, and making assumptions explicit.
3. Evaluating the reliability, relevance, and adequacy of the evidence supplied to support an argument.
4. Constructing an argument based on the principles of sound reasoning studied in the unit.

C. Scheduling the Unit

1. This unit places within the context of argumentation the skills of defining studied in the previous unit. The ability to define precisely is seen as one of the prerequisites of stating an issue clearly. The unit therefore follows logically from Unit 18. Moreover, as the unit isolates and defines the rudimentary elements of fair argument, it prepares for the critical analysis of Mencken's argument in Unit 20. Thus, the three units—18, 19, and 20—form a sequence, the latter two specifically directed at examining argumentation.

2. Students waste much effort attempting to determine what they want to say, developing false starts, and supporting unexamined opinions. There are a number of ways to combat these tendencies: writing and critically examining thesis statements, constructing outlines from which to write, determining the structure of the argument to be developed (see Josephine Miles's "Essay in Reason," *Educational Leadership*, February, 1962, pp. 311-314). This unit offers another way to help students overcome

wasted effort, for while it encourages taking sides, it illustrates how to avoid the shoddy development that results from overgeneralizing. The students are interested in the issues of the day, but can waste their efforts coping with them unless they have specific skills to think through to a reasonable conclusion.

3. As the unit selection focuses interest on the nature of language itself, the unit could be used to complement any work the class does on the history of language, the symbolic process, language structure, or language as a system. If *The Miracle of Language* is one of the class's texts, the unit could obviously be used as an extension of the text.

II. MOTIVATING THE UNIT

A. Background—Author and Selection

1. AUTHOR: Charlton Laird (1901-   ) is a professor of English at the University of Nevada. Author of fictional and scholarly works, his main interests in recent years have been historical linguistics, structural linguistics, and modern rhetoric. A tireless and stimulating writer, he has helped to make language study an entrancing subject. His writing has a zest and joy that enables the layman to see the drama in scholarly subjects. These qualities are exhibited to good advantage in *The Miracle of Language* (1953), a popular account of the history of language, particularly English, and of some of the major problems confronting contemporary language study. Among Laird's other books are *The World through Literature* (1951), *Laird's Promptory* (1948), *The Tree of Language* (with Helene Laird, 1957), and *A Writer's Handbook* (1964).

2. SELECTION: *The Miracle of Language* recounts in lively fashion the history of the English language——its place in the Indo-European language family, its beginnings, its vocabulary influences, its principles of change. It also contains chapters on the problems of phonology, morphology, syntax, lexicography, usage, and meaning. As Laird admits, his book is a popular account, but one that carefully avoids oversimplification and manages to communicate the fascination of language study. It is a must for anyone who wants a painless introduction to many of the topics now seriously considered in curriculum reformation.

   The account of the difficulties of determining how language was invented occurs at the beginning of Chapter 2 of the book. A brief essay in itself, it also serves as an introduction to an explanation of linguistic families, especially of the Indo-European family, and of the relationship of modern languages to one another and to protolanguages. Thus, the chapter works as far back to Og and his initial "Bup" as scholarly investigations will enable us to go.

B. Setting the Stage

1. One way to start this unit would be to engage the class in a discussion of an issue or a controversial statement, purposely starting with conclusions ("What's your opinion of . . . ?") and working backward to reasons and then to the answering of objections. The purpose here would be to illustrate how much confusion is created when the issue is not defined specifically and how difficult it is to answer objections when the boundaries of the discussion have not been agreed on and the evidence adduced has not been tested. The class could then turn to the unit as a way of eliminating some of this confusion. Possible topics for discussion would be local school issues, topical political issues, controversies generated from literary works studied by the class (e.g., "Is Hamlet mad?" "Is Lord Jim a coward?"), provocative statements from Bernard Shaw's "The Revolutionist's Handbook" suggested as the basis for Additional Writing Topics in Unit 13, or other statements from this source of contention, such as "The love of fairplay is a spectator's virtue, not a principal's"; "Those who minister to poverty and disease are accomplices in the two worst of all crimes"; and "It is dangerous to be sincere unless you are also stupid."

2. Another way to start the unit would be to put on the board some definitions of man—such as, "Man is a featherless biped"; "Man is a thinking reed"; and "Man is a languagized mammal"—and engage the students in a discussion of the appropriateness of the definitions. This procedure would tie in with the previous unit, emphasizing the necessity for selecting essential attributes in a genus-difference definition. It would also lead to interest in the centrality of language in human society and would be an indirect way of getting at the assumptions behind arguments, for our definition of man often underlies the position we take on social questions.

3. A variation on the above procedure would be to ask the students to write a definition of language or to write an explanation of how language was created. Have some of these definitions or explanations read for discussion and criticism by the class. Illustrate how difficult it is to get any sensible discussion when the key terms have not been defined, or when we have no evidence to adduce. Do we mean the spoken language or the written language? Do we mean language as a structural system or as a social instrument? This procedure will help to highlight some of the material to be studied and will lead to the unit selection.

4. Still another approach would be to take conflicting interpretations of a given event—say an action of the President praised by his party and damned by the opposition—and ask students to account for these conflicting interpretations. The action is the same. How, assuming the commentators are men of good will, can the assessments of the act be in such disagreement? What would have to be done to clear up the confusion? Then lead to the unit as a way of eliminating much confusion at the outset.

III. TEACHING THE UNIT

A. General Points of Interest and Emphasis

1. This unit is an introduction to argumentation and merely specifies some of the fundamental steps one must take if he wants to secure a reasonable hearing for his argument: defining the issue, supplying evidence, answering objections. The next unit takes up some of the formal ways of arguing: induction, deduction, analogy. You might at this point, however, wish to introduce the students to some of the other elements of argumentation, especially fallacious ways of arguing. Helpful references would be, in addition to those mentioned in the suggestions for teaching the previous unit, Richard Altick's *Preface to Critical Reading* (Holt, 1960) and Stuart Chase's *Guides to Straight Thinking* (Harper, 1956).

2. After reading the unit selection through with the students, ask them to define the issue. What is the argument about? Have them stick to the text. Ask them to point out the sentences in the first paragraph that help us understand what the issue is, what Laird is against. What is the key word in the first paragraph? How do they know it is the key word? This preliminary analysis will help prepare the students for following the analysis carried on in the body of the unit.

3. To generate involvement in the content of the unit selection, ask the students what they think the various theories (Ding-Dong, Ee-Ee, etc.) are. Capsule explanations of some are contained in the text. But the onomatopoeia in the theory names should help the students guess what the theories are. Brief explanations of the major theories are contained in Gerd Fraenkel's *What is Language?* (Ginn, 1965).

4. While the class is studying the unit, have the students bring examples of poorly defined arguments to class. Any number can be found in the letters-to-the-editor section of the daily newspaper. Students can then analyze for the benefit of the rest of the class the inadequacies of the statement of the issue: overgeneralizing, ambiguous key words, faulty assumptions.

5. Other unit selections that the students can examine for statement of issue and supplying of evidence are the excerpt from Orwell's "Such, Such Were the Joys..." (Unit 6), the excerpt from Stefansson's *The Standardization of Error* (Unit 7), the excerpt from Highet's *Man's Unconquerable Mind* (Unit 11), and Mencken's "The Hope of Abolishing War" (Unit 20).

B. Special Observations for Levels A, B, and C

1. *Introductory Matter:* The students will notice that the introductory paragraphs of the unit stress the necessity for defining in argumentation. This stress, of course, ties in with the previous unit, and it would be appropriate to review the methods of defining at the beginning of the unit. Ambiguous words are a major source of confusion in argumentation, and the way to clarity is precise defining. The students may also notice

that the introductory paragraph contains a definition; it would be appropriate to have them judge the efficacy of this definition according to the standards they studied in the previous unit.

- 2. **Practice 1. Levels A and B:** This exercise is rather difficult, and you should not expect your students to do a very thorough job of making the propositions clearer and more specific, especially if they do the exercise as an impromptu. The main difficulties will be with the key words—such as "government," "grammar," and "change"—and the assumptions. The key words they will tend to think of as understood. Give them some help by drawing out in discussion the various conceptions or misconceptions of, say, grammar (word classes, sentence parts, usage, punctuation). Then try to elicit some understanding about assumptions. There is an assumption about human nature behind the government proposition and the changing human nature proposition that should not be too difficult to draw out. Discussion and analysis of the paragraphs the students write should increase the students' understanding of the requisite steps in stating an issue clearly.

  Level C: The questions should help the students expand the proposition into a more specific statement. Indicate to them that the expanded statement will be more than one sentence. They may have trouble explaining what they mean by education; this may be too difficult an abstraction for them to cope with. Their definition will, in any case, be implicit in their examples. Before they write, discuss and put on the board a few concrete examples of each key word.

- 3. **Practice 2. Level A:** The word to clear up in item **a.** is "free"; it means of course free *from* ignorance. For item **b.** the question to ask is "How?" Refer the students to Hayakawa's comments on "truth" in Unit 12 and to Russell's observations on the difficulties of changing imaginative constructions (Unit 10).

  Level B: The issue at stake is the value of imagination and sympathy. The key word to clear up is "sentimental."

  Level C: This Practice is an extension of Practice 1 and allows the students to express their opinions and to support them with reasons. In so doing, however, they may have to recast the paragraphs they wrote for the first Practice. To avoid repetition, they could confine the first paragraph to explaining what the question means and to defining the key terms.

- 4. **Practice 3. Levels A, B, and C:** Why, first of all, would anthropologists want to find a primitive language? After answering this question, the students should not have much trouble with the analysis. They can use the analysis of Laird's second paragraph as an example. What does Laird mean by "elaborate"? Why is the decaying of the languages of primitive people important?

- 5. **Practice 4. Levels A, B, and C:** The students will not be able to answer some of the questions with anything near certainty because, for one thing, they do not know enough about the subject. Make it clear, however, that they can at least depend on his examples, and they can determine the concreteness of these. Get them to explain what they would have to do to test the evidence adequately. Relevance is not in question here, but reliability and adequacy are. The authority is mostly Laird's, although he does refer to Herder. Ask the students how they could test Laird's authority.

- 6. *Practice 5. Levels A and B:* This is a warm-up for the writing Problems. Have the students do the Practice as an impromptu, and then discuss and criticize some of their papers with emphasis on the principles of argumentation studied.

- 7. *Problem 1. Levels A, B, and C:* Before the students write their analyses, review the techniques of defining, the means of specifying (see Unit 5), the kinds of evidence, and the tests for evidence. In the Level A and B passages there are assumptions about correctness in speech and naturalness; in the Level C passage there is an assumption about taste. You may want to explore these a bit before the students write. A good way to get at assumptions, incidentally, is to show the students a series of cartoons (ones from *The New Yorker* work well) and ask them what assumptions about human nature lie behind the jokes.

- 8. *Problem 2. Levels A, B, and C:* The unit has led to this composition assignment, and the students should regard their essays as a proof of their understanding of the unit. Give them ample time to write the essays. Discuss the suggested topics. What, for example, is meant by " 'rules' of grammar"? If they want to write on topics of their own, have them first write a statement of their issue and their position on it together with an outline of the rest of the essay. Have the students determine at the outset the kinds of evidence they will have to supply to support their positions. It may be that some will find themselves trying to support positions for which they cannot get adequate or reliable evidence.

IV. EVALUATING THE UNIT

The students should probably be evaluated primarily on the compositions they write in response to Problem 2. The review before the Problems and the directions to Problem 2 should give the students ample indication of the standards by which their papers will be judged:

Is the issue stated specifically?
Are the key words defined so that their meaning is not ambiguous?
Are assumptions about purpose, function, and essence clearly understood?
Is the writer's position supported with evidence?
Are fallacies avoided?
Can the evidence be verified?
Does the writer consider evidence that conflicts with his view?
Is the essay a reasoning toward, a thinking through?

V. ADDITIONAL WRITING TOPICS

A. A controversial clause of the Fifth Amendment of the United States Constitution declares that a witness shall not be compelled to testify against himself. Write an essay in which you explain the meaning of this clause, attempt to account for its intention, and explain why it is controversial. Apply it to various specific situations: testifying at a criminal trial, testifying before a grand jury, testifying before a Congressional committee. Defend or attack its use.

B. Henry Ford said, "History is bunk." On the other hand, Machiavelli said, "Wise men say, and not without reason, that whoever wishes to foresee the future must consult the past; for human events ever resemble those of preceding times. This arises from the fact that they are produced by men who have been, and ever will be, animated by the same passions, and thus they must necessarily have the same results." Write an essay in which you attempt to explain how these two conflicting views on the value of history could exist (with Ford's comment, you do not have much to work on). What could Ford mean by "history"? What assumptions are behind each observation? Supply, if you can, specific events that would illuminate each view. With which view do you agree? Support your agreement with reasons and evidence.

C. "Do you think that the things people make fools of themselves about are any less real and true than the things they behave sensibly about? They are more true: they are the only things that are true."

—George Bernard Shaw

Write an essay in which you, first, expand this observation so that it is specific and the key words are defined (remember Hayakawa's comments on "truth" in Unit 12), then support or attack the observation by applying it to concrete situations that will illustrate its validity or lack of validity. Whichever position you take, explain why the opposing position is inadequate.

UNIT 20 — REASON TOWARD A CONCLUSION

Selection from "*The Hope of Abolishing War*," from
MINORITY REPORT by H. L. Mencken

(Student Text—A-Level, p. 125; B-Level, p. 124; C-Level, p. 121)

I. PREPARING TO TEACH THE UNIT

A. Purposes of the Unit

1. To illustrate how to use the argument from analogy.
2. To illustrate how to argue inductively.
3. To illustrate how to argue deductively.
4. To help students understand the interdependence of these three forms of argument.

B. Skills Students Will Practice

1. Analyzing and evaluating the applicability of analogies.
2. Using analogies to support a position.
3. Constructing generalizations based on an inductive process of thought.
4. Criticizing faulty inductive arguments.
5. Constructing deductive (syllogistic) arguments.
6. Evaluating the validity of deductive (syllogistic) arguments.
7. Using the skills of analogy, induction, and deduction to construct an essay defending an argumentative position.

C. Scheduling the Unit

1. This unit follows naturally from Unit 19. Unit 19 helps students learn how to set up an argument, and it identifies some of the basic requirements of fair arguing. This unit identifies and explains three formal methods of arguing and therefore is a logical extension of the previous unit.
2. Like Unit 19, this unit can be used at any point in the semester when the students are experiencing unusual difficulty supporting their theses or defending their positions. Students need to know how to evaluate opposing views and conflicting arguments, or they might fall into the complacent mindless habit of feeling that one opinion is as good as another, a habit which is doubly fatuous: fearing to criticize an opinion because "every man's opinion should be respected" or dismissing an opposing view because "it's just your opinion." From this unit students will learn some of the skills that will help them evaluate the validity of arguments.

146

3. Many composition courses include units on logic in which students study directly such topics as categorical propositions, the forms and rules of the syllogism, scientific reasoning, and logical fallacies. This unit could, of course, form part of the class's study of logic.

4. If you generate composition work in your class by means of topical discussions, you might very well make this unit part of the discussion of the possibility of abolishing large-scale war. Everybody, of course, is against war; but until recent times few have seriously entertained the possibility of outlawing it. Walter Millis has written a number of articles for *Saturday Review* and other journals describing the procedures for and consequences of outlawing war as a means of settling disputes. And Herman Kahn has calculated rather precisely the cost—in human, natural, and civilized resources—of conducting a thermonuclear war. The subject has much topical interest and might be one you could wish the class to consider.

II.   MOTIVATING THE UNIT

A. Background—Author and Selection

1. AUTHOR: H. L. Mencken (1880-1956) started his career as a newspaperman for the Baltimore *Herald*. From 1906 on he contributed regularly to the Baltimore *Sun*. He also wrote satirical criticism for *Smart Set*, and in 1924 he and George Jean Nathan founded the *American Mercury*. It soon became one of the most influential social and literary journals of the time. In contrast to the present form of the *Mercury* (Mencken left in 1933), it advocated the *avant garde* and acidly criticized the *status quo* and the complacent conservatism of those in power.

   Many of Mencken's magazine and newspaper writings have been collected and published in book form. Perhaps the most famous of these books are his *Prejudices*, six books issued as a series from 1919 to 1927. Among other books by Mencken are critical biographies of Nietzsche and Shaw as well as his three-volume autobiography (*Happy Days*, 1940, *Newspaper Days*, 1941, and *Heathen Days*, 1943). The anthology *Mencken Chrestomathy* (1949) contains a wide selection from his writings.

   Mencken had a genius for exposing cant, hypocrisy, and fatuous self-righteousness. Politicians, fundamentalists, pompous academicians, and the middle class were his natural targets. He coined the term *booboisie* to express his contempt for the middle class. His writings championed the new realism of the early 20th century and paved the way for such writers as Theodore Dreiser, Sherwood Anderson, and Sinclair Lewis. He was the Dr. Johnson of his time and helped launch a new age of social realism in American letters.

   Mencken also had a scholarly interest in American English as a language distinct from British English. His *The American Language*, first published in 1919, revised a number of times, and recently edited by Raven McDavid, Jr. and reissued, is a classic in the field.

2. SELECTION: *Minority Report* (1956), the book from which the brief discussion of the hope of abolishing war is taken, is a selection of observations from Mencken's notebooks. In the Preface, Mencken explains that from the outset of his career as a writer, he had the habit of setting down notions as they came to him. These served as the basis for innumerable books and articles, but he always had a greater number of notes than he had time to develop. Toward the end of his life, therefore, he selected a number of observations from his notebooks for publication in book form. Familiar targets in the book are relations between the sexes, the absurdities of the law, the inanities of government, and the unrealities of religion. War is a recurring subject in the book with Mencken usually trying to relate its occurrence to innate propensities in man. The book has no noticeable organizational scheme; the observation on abolishing war is entry 76 of a total 432 entries, and it is immediately preceded by an entry on the New Deal and followed by an entry on the ugliness of some art. It is the type of book, therefore, that one reads a bit at a time. Mencken's observations are, as usual, provocative, stimulating, and contentious.

B. Setting the Stage

1. One way to start this unit would be to conduct a class discussion on ways of arguing. What *forms* do arguments take? Students will eventually come up with comparison (*this* is like *that; that* doesn't work, so *this* won't), with the scientific method (we gather evidence to reach a generalization or to support a hypothesis), and with arguing from a principle (we identify a standard or a criterion and then relate the action or event to it). This abstract characterization of the forms of arguing can then be given concreteness by your asking the students to take the compositions they wrote in response to Problem 2 of Unit 19 and identify their arguments as examples of analogy, induction, or deduction. Some specimens could be discussed by the class. Does the analogy hold up? Is enough evidence adduced? Is the principle dubious? This discussion and analysis will generate interest in how to judge the efficacy of such arguments and will indirectly illustrate the interdependence of these forms of arguing. The class can then turn to the unit for clarification and specific analysis.

2. A slightly different approach would be to take an editorial from the school newspaper and have the class analyze its arguments. Are comparisons used and for what purpose? Do they fit? What evidence is cited? What conclusions are derived from the evidence? What principles are explicitly or implicitly used to support the recommendations given in the editorial? The students may find the editorial wanting. The forms of arguing can be identified, and the students can then turn to the unit to learn how to use these forms effectively.

3. Another way to approach the unit would be to lead a class discussion

related to the content of the unit selection: one on the causes and preventions of war. What are the causes of war? economic (the Marxian view)? genetic (Mencken's view)? other? Is war inevitable? Can it be abolished? What would this mean? What does the history of our own country tell us? The students can call on their reading of such works as *The Red Badge of Courage, A Farewell to Arms, All Quiet on the Western Front, The Cruel Sea,* and *The Caine Mutiny.* Aside from Mencken's observations, background material would be the series of articles by Walter Millis in *Saturday Review,* views by Edward Teller and Herman Kahn, and the essay on war by Edmund Wilson in his *A Piece of My Mind* (Farrar, Straus, 1956). This approach has more than the usual justification in that exception is taken to Mencken's view in the body of the unit, and the unit asks the students to evaluate Mencken's position.

III. TEACHING THE UNIT

A. General Points of Interest and Emphasis

1. It is important for the students to realize that the unit *introduces* them to the three forms of argument: analogy, induction, and deduction. They will, however, still have much to learn about the forms after they have finished the unit (another instance of education's being a continuous process). For example, they will still need to learn that analogy never demonstrably *proves* anything; its purpose is to illuminate and clarify, but it does not constitute proof. To understand this limitation, students need to know what demonstrable proof is. Also, we seldom practice induction in a random fashion; we usually gather evidence to verify a working hypothesis. And deductive statements have certain prescribed forms and logical limitations that the student will eventually have to study. If you wish to take up these aspects of reasoning in a somewhat more formal manner than the unit does, the section on "Patterns of Clear Thinking" in Richard Altick's *Preface to Critical Reading* (Holt, 1960) and Manuel Bilsky's *Logic and Effective Argument* (Holt, 1956) will serve as good references.

2. After your introductory discussion of the forms of arguing or the possibility of outlawing war, have the students read through the Mencken selection and conduct a preliminary analysis of his methods of arguing. What view is Mencken opposing? What is the form of the argument he is attacking (remember the fallacy, faulty analogy)? How does he organize his attack? What kind of reasoning does he use? comparison? specific evidence? general principles? Where? Anticipate writing Problem 2 by asking the students what they would have to do to refute Mencken's arguments. In this fashion the students will get an overview of the unit and the specific elements of argumentation they will analyze.

3. Here, as in other units, you might encourage the students to bring to class examples from the popular press and elsewhere of material exemplifying the emphases of the unit. Illustrative analogies and inductive

and deductive arguments found by various students could be analyzed and criticized by the class.

4. In lieu of the students' finding examples of the forms of argument in current journalistic material, they can examine the following unit selections for analogy, induction, and deduction: the excerpt from Saint-Exupéry's *Wind, Sand, and Stars* (Unit 8), the excerpt from Highet's *Man's Unconquerable Mind* (Unit 11), and the excerpt from Chesterton's "The Ethics of Fairyland" (Unit 16).

B. Special Observations for Levels A, B, and C

1. *Introductory Matter:* The chart on the process of reasoning should make clear to the students that while analogy is a form of comparison, it is also a form of classification. A little prodding should help the students recall how crucial classification is to thinking. Naming, concept formation, metaphor, control of language—all depend on classification. And the students should readily recall how often they have dealt with classification in previous units—in Units, 7, 8, 9, 16, and 18, for example. The students can test the applicability of the chart by analyzing how they came to use and do use some of their cant expressions, e.g., "a square," "a creep," "it's tough." Or they can keep a journal of the steps in reasoning they go through in the writing of an essay.

● 2. *Practice 1. Levels A, B, and C:* The point about exaggerating or over-extending analogies is, of course, a way of emphasizing that analogies do not constitute proof and a way of cautioning against false analogies. A familiar example from the political world is "Where there's smoke, there's fire." The implicit or explicit analogy is: Smoke is to fire as accusation, suspicion, or innuendo is to proven guilt. Fire, of course, has very little relation to treason, subversion, or improbity. The proportional method of stating an analogy may be helpful to the students. For example, the analogy in item **b.** of Level A could be summarized as: Exercise is to physical health as studying mathematics is to mental health. In Levels A and B, where the student is asked to criticize the analogies, the point to stress is that the proportion is extended to include characteristics not in the two ratios; significant dissimilarities are overlooked.

   Level C: Discuss the students' explanations. Is **a.** or **b.** more loosely reasoned?

● 3. *Practice 2. Level A:* You may need to point out to the students that they need not quote the lines by Pope or Emerson in their paragraphs; they need only use the ideas stated in the quotations. These are not meant to be valid analogies; discussion of the students' paragraphs should clarify the distinctions between natural functions and socially organized functions and between lack of comprehension due to genius and misunderstanding caused by incompetence.

   Level B: There are implied syllogisms in the analogies here. You may want to return to these items after the class has completed section **C.**

Students should be able to draw on their understanding of overgeneralizing and the difference between an essential and an accidental attribute (definition) when they come to criticize the conclusions they are forced to draw.

Level C: After doing this exercise, the students should have a sound understanding of the dangers of assuming that because two items are alike in some respects, they are alike in all respects. The students may think item **b.** a good idea. It will take a little persuading to get them to acknowledge the differences between students and the electorate.

- 4. *Practice 3. Levels A and B:* If the students restrict themselves to drawing a universal conclusion, they are likely to concentrate on the innocuous. Suggest that they can draw conclusions of the "most" sort. Then they can entertain such propositions as "Students of this class are conformists"; "Parents of adolescents propel their children into social maturity." Some discussion of possible topics before the students begin writing will be helpful.

  Level C: The point to be stressed here is that the sampling is not large enough.

- 5. *Practice 4. Level A:* Item **a.**—restricted sampling; fallacy of ambiguity ("instructed," "unique"). Item **b.**—accidental attribute. Item **c.**—no necessary connection; form of *post hoc* fallacy and of "one cause" fallacy.

  Level B: Item **a.**—restricted sampling. Item **b.** restricted sampling; causes and essential attributes need to be specified. Item **c.**—accidental attribute.

  Level C: Item **a.**—restricted sampling; fallacy of the single cause. Item **b.**—restricted sampling (baby boom may have been confined to three non-sequential years); "more" not specified (may not be numerically significant).

- 6. *Practice 5. Level A:* Item 1—Conclusion: C is not B. Example: No right-thinking person is seriously influenced by television commercials; Doris Jones is a right-thinking person; therefore, she is not seriously influenced by television commercials. Item 2—This need not be confusing; it means the same as "No A is B." A three-part verbal argument could be: Spiders are not insects. The black widow is a spider. Therefore, the black widow is not an insect. Or, more concretely, because it permits reliance on personal observation: Spiders do not have six legs. This crawling thing has six legs. Therefore this crawling thing is not a spider. Item 3—this is the same as the example; the A and B are merely transposed. Example: All metals are elements; all iron is metal; therefore, iron is an element.

  Level B: Examples are provided for items **a.** and **c.** and the students should have no trouble with them. Item **b.** should be handled the same way as item 2 in Level A. In addition, it means the same as item **c.** and, therefore, the example and diagram for "No A is B" will help the students work out their sentences.

  Level C: Conclusion: Therefore, a world court would not be an effective legal system. Some leads for item **b.**: World courts could be backed by force (e.g., Korean War). Judges in city, county, state, and Federal courts have personal interests and local loyalties; yet the legal system seems to be effective.

- 7. **Practice 6. Level A:** Example of another deductive argument from Mencken's essay: To be effective, any legal system must be backed by force; a world court would not be backed by force; therefore, a world court would not be an effective legal system.

  Level B: Item **a.**—same problem as in the example: "tools" is undistributed (there can be tools that are not shovels), called fallacy of illicit major term. The minor premise is incorrectly stated; if it were reversed: "All tools are shovels," the conclusion would be an example of valid reasoning, although untrue. To make the argument hold, we need a new minor premise, such as "This object is a pencil." Item **b.**—the conclusion is not valid because the major premise does not state that only trees are green. The middle term is undistributed, i.e., all members of the class *green* are not included in the premises. Strictly speaking, nothing follows from these two premises.

  Level C: Item **a.**—There can be some Englishmen that are not Americans. Item **b.**—fallacy of the illicit major term; i.e., there can be vehicles of transportation that are not trains.

- 8. **Problem 1. Levels A, B, and C:** Review the section on analogies before the students do this assignment. Remind them that analogies are useful for clarifying but that they do not conclusively prove anything. Taking *this* to be exactly like *that* is what leads to faulty thinking; there are always differences. Have the students review the limitations they found in the analogies in Practices 1 and 2. After the students have written their paragraphs, have the class discuss briefly the limitations they found in the analogies.

- 9. **Problem 2. Levels A, B, and C:** Here you can have the class return to the discussion of the content of the unit selection. Bring other writers on the topic (Millis, Wilson, etc.), and have the class outline supporting and opposing views. These you can list on the board so that the students will have a skeleton to follow. Inasmuch as analogy is a weak form of argument, caution them to emphasize inductive and deductive arguments.

IV. EVALUATING THE UNIT

What the students accomplish in this unit can influence their writing from now on. It is a little artificial, therefore, to use one composition (Problem 2) to evaluate their achievement, but it is pedagogically efficient. One way to help determine how well the students have assimilated the material in the unit is to have them turn in a gloss of the forms of argument they used along with the composition. As for the standards by which the compositions will be judged, these should be clear to the students from the admonitions in the unit:

Do not everextend an analogy.

Analogies do not constitute proof.

Avoid overgeneralizing and insufficient sampling in inductive arguments.

In deductive arguments the terms (A, B, and C) must not be ambiguous and must be used consistently.

Conclusions must not be greater than the premises will allow.

Remember, deductive arguments may be valid, that is, correctly formed, but still not true. The premises and conclusion must be related to fact.

V. ADDITIONAL WRITING TOPICS

A. Write an analysis of the following famous extended analogy from John Donne's "Meditation 17." What is man compared to? What analogy is rejected? What part of the analogy is developed? What conclusion is arrived at? Try to schematize the relations, e.g., man is to mankind as .... Put man and references to man in one column and the items he is compared to in another column.

No man is an island, entire of itself; every man is a piece of the continent, a part of the main. If a clod be washed away by the sea, Europe is the less, as well as if a promontory were, as well as if a manor of thy friend's or of thine own were. Any man's death diminishes me because I am involved in mankind, and therefore never send to know for whom the bell tolls; it tolls for thee.

B. A friend of yours from a foreign land is taking a course in sociology and needs some firsthand information on American family habits. He writes you requesting information on the following topics:

How are decisions arrived at in the family?

What activities do families engage in together?

What activities, if any, are regarded as strictly adult pastimes?

At what age are children allowed to date?

What restrictions, if any, are put on dating?

What punishments are inflicted for the breaking of family rules?

What responsibilities are given to adolescents in the family?

From your friends and acquaintances gather evidence on these topics. Put your findings in the form of a report to your friend, drawing those conclusions that seem warranted from the evidence.

C. Select a lengthy advertisement from a magazine like *The New Yorker* or *U.S. News and World Report*. Write an analysis of the advertisement in which you show how analogy and deductive reasoning are used. What appeals to general principles are made? What fallacies do you find? Explain them. Do you find any instances of name-calling, overgeneralizing, appealing to authority or to prestige, card-stacking, and jumping on the band wagon? Explain them.

UNIT 21 — USE SOURCE MATERIALS RESPONSIBLY

Selection, *"The Evil that Lurks in the Heart"*-
Granville Hicks reviews *THE SPIRE*
by William Golding

(Student Text—A-Level, p. 137; B-Level, p. 136; C-Level, p. 132)

I. PREPARING TO TEACH THE UNIT

A. Purposes of the Unit

1. To encourage students who use source materials to consider the demands of their audiences.
2. To caution students about their responsibilities to the sources they use when composing papers.
3. To explore the ways writers organize material from written sources to meet a particular purpose.

B. Skills Students Will Practice (while using source materials)

1. Assessing their responsibilities to their sources.
2. Selecting material from their sources to meet the demands of their controlling idea.
3. Suiting topics to the needs of their audiences.
4. Writing a paper based on information from source materials, giving close attention to audience, source, and idea.

C. Scheduling the Unit

1. This unit is not part of a larger sequence; it can be scheduled independently at any time. Since its subject is the use of written source materials, the unit would be an appropriate introduction to a writing assignment that requires some research—a formal paper or a book review.
2. Because the emphasis in this unit is on reporting information accurately and objectively, it might best follow units that provide the preliminary or utilitarian skills for handling source materials: Unit 7, "Compress and Expand Your Information"; Units 1 and 2, which stress economy in writing; and Units 18, 19, and 20, all of which deal with the handling of ideas through reasoning. (See also suggestions in II, B, 2)
3. If you reserve a place in your course of study for stress on the problem of basing writing on sources of information outside the writer, you might —in addition to the uses suggested in points 1. and 2.—teach this unit in connection with the material in some college casebooks in controlled research published by various companies, or with one or more of the new *Casebooks in Objective Writing* now being published by Ginn expressly for use with high school students.

II. MOTIVATING THE UNIT

A. Background—Author and Selection

1. AUTHOR: Granville Hicks, who is currently most widely known for his weekly book reviews in *Saturday Review*, was born in Exeter, New Hampshire, in 1901. He graduated from Harvard in 1923, continuing for two additional years at Harvard Theological School. In 1925 he decided against the ministry and accepted a position at Smith College, where he taught Biblical Literature and English until 1928. During these years he was also literary editor for *Universalist Leader*, and the reading he did for this periodical stimulated his first book, *Eight Ways of Looking at Christianity* (1926). In 1929, after he had received his M.A. from Harvard, he became assistant professor of English at Rensselaer Polytechnic Institute. In 1936-1937, a Guggenheim Fellowship enabled him to study recent British literature, after which he served as Counsellor in American Civilization at Harvard in 1938 and 1939.

   Hicks has contributed articles to many periodicals—*Mercury, Forum, Nation*. He was literary consultant to *The New Leader* from 1951 to 1958, and he has been a contributing editor for *Saturday Review* since 1958. His published works include *Only One Storm* (1942), *Behold Trouble* (1944), *Small Town*, (1946), *There Was a Man in Our Town* (1952), and *Where We Came Out* (1954); he edited *The Letters of Lincoln Steffens* with Ella Winter, (1938), and *The Living Novel* (1957).

2. SELECTION: The selection is printed in its entirety from the April 18, 1964, *Saturday Review*, where Granville Hicks's "Literary Horizons" appears every week. Often, as in this case, "Literary Horizons" is limited to the review of one book; but sometimes Hicks discusses a common theme that involves many books, or he delineates a movement in contemporary literature or surveys the novels of a year's time. His critical views reflect the influence of sociologists and impressionistic critics. At Smith he was influenced by Newton Arvin and consequently Van Wyck Brooks. *Time* has called him a "Yankee moralist." He is one of the group of liberal literary critics—the line that begins with V. L. Parrington. This review is typical of his criticism—clear, beautifully ordered, persuasive.

B. Setting the Stage

1. If the class has just finished reading *Lord of the Flies*, a discussion of Golding would lead naturally into Granville Hicks's review. This unit involves so much reference to the review that it would undoubtedly have more meaning to the students if they were familiar with at least one of Golding's novels.

2. This unit would serve usefully as a general preparation for any composition of length that requires the use of written source materials. Units 10, 11, and 12—which concern paragraph development and transitions

155

between paragraphs—will also help students compose long papers and reports. These three units, then, might be reviewed briefly as a way of getting into the special skill of this unit.

III. TEACHING THE UNIT

A. General Points of Interest and Emphasis

In the **B.** section of "The Craft of Writing" there is a brief reference to plagiarism. If the class has not already had thorough exposure to the ground rules of exactly what constitutes plagiarism, this part of the unit should be given fuller treatment than it receives here. All students know that word-for-word copying constitutes plagiarism unless the source passage is put in quotation marks (or indented) as well as footnoted. Many of them do not, however, realize that one has to footnote a paraphrased idea that he has borrowed from another author and that even unusual metaphors or striking phrases or special terms must be footnoted when they are borrowed. You might have the students compare the treatment that various style manuals give this important subject.

B. Special Observations for Levels A, B, and C

1. *Introductory Matter. Levels A, B, and C:* Although responsibility to audience is treated first in this unit, audience is not the writer's fundamental consideration. Writers should, of course, give first and primary attention to their content——and in this case, the content is a combination of the printed source and the writer's controlling idea, which is his interpretation of the source. This duality of content poses a delicate question for a student writer: He must be true both to himself and to his source and, in addition, he must be aware that his audience may include persons who will have read his sources.

   These facts will place a definite strain on those students who have frequently given no thought at all to their audience, who have done most of their writing to meet course requirements, and who have been in the habit of writing only for the impersonal red pencil that makes marginal notes and affixes the grade. It may help them here to learn to visualize and be consciously concerned with the minds that receive their communication.

- 2. *Practice 1. Level A:* You may wish to have students make notes on the questions and then compare answers in discussion.

   a. There are almost unlimited answers to this question—for the entire essay is intended for a well-read audience. Hicks assumes that his readers are familiar with Golding's works (paragraphs, 1, 9, 10); he develops his essay around the idea of inherent evil—certainly a difficult topic (paragraphs 1, 8, 9, 10); he expects his audience to understand phrases like "respect for human limitations" (paragraph 4), "to see people as people, not as instruments" (paragraph 4), "the given nature of man" (paragraph 8) "faithless *homo sapiens*" (paragraph 9).

b. Ask students how this review handles plot, the key to meeting the needs of both the readers and nonreaders of the novel.

Level B:

a. Golding's other books are mentioned in paragraphs 1, 9, and 10; his philosophy is mentioned in the same places and in paragraph 8.

b. Paragraph 10, and perhaps by implication, paragraph 1 make judgments.

c. See Practice 1, Level A, question **a.** above.

d. See Practice 1, Level A, question **b.** above.

Level C:

a. See Practice 1, Level A, question **a.** above.

b. Paragraphs 2, 3, 4, 5, 7 (approximately 60 per cent) refer to plot events directly or indirectly.

c. The idea is summarized in Forster's comment and in the closing sentence in paragraph 1.

- 3. *Practice 2. Level A.*

  a. If any students have read *The Spire*, it would be particularly interesting to hear them discuss this question. But it will also be interesting to hear the responses to the Practice by those who have read only the unit selection.

  b. Students should consider their different teachers and whether their demands vary, their school publications, the letters-to-the-editor they have written, and their personal letters (and here is where audience can really make a difference). Some students may ask why the audience factor is not made a part of every paper they are asked to write.

  Level B:

  b. People who have done very little reading would still be interested in Jocelin's fanaticism. One could compare Jocelin to historical fanatics—in politics, religion, and science.

  Level C: See Levels A and B above. You may want to conduct a preliminary discussion of the requirements of the different audiences listed.

- 4. *Practice 3. Level A:*

  a. Hicks discusses Golding's central theme in paragraphs 1, 8 and 9; he states the theme of *The Spire* in paragraph 2 and refers to it also in paragraphs 4 and 5.

  b. Jocelin is described in paragraphs 2, 3, 4, 5, 6, and 7; minor characters are described in paragraphs 4 and 7.

  c. The plot is given deftly in paragraphs 2, 3, 4, 5, 7, but the interest is character, not plot.

  d. Setting is mentioned in paragraph 2.

  e. Point of view is the subject of paragraph 6.

  f. Paragraphs 1, 9 and 10, refer to Golding's other works.

  g. Evaluation occurs in paragraph 10. Paragraph 6 mentions the "particular power" of the novel; paragraph 7 quotes passages from a "fine scene."

  h. Style is discussed in paragraphs 6 and 10; paragraphs 4 and 7 quote conversations, and paragraph 2 gives us a passage from the beginning of the novel.

  Level B and C: See Practice 2, Level A, question **b.**

- 5. *Practice 4. Level A:* Students will profit from close examination of this remarkably well-knit review. The last sentence of paragraph 1 states the controlling idea: "The preoccupation with evil is reflected in everything he has written." References to this theme occur in *every* paragraph except 3—and perhaps even there with the mention of Jocelin's tensions (which are the result of his evil passion).
  Levels B and C: See Practice 3, Level A.
- 6. *Practice 5. Level A:* The first passage, from a review by Nigel Dennis in *The New York Times Book Review*, April 19, 1964, leads one to expect a discussion of style, the compression and energy in this novel. This first paragraph does not, however, state the theme of the review, which concerns primarily the symbolic character of the novel.

  The second passage is from Richard P. Brickner's review in the May 23, 1964, issue of *The New Republic*. These two first paragraphs lead us to expect a discussion of symbolism, a comparison of Jocelin to Ahab, and an unfavorable judgment of the novel. All three of these expectations are fulfilled in the review. You may want to read and discuss several of the student paragraphs, stressing the reasons they advance for choosing their particular controlling ideas.
  Levels B and C: See Practice 4, Level A. Discuss the student paragraphs comparing the varying choices of particular paragraphs—any one of the sequence of paragraphs 4 through 9 may be chosen.
- 7. *Problems 1 and 2. Levels A, B, and C:* If all the students write on the same book, you could duplicate the best review and give it the same kind of analysis that you have given Hicks's review. If the review is good enough, this would be a profitable experience for the class. In any event, it should be profitable to devote perhaps a full class discussion to the questions and directions in Problem 1 before proceeding to Problem 2. Or, instead of discussion, this can be a work period with individual questions being answered on a person-to-person or small-group basis.

IV. EVALUATING THE UNIT

Students could compose a list of evaluation questions while they are working on Problem 1. Such a list (assuming that the audience is their English class and that all students have read the book) might read as follows:

A. Did the review interest the audience? (Did it avoid too much elaboration on plot? Did it present ideas of substance? Did it lead the audience to think beyond the book?)

B. Did the writer do justice to the book? Was the source reported accurately and interpreted creditably?

C. Was there a controlling idea that gave the review a coherent organization?

158

V. ADDITIONAL WRITING TOPICS

A. Select a novel with which you are very familiar. Read two reviews. (Consult periodicals such as *The New Republic, Time, Saturday Review, The New York Review of Books, The New York Times Book Review,* and *The New Yorker.*) Write an analysis in which you compare the treatment of the novel in these two reviews. State your preference and give reasons for it.

B. Using the same novel, write a theme in which you explore the different ways you would discuss this book if your audience happened to be: (1) your history teacher, (2) a person who has read very little, (3) a person who has read widely, (4) a person who has written several novels, (5) a psychologist, (6) your twelve-year-old brother.

C. Select a topic for which you might find several sources of information, e.g., the right of students to demonstrate on or off campus, or changing recreational habits in your community. Read as much pertinent source material as you can find in two hours. Then develop a controlling idea and write a paper which will evidence your responsibility to your sources, your purpose, and your audience.

UNIT 22 — COMBINE THE FORMS OF WRITING

Selection from *THE IMMENSE JOURNEY*
by Loren Eiseley

(Student Text—A-Level, p. 145; B-Level, p. 143; C-Level, p. 140)

I. PREPARING TO TEACH THE UNIT

A. Purposes of the Unit

1. To make the student aware that the traditional "four forms of discourse" —narration, description, exposition and argumentation—do not appear as separate entities in normal writing.
2. To show that two or more of the four forms of discourse are normally present in any writing, even though the author's purpose may primarily be to tell, to describe, or to explain.
3. To define the term *exposition* not only as explaining or reasoning about ideas, but also as the writer's way of interpreting, revealing, and unfolding experience. In this sense, exposition becomes the most exalted of all the forms of writing.
4. To make the student aware that the degree of exposition in any type of writing is a measure of the degree of emphasis the writer gives his purpose, hence also a measure of the degree of subjectivity the writer imparts.
5. To define persuasion as an element present in all forms of writing.

B. Skills Students Will Practice

1. Recognizing narration, description, and exposition in writing, separately or in combination.
2. Analyzing the use of the forms of discourse as they relate to and reflect the writer's purpose.
3. Relating the degree of exposition in writing to the degree of objectivity or subjectivity practiced by the writer: In writing that is primarily objective, exposition remains on the level of explaining or "reasoning about"; in writing that is primarily subjective, exposition adds the dimension of the writer's interpreting or translating experience.
4. Writing papers utilizing varying emphasis on narration, description, or exposition, separately or in combination.

C. Scheduling the Unit

Because several of the preceding units involve indirectly the use of narrative, descriptive, or expository techniques as the writer pursues directly other skills, this unit may best be presented late in the school

160

year. If the printed sequence in the book is generally being followed, this
unit should perhaps be taught no earlier than its present position, following the units on emphasis and critical thinking, taking its place in the
block of units—numbers 22, 23, 24, 25—which deal primarily with the total
effect of a passage.

II. MOTIVATING THE UNIT

A. Background—Author and Selection

1. AUTHOR: Loren Eiseley (1907-   ) is a native of Lincoln, Nebraska.
   He was born into what is now characterized as a "disadvantaged" or
   "culturally deprived" family (his father was a day laborer; his mother
   was totally deaf and unable to communicate with her neighbors). "We
   never had visitors . . . . We were, in a sense, social outcasts . . . . We were
   simply shunned as unimportant and odd." (*The Mind as Nature*, 1962,
   pp. 19-20.) From these beginnings Loren Eiseley rose to be chariman of
   the Department of Anthropology at the University of Pennsylvania,
   Curator of Early Man in the University Museum, Provost of the University, and now head of the Department of History and Philosophy of
   Science in the Graduate School of Arts and Sciences. He has contributed
   articles to many periodicals, including *The Saturday Evening Post,
   Harpor's Magazino*, and *Sciontific Amorican*, and his books *Tho Immonso
   Journey* (1957), *Darwin's Century* (1958), and *The Firmament of Time*
   (1960) have gained him a wide popular audience. His latest book, *The
   Mind as Nature*, was published as a part of the John Dewey Series—a
   series of annual lectures sponsored by the John Dewey Society and the
   National Society for College Teachers of Education.

2. SELECTION: The unit selection is from the next to the last chapter in
   The Immense Journey, a book completed by Eiseley when he was forty-
   five years old and which is described on the jacket as a "blend of
   scientific knowledge and imaginative vision." It is certainly that and
   more, because it represents also a sensitivity to language possessed by
   few men. The book probes the secrets of life on this planet—to scientific
   fact and interpretation, Loren Eiseley adds statements of his convictions
   about the meaning of existence, and reveals a sympathy for all forms of
   life. The unit selection epitomizes his philosophy: The essence of life
   is above and beyond man's tampering.

B. Setting the Stage

1. Draw out through class discussion the students' ideas concerning
   narrative and descriptive writing. The students' concepts of narration
   and description will very likely be accurate; they will associate narration with *time* and description with *place* or space and they will be aware
   of—or they will comprehend easily when you point it out—the dynamic-

static relationship of these two natural ways for the human mind to record experience through language. The students will also be able, of course, to furnish many examples of each kind of writing. If you wish, you might review the narrative and descriptive elements in several of the unit selections elsewhere in the text: Units 2 through 6, and Units 8, 12, 13, 23, 24 and 25 all contain direct examples.

2. To prepare the class for the two-level definition of exposition developed in this unit, turn to the selection on the making of tappa from Melville's *Typee* (Unit 12) and note the explanation of a process—one of the most common types of explaining. Lead the class then to a discussion of processes they know about—they might present orally several different processes: from explaining how to modify a car to convert it into a drag-racer, to how to design a stage-set to produce a suitable background for a play or even create a mood. This last kind of activity will lead directly to our second-level definition of explaining—a *revealing* of a purpose or of a principle of life, the element we respect most in writing. In this sense, lyric poetry is exalted exposition; we value Emily Dickinson's "The Brain—is wider than the Sky," and Robert Frost's "Something there is that doesn't love a wall," because of the deep and perhaps dimly felt principles these lines of poetry *explain*—reveal, unfold, make understandable to us.

III. TEACHING THE UNIT

A. General Points of Interest and Emphasis

1. Before you do much with the unit selection, you may want to have two or three members of the class read Eiseley's *The Immense Journey* prior to your assigning this unit so that they can discuss various aspects of the book—perhaps in a panel. The panel might read aloud from the book to give the class the flavor of Eiseley's style of writing and to reveal his all-encompassing grasp of the secret of life viewed against the background of geologic time. Eiseley shares with Rachel Carson the ability to make clear the large and deep relationships of an intricate and myriad array of scientific detail. An excellent introduction to Eiseley's feeling for life is his description of floating on the Platte River in Chapter 2.

   A reading of Eiseley's discussion of the extent of man's reliance on machines, pp. 89-90 in *The Immense Journey*, will help prepare the students for the central point in the unit selection: There is a quality and a meaning in living things that will never be usurped by the machines men create.

2. Read the unit selection aloud, without interruption, to get the feeling of Eiseley's prose and his simultaneous portrayal of images and ideas. On the basis of this reading, ask the students what images they see in their

mind's eye, and what ideas Eiseley reveals. Compare paragraphs 9-12 with the preceding paragraphs. Has Eiseley prepared his readers for his introduction of the newspaper headlines in paragraph 9? It would be helpful at this time to read and discuss the first part of the chapter, "The Bird and the Machine," from which the unit selection is taken, for here Eiseley makes absolutely definite his attitude concerning the relationship of life to man's machines.

3. After reading the unit selection for the image/idea content, you might lead directly into the skill of the unit by asking: What happened step by step in the selection? Is this narration? Where did the event take place? How did the participants look and move? Is this description? What is Eiseley attempting to reveal to us? What is his point? Is this exposition?

4. We have already referred to various unit selections in the text that contain narrative and descriptive elements. (II,B,2). You might wish to return to these selections to discuss the expository element, the author's revealing of ideas. In Unit 6, Orwell reveals the almost fiendish quality of the adolescent society in an English boy's school; in Unit 8, Saint-Exupéry reveals his belief in man's reliance on and love for machines; in Unit 24, Joseph Conrad reveals man in relation to nature, and so also Crane in the selection in Unit 25. Brief looks at the expository element in these selections or in the reading the class has done outside the text will help prepare the student for the composition skill of this unit.

B. Special Observations for Levels A, B, and C

- 1. *Practice 1. Levels A, B, and C:* The text treatment on all three levels, together with the examples provided in the practice in Levels B and C, should make it easy for the students to proceed with the assignment on their own. But you might want to have many of the statements read aloud and discussed before the students proceed to Practice 2. Not all levels of students may specify sufficiently. The B- and C-Level students will benefit from a discussion of the narrative and descriptive elements in *all* the sentences in the Eiseley paragraph.

- 2. *Practice 2. Levels A and B:* Because narration and description are to be incorporated separately, it will be good discipline to hold the students to bare narration in their initial paragraphs. Read several of the narrative accounts and strike out all descriptive details possible. Then, when the students purposely add descriptive matter, their paragraphs should take on a much greater image-making quality.

  Level C: Both narrative and descriptive details are asked for in the first draft because our main purpose is to get these students to produce a paragraph. Then, when you read the paragraphs aloud, you can suggest the addition of either narrative or descriptive detail to give the image greater delineation.

- 3. *Practice 3. Levels A, B, and* C: The writing of this Practice should be preceded by a careful class reading and discussion of section **B.** of the text. The text treatment is purposely lengthy so that the students may follow the introduction of difficult and subtle concepts different from the usual presentation of exposition and its relation to the degree of subjectivity and objectivity in a passage. The definition of "persuasion" here is also different from the time-honored one. We are all aware that a "new rhetoric" is entering into our study of our native language, just as various new approaches to grammar are being investigated so that we may describe with greater precision the structure of a language more complex than our former instruments seemed to indicate. So also with rhetoric (and there is no virtue merely in looking for a new rhetoric as though it were a matter of keeping in style); the need for a new rhetoric arises from the fact that we now require a more precise set of values if we are to describe the relation between man and that world of experience he endeavors to convey to others through language. The old *trivium* of "invention," "disposition," and "elocution" still applies, of course, but not in any discrete or static fashion. The complexities of a modern civilization with its widely diverse audiences, a world of ideas and material inventions increasing one-hundred-fold every five years or less, and a burgeoning knowledge of the psychology of man and his language all combine to make classical rhetoric inadequate.

  Because of the nature of section **B.**, you may want to complete Practice 3 entirely on an oral basis. A discussion of student ideas could round out the class's understanding of the concepts in section **B.**

- 4. *Practice 4. Levels A, B, and* C: With a thorough discussion of section **B.** and Practice 3 preceding this, the students should be well prepared to carry out the assignment: to relate *purpose* to a familiar and personal content. This is the key assignment preparatory to the completing of the Problems, because it involves narration, description, exposition, and persuasion—as defined in this unit. Because it serves as the basis for Problem 1, Level A, and Problem 2, Levels B and C, you may want to discuss and criticize these paragraphs thoroughly before proceeding.

- 5. *Problem 1. Level* A: Probably the best papers will be those that increase specificity through the use of additional narrative and descriptive detail in support of an increased emphasis on the expository element.
  Levels B and C: You may want to review the paragraph skills in Units 7, 10, and 12, before these papers are attempted. Students who wish to add an expository element should be encouraged to do so.

- 6. *Problem 2. Level* A: The purpose here is expository—in both the sense of explaining and the sense of revealing a basic belief or a general principle. The assignment requires a conscious attempt to persuade; thus, the students should select topics they are strongly interested in.
  Levels B and C: See suggestions for Problem 1, Level A.

IV. EVALUATING THE UNIT

Students will appreciate being evaluated on the *control* they exercise over narrative, descriptive, and expository elements and, most of all, on the degree to which they enlist narration, description and first-level explaining to achieve a worth-while purpose. This unit should evoke statements of strongly felt beliefs and the final papers can be evaluated on the unmistakable emphasis with which these beliefs are revealed.

V. ADDITIONAL WRITING TOPICS

A. Collect editorials from your local or regional newspapers which take opposing sides on a political or social issue. Analyze the various editorial statements, and write a paper in which you state your personal belief concerning the issue, referring to the editorials and telling and describing any personal experiences you have had which have influenced your viewpoint.

B. Write a paper comparing the level of expository writing in the selection from Melville's *Typee* (Unit 12), Orwell's "Such, Such Were the Joys..." (Unit 6), and Laird's treatment of the origin of language from *The Miracle of Language* (Unit 19). In which selection does the writer reveal most strongly an underlying conviction about his topic? In which selection are narration and description used most effectively to support the writer's underlying purpose?

C. Discuss the author's underlying purpose in a short story, a novel, or a poem you have read recently. Explicate passages or lines in the work to bring out the narrative, descriptive, and expository elements in this material.

UNIT 23 — CREATE IMAGES THROUGH METAPHOR

Selection from *"The Crumbs of One Man's Years"*
in *QUITE EARLY ONE MORNING*
by Dylan Thomas.

(Student Text—A-Level, p. 153; B-Level, p. 151; C-Level, 147)

I. PREPARING TO TEACH THE UNIT

A. Purposes of the Unit

1. To make students aware of the difference between the denotative and connotative uses of language.
2. To establish metaphor as a fundamental cognitive operation as well as an important linguistic device.
3. To reveal the power of metaphoric language to convey complex, rich, and original thoughts.
4. To reveal the economy which results from a writer's effective use of metaphor.

B. Skills Students Will Practice

1. Recognizing the emotional impact inherent in figurative language.
2. Recognizing the highly concentrated, thought-packed quality of metaphor.
3. Constructing metaphors by finding similarity in dissimilar items.
4. Creating descriptive prose which includes the imaginative device of metaphor.

C. Scheduling the Unit

1. This unit can be effective as part of an extended study of prose style or of the nature of language as symbolic process.
2. There are various ways this unit can serve as a bridge between literature and composition. For example, you might teach it as part of the introduction to the study of a short story or novel that is especially rich in texture or ornate in style; it will, for example, enhance the student's reading of a work by William Faulkner, Katherine Anne Porter, Herman Melville, Joseph Conrad, Charles Dickens, or Thomas Wolfe. Also, this unit will provide a transition as you move from prose fiction into poetry. It will allow the student to see that poetry often differs from prose only in degree and that poetry, like its main tool, metaphor, is first of all a way of knowing.
3. You might teach this unit in conjunction with Units 8, 9, or 14, all of which have a high metaphoric content. It would be most interesting to

make it possible for students to discover the close relation between
Saint Paul's Epistle to the Corinthians and Dylan Thomas's passage:
the similarity in the metaphor; the quality of charity which is directly
stated in one, and implied in the other; the revealing of the emptiness of
vanity. (See also II, B, 1 for further suggestions for use with other units.)

II. MOTIVATING THE UNIT

A. Background—Author and Selection

1. AUTHOR: Dylan Thomas (1914-1953) was one of the greatest lyric poets
   of this century. Thomas was born in Wales, the son of a schoolmaster
   who taught many of the leading figures of Welsh literary life. During his
   life, he worked as a journalist, a broadcaster, a writer of sketches,
   short stories, and film scripts. Though some of his poems are difficult
   to comprehend, he achieved and has retained a wide popular fame. His
   reading tours in America and the recordings of such works as *Under
   Milk Wood* and "A Child's Christmas in Wales" reveal his magnificent
   voice and account, in part, for the acclaim his works have received.

      Dylan Thomas defined poetry as "... the rhythmic, inevitably narra-
   tive, movement from our overclothed blindness to a naked vision." At
   the heart of the impassioned, symbolic exuberance of his language there
   is always a childlike innocence, a deep simplicity. His work shows the
   influence of Joyce, Freud, and Hopkins, but perhaps the Bible was the
   strongest influence on his poetry. Conrad Aiken's remark about Thomas
   is particularly relevant to our unit selection. "... a born language-lover
   and language-juggler ... a genius for word-magic ... he is a chameleon of
   colors."

      The separate works of Dylan Thomas include: *Eighteen Poems* (1934),
   Twenty-Five Poems (1936), *The Map of Love* (1939), *Portrait of the
   Artist as a Young Dog* (1940), *Twenty-Six Poems* (1950), *Under Milk
   Wood* (A Play for Voices, 1954), and *Quite Early One Morning* (1954).

      Some critical and biographical studies include: *The Poetry of Dylan
   Thomas* by Elder Olson (University of Chicago Press, 1954), *Dylan
   Thomas in America* by J. M. Brinnin, (Little, Brown, 1955), A *Grammar
   of Metaphor* by C. Brooke-Rose, (Dufour, 1959); *Dylan Thomas* by G. S.
   Fraser (London House, 1959).

2. SELECTION: *Quite Early One Morning* is a collection of diverse prose
   sketches which Thomas wrote during a ten-year period—1943 to 1953.
   The English edition consists solely of material written for radio broad-
   casts, but the American edition (*New Directions*, 1954) includes a number of other stories and articles originally published in magazines.

      The unit selection is an excerpt from "The Crumbs of One Man's
   Years," a prose piece written in 1946 for the Welsh division of BBC.
   Composed at the year's end, "The Crumbs of One Man's Years" renders

Thomas's recollections of some fleeting but poignant events. The paragraph which immediately precedes our unit selection establishes London as the setting and also reveals the informal episodic style that characterizes this essay: "And on one occasion, in this long dissolving year, I remember that I boarded a London bus from a district I have forgotten, and where I certainly could have been up to little good, to an appointment that I did not want to keep."

B. Setting the Stage

1. Reading the unit selections for Units 3 and 4—"Render Sensory Experiences" and "Combine Fact and Feeling"—will give the students an excellent introduction to connotation and metaphor. In fact, these units might well be taught in conjunction with this metaphor unit, as part of a sequence of lessons on the uses of imagination in a developing prose style.

2. In order to familiarize the class with the wide relevance of metaphor, discuss the many ways figurative language surrounds them. Draw on their experience with mass media for examples of the connotative diction of the "image-makers." A possible homework assignment would require the student to identify metaphors in magazine and television advertisements.

3. Another method for helping the students discriminate between the denotative and the connotative aspects of language is to read them a textbook or dictionary definition of a specific bird, tree, flower, or season and then read them a lyric poem about the same subject.

4. During this preliminary period of discussion, be sure to explain the basic distinction between words and images, stressing the process by which words stimulate the reader to call forth images in his mind. Point out the way metaphors often join an abstract word ("love" or "spring") to a sense-image (a "red rose" or "nimble and crocus"). This process activates the reader's memory and imagination; it makes him "feel his ideas."

5. *Kennings*, the compound metaphors which were used in Old English and other Germanic tongues as synonyms for simple nouns, will provide an imaginative introductory assignment for the student. A few examples of this primitive and powerful figure of speech are "whale-road" for "sea," "whale-traveler" for "ship," "battle-adders" for "arrows," and "world-cradle" for "sun." *Beowulf* contains a number of excellent examples of kennings. Write several of these figures of speech on the board and then have the students try to discover what it is that each kenning describes. You may wish to give a short writing assignment, requiring the student to construct some original kennings.

6. Metaphor is man's way of viewing the universe as a coherent organism, of establishing interlocking relationships among apparently disparate orders of existence. It attempts to see "the world in a grain of sand." But in a mixed metaphor two or more incompatible items are joined together in a way that does violence to our sense of logic. The effect can

be absurdly comic: "When we open that Pandora's box, we shall find a bunch of Trojan horses"; "The British lion will never pull in its horns"; "He is to be congratulated on producing a very tasty rehash of several questions which have been fully ventilated in the Parliament"; "We are leaving no stone unturned by keeping our ear to the ground." One way to motivate a student's interest in the structural properties of a metaphor would be to mimeograph a number of mixed metaphors and discuss them with the class, calling on members of the class to analyze each structure for its incongruous identification.

III. TEACHING THE UNIT

A. General Points of Interest and Emphasis

1. The teacher will find a wide range of performances on this unit. Metaphor is to be regarded as much a mental operation as a linguistic skill. Ancient philosophers and literary critics and modern psychologists and linguists have agreed that metaphorical power is intimately associated with intelligence and with intellectual discipline. Since metaphoric ability is largely a quality of mind and perhaps reflects a particular *kind* of intelligence, you should anticipate vastly different results from student to student. The unit will, at best, make only an initial inroad for the highly "literal-minded" student; he will undoubtedly increase his ability to read and to appreciate metaphor, but he may show only a minimal skill in writing metaphors. On the other hand, the "intuitive" student may create some authentically original thought and language.

2. For brief but thoughtful discussions on the nature of metaphor, see *Theory of Literature* by René Wellek and Austin Warren (Harcourt, 1949) and *English Prose Style* by Sir Herbert Read (Beacon Press, 1955). For an extensive analysis of metaphor in thought and language, see Ernst Cassirer's *Language and Myth* (Dover, 1946) and Susanne Langer's *Philosophy in a New Key* (Harvard University Press, 1942). Walter Ong's essay "Metaphor and the Twinned Vision," published in the Spring, 1955, issue of *Sewanee Review*, is one of the clearest and most profound studies ever written on this subject.

B. Special Observations for Levels A, B, and C

- 1. *Practice 1. Level A:* First read a poem to the class—Wordsworth's sonnet "Composed upon Westminster Bridge" would serve very well. Then call on several of the students to describe orally the scene they see in their mind's eye.

  Levels B and C: In order to be sure that students clearly understand this assignment, discuss with them some of the connotations stimulated by "loaded words" used in contemporary politics ("communists," "ultraconservative," "radical left," "subversive," "appeasement," "welfare state," "conform," "reactionary") and slang ("square," "far-out," "in," "swinger," "tough").

- **2. Practice 2. Level A:** Using some of the terms suggested in the Practice, write on the board a sentence containing a metaphor. This should help the student make a natural entry into what otherwise could become a difficult or mechanical exercise. When the students have had time to generate their sentences, use the board or opaque projector to illustrate the most successful products. Take the time to analyze these sentences with the class, stressing the structure and the effect each metaphor creates.

  Levels B and C: To emphasize the radical differences between the original and altered version, ask a competent reader in the class to read both of them aloud. When the students have completed their paragraph of analysis, have them read one another's papers.

- **3. Practice 3. Level A:** To illustrate the positive ways a metaphor stimulates personal reaction, call on a number of students to read their paragraphs.

  Levels B and C: See suggestions for Practice 2, Level A. In addition, have the class compose a sentence as a group—let them decide which of the metaphors they create is superior; in general, C-Level students will require more discussion.

- **4. Practice 4. Level A:** Read and discuss this paragraph with the class. Point out the clumsy wordiness and high ratio of weak, general verbs and nouns which characterize the threadbare quality of prose here. Elicit suggestions from the class for improvement of the word choices in the first sentence.

  After the student paragraphs have been completed and discussed, you may want to let them know that the paragraph is a mutilated version of Dickens's "A Christmas Carol." If you have had time to ditto copies of the original version to put in the students' hands, they can profit from comparing the text paragraph, the original, and their versions.

  Levels B and C: See suggestions for Practice 3, Level A.

- **5. Practice 5. Levels B and C:** See suggestions for Practice 4, Level A.

- **6. Problem 1. Levels A, B, and C:** Before the students write, it might be well to read once more the Dylan Thomas selection and discuss the metaphors that may not have come to the attention of various members of the class: What different metaphorical equations does the ambiguous "shooting green spring morning" permit? Is Thomas evoking an image of "sprouting green plants," or "a fine green morning for shooting," or "a fine morning for shooting on the green," or any number of other images, more Thomasesque, even more elusive? What about "shaggy"? Does it mean "unkempt," or does it actually point to that Panlike quality which becomes more apparent with "winks and pipes of cloven-footed sandwichmen"?

Or, you might go outside the unit selection. You might put on the board a metaphor from a different field of study, such as this statement from a high school biology workbook: "The surface of the earth is covered with a seamless web of life." This procedure will help emphasize once more the mental operation that must go on before a writer can put into words a fresh, creative metaphor.

- **7. Problem 2. Level A:** This is purposely an extension of Problem 1, but mainly, of course, in the way it pulls the students from the preceding assigned area of visual movement to any area the students may select. These papers will benefit from a reading and discussion of many of the Problem 1 papers.

  Levels B and C: The students will all have a wealth of experiences to draw from here. The principal hurdle will be their tendency to use mixed and dead metaphors in imitation of the cliché-ridden world of the used-car advertising writer. It might be profitable to have the students bring to class examples of advertisements from both national magazines and local newspapers and discuss the differences between the creative metaphor of the former and the flat clichés common in the latter.

IV. EVALUATING THE UNIT

A. The student should use the following guideline in evaluating a metaphor: Does it illuminate or obscure his subject and his intention?

B. Perhaps the best test for an effective metaphor is to diagram or sketch it. When extended metaphors of a John Donne, a William Shakespeare, or a Dylan Thomas are visualized or charted, they have an inherent logic. Often it is a "logic of feeling," an intuitive adequacy. To demonstrate this truth, simply contrast a metaphor by a skillful writer with one by Edgar Guest.

V. ADDITIONAL WRITING TOPICS

A. Write a paragraph based on the comparison of the ages of man to the seasons of the year.

B. Use a metaphor (or a series of them) that will identify the action of a particular athlete with the movement of a machine or an animal.

C. Use a force in nature to describe a state of mind: a zephyr, a hurricane, a flood, an earthquake, a volcanic eruption, a downpour of rain.

UNIT 24 — ACHIEVE TONE IN DESCRIPTION

Selection from "*The Lagoon*" by Joseph Conrad

(Student Text—A-Level, p. 158; B-Level, p. 156; C-Level, p. 152)

I. PREPARING TO TEACH THE UNIT

A. Purposes of the Unit

1. To help students recognize tone in writing.
2. To analyze some of the qualities in writing which produce a unified tone.
3. To enable students to achieve the quality of tone in their writing.

B. Skills Students Will Practice

1. Getting the grasp on content which will enable them to determine the tone they wish to convey in their writing.
2. Selecting the details in a scene that will enable them to produce a definite tone.
3. Utilizing effects of color, sound, rhythm, and contrast to achieve tone.
4. Writing a composition in which they attempt to create in the reader a definite emotional response or attitude.

C. Scheduling the Unit

1. This is the first unit in this book in which we deliberately approach the quality of tone in writing. Because "tone" is variously interpreted as "the total emotional context...of any passage of writing" (Richard Altick, *Preface to Critical Reading*, Holt, 1960, p. 233) or the term used "to refer to the implicit evaluation which the author manages to convey behind his explicit presentations" (Wayne Booth, *The Rhetoric of Fiction*, University of Chicago Press, 1961, p. 74) or "the general feeling which suffuses and surrounds the work," arising "ultimately out of the writer's attitude toward his subject" (Fred B. Millett, *Reading Fiction*, p. 11; quoted in Booth, *Op.cit*, p. 74), it will be best not to schedule this unit early in the year. It does not, however, follow any small sequence within the text, and thus it can be taught earlier, if the class and the time seem right.
2. For example, this unit would support the teaching of Unit 4, in which the delightful tone of E. B. White's essay about the Model T is achieved by his combination of feeling and fact. It would also give additional meaning to Unit 7 in which Stefansson's satiric tone is purposely kept in the background except for the Level A version. And, of course, the connections are strong between this unit and Unit 16, "Emphasize with Paradox"; Unit 22, "Combine the Forms of Writing"; and Unit 23,

"Create Images Through Metaphor," in which the tone Dylan Thomas achieves through metaphor *is* the meaning.

3. The unit could be scheduled to support emphasis on literature, at a time when the class is reading, for example, poetry, the short story, or the play. Discussions of the tone—whether defined as the writer's "tone of voice" or "the feeling arising from the author's attitude"—of Albert Camus's "The Guest" or Robert Frost's "Stopping by Woods on a Snowy Evening," or John Millington Synge's *Riders to the Sea* could be given a broader base through the use of this unit.

II. MOTIVATING THE UNIT

A. Background—Author and Selection

1. AUTHOR: Joseph Conrad was born Józef Teodor Konrad Nalecz Korzeniowski at Berdyczew, Poland, in 1857. He died of a heart attack in England in 1924, one of the most renowned of modern writers of English prose. Just before his death he had declined a knighthood.

Conrad's early years with his parents were filled with turbulence and danger; when Joseph was five, his father, a militant leader in the struggle to free Poland from the Russians, was condemned for his political activities to exile in Russia. Joseph's mother died when he was eight. He lived first with his uncle, then briefly with his father, who died when Joseph was twelve. By the time he was seventeen, Joseph had entered the French Marine service—"I verily believe mine was the only case of a boy of my nationality and antecedents taking a, so to speak, standing jump out of his racial surrounding and associations."

Conrad served on a succession of ships, advancing from seaman through the ratings to first mate, and finally to the command of a barque. He terminated his years at sea in 1894, at thirty-seven, and devoted the rest of his life to writing. During his years aboard ship, Conrad had amassed the experiences which served him as material for a long list of stories of the sea and the jungle—*Almayer's Folly* (1895), *The Nigger of the Narcissus* (1897), *The Lagoon* (1898), *Lord Jim* (1900), *Youth* (1902), *Heart of Darkness* (1902), *Typhoon* (1903), *Nostromo* (1904), *The Mirror of the Sea* (1906), *The Secret Sharer* (1912), *Chance* (1914), *Victory* (1915), and *The Arrow of Gold* (1919)—titles which established him as a leading short-story writer and novelist. Polish was Conrad's native language; he learned to speak and write French fluently as a youth; and he learned his English by reading the newspapers and listening to the speech of fishermen, shipwrights and sailors. Before he died, however, he had become a master of English prose style, a friend of John Galsworthy and H.G. Wells. In the year of Conrad's death, Ernest Hemingway wrote, "If I knew that by grinding Mr. [T.S.] Eliot into a fine dry powder over Mr. Conrad's grave Mr. Conrad would shortly appear . . . and commence

writing, I would leave for London early tomorrow with a sausage grinder."
(Frederick R. Karl in *A Reader's Guide to Joseph Conrad*, Noonday, 1960, pp. 3-4). Karl also states that "next to Joyce and perhaps Faulkner, [Conrad] is at present the most discussed of any modern author writing in English."

Two salient biographies are G. Jean-Aubry's *Joseph Conrad: Life and Letters* (Doubleday and Dent, 1927), and Jocelyn Baines's *Joseph Conrad, A Critical Biography* (McGraw-Hill, 1960). Two helpful introductions to the work of Conrad are Frederick R. Karl's work cited above, and F. M. Cushwa's *An Introduction to Conrad* (Odyssey, 1933).

2. SELECTION: The unit selection is from the beginning of Conrad's story; only two introductory sentences precede it. The story, one of Conrad's masterpieces, takes the white man to the house of Arsat, a Malay he had befriended in the past. When the canoe reaches Arsat's hut on the shore of a stagnant lagoon, the white man finds Arsat's wife burning with fever. During the night with the woman slowly dying, Arsat tells the white man how he and his brother captured the woman from their ruler and how he chose to escape with her rather than go to the help of his brother who died trying to gain time for the runaways by fighting their pursuers. When morning comes, the woman has died; the white man and his crew return to their trip on the river, and Arsat has decided to return to his tribe to avenge his brother's death.

The tone of the unit selection is the tone of the story. The action throughout the story is *sotto voce*: The woman dies without regaining consciousness, and Arsat recounts the violence of her capture and his brother's death in the half-light of reminiscence. The lagoon—stagnant, cut off from the world on all sides by the dark and towering jungle—is untouched by the history enacted there.

B. Setting the Stage

1. If you have a record player available, you might introduce this unit by playing sections of various compositions, each representing a characteristic tone, ranging from the ringing electric quality of "Seventy-six Trombones" to the gentleness of Debussy's "Serenade for the Doll" and from the chaotic questioning of Prokofiev's "Sonata No. 7" to Duke Ellington's "Mood Indigo." Ask students to describe the emotional effect each piece has on them—is it also possible for words to produce emotional effects? Is there a "tone of voice" in literature comparable to the tone of a trumpet or a violin? Is there also an emotional tone in writing comparable to the emotional tone of band music, jazz, the blues, or "Here Comes the Bride"?

2. Bring to class several poems or prose passages which represent to you an attitude on the part of the author which creates an emotional response in the reader. Students will react to the ironic tone in Swift's *A Modest Proposal*, the tone of utter despair in William Morris's "The Haystack in the Floods," or the tone of happiness in Robert Browning's "Pippa's

Song." Discuss first the total reaction a student has to a passage, then explore some of the qualities in the language that help to produce the dominant tone.

III. TEACHING THE UNIT

A. General Points of Interest and Emphasis

1. Before the students start the unit, sketch briefly the biography of Conrad, relating "The Lagoon" to the author's experience as second mate on the steamship *Vidar* which sailed from Singapore to Borneo and along the coasts and rivers of Borneo, Celebes, and Sumatra. It was during this time, according to Cushwa (cited above, p. XII), that Conrad first began to write (1887-1888). "The Lagoon" came out in 1898, after Conrad had been living and writing in England for four years.

2. Discuss the complete story. If students have read it, ask them what effect it had on them: Did it point up relationships between man and nature? between the civilization of the white man and the civilization of the Malay? Is the tone of the story similar to or different from the tone of the unit selection?

3. Read the selection aloud, then ask various students to read it aloud, interpreting the feeling the passage gives them.

4. Discuss "The Craft of Writing" as an attempt to introduce the nature of the quality of tone. Apply the statements in the text to the selection—do the students accept the analysis of tone? Do they agree with the interpretation of the tone of the passage? The Level B and C versions distinguish for the student the difference between the *content* or subject of the passage (man in relation to nature) and the *tone*, which in all levels is defined as one of heavy, brooding stillness.

5. Other passages in the text exhibiting a definite tone are named in I, C, 2 above.

B. Special Observations for Levels A, B, and C

- 1. *Practice 1. Levels A and B:* Before the students write, you may want to remind the students that a basic quality in humor is *incongruity*; the person or thing or idea out of place, not in harmony, invariably defeats seriousness (e.g., the circus clown with his tiny Mexican hairless dog at the end of a one-inch thick rope). The happy bird song here would be incongruous. Everyone should benefit from a reading and discussion of the paragraphs.

  Level C: Additional details the students might list: "water that shone smoothly like a band of metal," "Nothing moved on the river," "the portals of a land from which the very memory of motion had forever departed." Students may point out also that "*every* tree, *every* leaf, *every* bough, ..." intensify the feeling of stillness. Because it may be difficult for some Level C students to admit they appreciate tone in a selection, you may want to suggest that they hand in their sentences anonymously so that you can read and discuss them freely.

- 2. *Practice 2. Levels A and B:* Color is included only in the Level A text. The one word in Coleridge can be compared nicely to the one direct color word in Conrad; also, the implications of color in both selections can be compared and contrasted: flatness in Conrad, darkness in Coleridge. In order to discuss sound effects, it may be best to read and discuss many of the student paragraphs. In this area of language, and it is a basic area, we are caught between the science of language and aesthetic appreciation of language. The linguist will point out that the letter *s* is not a sound, but only a grapheme (visual symbol) representing a *phone* or *phoneme* (a sound carrying intelligible differences from other sounds). Some of the sounds represented by *s* in the two sentences referred to in the text should be represented by the symbol *z* (his, rose). But our goal here is the *effect of sound on meaning* and although there are studies by Sapir and Newman which reveal that people attach the meaning of *small* to vowels articulated near the front of the oral cavity and *large* to vowels articulated near the back of the oral cavity, and although the proponents of modern grammar are admitting meaning as an added element in their examination of sound distribution and syntax, the area is still a subjective one. The main value in these Practices is the increased sensitivity of the students to the sound of language.

    Level C: It will be best to conduct this Practice entirely on an oral basis. Make it a preparation for Practice 3. Read aloud together the sentence beginning ''In the stillness of the air...'' and the last sentence. Neither sentence will permit fast articulation—the shaping of the vowel sounds slows up the speaking mechanism. Have one or two students read certain sentences as fast as they can—the ludicrous effect will point up the connection between the sound of language and its meaning.

- 3. *Practice 3. Level A:* This is a challenging assignment, involving a good deal of creativity. The Level A students should be ready for it by this time. If you feel the need to caution them about ''overwriting'' before they start, you will have to decide whether this cautioning will obstruct the sincerely creative attempts you are hoping for.

    Level B: Because this is a subjective decision, any of the words is a possibility. The interesting element, of course, will be the reasons the students advance—this is the real value of the exercise. Again, a full discussion will benefit everyone.

    Level C: The suggestions for Practice 2, Levels A and B, should be helpful here, in addition to the discussion you conducted in Level C. You may want to go one more step and list on the board suggestions for sounds that may be repeated in each of the three topics. Stop short of repletion—the value is in the sounds students can bring up from their individual memories.

- 4. *Practice 4. Level A:* This should be a less difficult task than the one in Practice 3. Contrast is easier to isolate than is ''heat'' as opposed to "tranquillity." The students ought to proceed on their own here, but you may want to caution them they must first establish a dominant tone—only then is contrast effective.

Level B: The suggestions for Practice 3, Level A, and for Practices 1 and 2, Level C, may be helpful here. Also, of course, the two preceding Practices of Level A are direct preparation—this Practice is a capstone. The students may want to read their paragraphs aloud and stand up to class comments.

Level C: See Level B above. Because this is the capstone paragraph before the students reach the Problems, you may want to duplicate these paragraphs and distribute them for class criticism, or you might display them on an opaque projector for class discussion.

- 5. *Problem 1. Levels A, B, and C:* You will note that no mention of the number of paragraphs is made—the problem for the student is selecting a landscape from his memory, determining before he writes what details he will have to select to produce an impression of motion, and then, through his attitude toward his subject, to create a dominant tone. If his landscape is filled with the movement of rushing cars, his attitude may be that the scene is noisily repulsive, discouragingly materialistic, emotionally stultifying, or throbbingly prosperous. And, of course, any attitude can be portrayed ironically. You may even want to suggest that students write as briefly as they can and still establish an unmistakable tone.

- 6. *Problem 2. Levels A, B, and C:* This is, of course, a highly creative assignment. Students—A-, B-, or C-Level—who are not attracted by it may choose an alternate topic, either equally imaginative or more mundane. Tone is certainly a quality in good argument or in the primarily expository development of an abstract idea. Students who, by this time, want to leave description should have full freedom to pursue a topic involving, for example, their attitude toward a political question or the results of surveys on the effects of smoking cigarettes.

V. EVALUATING THE UNIT

The unit skill is a subjective one—many of the Practices involve oral-aural qualities. You may, therefore, wish to grade formally only the Problem assignments. Also, because by its nature tone is an element dependent on the reader's reception, the class may want to elect an evaluating committee to judge the value of the papers. Any grade should be based on the writer's success in establishing a unifying tone.

V. ADDITIONAL WRITING TOPICS

A. Write a paper analyzing the quality of tone in any one of the unit selections in the text. Does the author employ techniques other than those discussed in this unit?

B. Choose a topic you can develop briefly—the Halloween costumes your younger brothers and sisters wear, the essentials of a job—and write two paragraphs about it, displaying a different attitude in each paragraph. The tone you create may be friendly or unfriendly, serious or humorous, direct or ironic, mysterious or condescending, reverent or satiric.

C. Write a paper discussing the dominant tone in a novel, short story or nonfiction book you have read this year. Analyze the author's purpose in setting the particular tone you find in his work.

D. Put yourself in the place of the author of any of the unit selections in this textbook. Would you attempt to create the same tone the author created? Would you attempt a different tone? Rewrite one of the unit selections, giving it a tone opposite to, or at least different from, the tone of the original.

UNIT 25 — USE THIRD PERSON POINT OF VIEW

Selection from "*The Open Boat*" by Stephen Crane

(Student Text—A-Level, p. 163; B-Level, p. 161; C-Level, p. 157)

I. PREPARING TO TEACH THE UNIT

A. Purposes of the Unit:

1. To acquaint the student with point of view as a pervasive organizing principle of writing.
2. To show the student how purpose and subject determine the writer's point of view.
3. To provide students with some understanding of the uses of third person point of view.
4. To illustrate how the words a writer selects are determined by the point of view he has assumed.

B. Skills Students Will Practice

1. Establishing and maintaining a consistent physical and mental point of view.
2. Analyzing the differences between a summary and a scene.
3. Recognizing the differences between writing that *tells* and writing that *shows*.
4. Writing scenes in order to convey a vivid sense of actuality for readers.
5. Writing summary statements to provide a coherent framework for the reader's understanding of scenes.
6. Writing an essay which combines the advantages of both summary and scene.

C. Scheduling the Unit

1. Point of view is a matter of crucial importance in all forms of writing; hence, this unit has an all-inclusive quality about it. Since point of view is largely a question of the narrator's knowledge, attitude, and limitations, this unit might well be taught in conjunction with those units that deal explicitly with thought process in composition. Units 1, 2, 4, 5, 7, 8, 13, 14, 15, 16, 17, 22, 23 and 24 all emphasize the connections between language and thought, but perhaps Unit 25 relates most directly to Unit 4; "Combine Fact and Feeling", Unit 22; "Combine the Forms of Writing", and Unit 24, "Achieve Tone in Description."
2. Because point of view is a capstone unit in helping the writer establish his relation with his material, it may be taught earlier in the year than its printed position indicates, provided the ability of the class warrants.

3. Allow ample time for Unit 25, at least three to five full class sessions. Careful attention needs to be given to the physical post of observation and to matters of psychological distance in narrative art.

II. MOTIVATING THE UNIT

A. Background—Author and Selection

1. AUTHOR: Stephen Crane (1871-1900), American novelist and short-story writer, was one of the first genuine realists in American literature. Crane was influenced by 19th-century Russian novelists and by Flaubert and other writers of the French school of Naturalism. His novel *Maggie: A Girl of the Streets* (1893) is considered the first example of a naturalistic novel to be produced in the United States. His other works include *The Red Badge of Courage* (1895), his finest and most famous book; *The Black Riders* (1895), a volume of poems; *The Little Regiment* (1896); "The Open Boat," his greatest short story; *Active Service* (1899); *War Is Kind* (1899); *The Monster* (1899); *Wounds in the Rain* (1900), sketches of the Spanish-American War; *The O'Ruddy* (1903), finished after Crane's death by Robert Barr.

   Crane is a master of technique. His style embodies the combined powers of rich imagery and stark detail; his characteristic diction is understated and ironic, yet his settings are charged with wide symbolic significance. In Crane's best work, the conventions of realism and symbolism merge to engender a unique imaginative experience. Through his rigorous devotion to the art of fiction, Crane was able to create an illusion of reality unprecedented in American writing. Because of his bold technical experiments and his deep sense of organic form, he made a significant contribution to the structure of modern fiction. Joseph Conrad, the great English novelist, admired Crane's work and had a special affection for "The Open Boat." Ernest Hemingway, Sherwood Anderson, and Willa Cather are only a few of the many 20th-century writers whose style has been influenced by Stephen Crane.

2. SELECTION: "The Open Boat" had its source in the following personal experience: On January 1, 1897, Crane sailed from Florida on the *Commodore*, bound for Cuba as a war correspondent. The *Commodore* sank and Crane, with three members of the crew, spent thirty hours in a small, open boat waiting to be rescued. Crane described this ordeal in a dispatch which appeared on January 7, 1897, in the New York *Press*. Most of the newspaper account dealt with the departure, voyage, and sinking of the ship, but it also contained a hint of the artistic transformation these journalistic materials would undergo: "The history of life in an open boat for thirty hours would no doubt be instructive for the young, but none is to be told here and now."

   "The Open Boat" is far more than a factual account of shipwreck and survival; it is a work of art which relates random facts to a deep thematic structure. Crane's subtitle for "The Open Boat" gives an immediate clue to the difference here between fact and fiction: "A Tale Intended to be after the Fact: Being the Experience of Four Men from the Sunk Steamer *Commodore*." Unlike the newspaper version, this is "A Tale"; it is "after the Fact," and it is "the Experience of Four Men." "The Open Boat" develops an ironic theme consistent with the philosophy of naturalism; it is the story of man's fate in an indifferent universe. Representing helpless humanity, the men in the open boat face death at sea, and they experience a "cosmic chill." But Crane goes beyond this conventional structure; he moves inside the minds of the men. As a concealed narrator, he shows us their inner response to crisis, dramatizing their thoughts about life and death, unfolding their growing realization of the sacredness of the human community. Theirs is a spiritual ordeal, and they are bound together in love and understanding.

The unit selection is the opening passage of the story. This passage, regarded by many critics as one of the greatest introductory sections in all of fiction, establishes the physical point of view. The reader finds himself immediately located in the boat, sharing the experience of the protagonists. The concluding paragraph of "The Open Boat" summarizes the whole story's mental point of view:

> When it came night, the white waves paced to and fro in the moonlight, and the wind brought the sound of the great sea's voice to the men on shore, and they felt that they could then be interpreters.

B. Setting the Stage

1. Initially, spend some time discussing the way "point of view" and "opinion" or "belief" are often confused in popular usage. Emphasize the meaning of point of view as the position from which something is seen, or as the rhetorical stance by which an attitude is expressed, limited, or focused.

2. Generate a discussion of the myriad situations in life which illustrate the significance of point of view. You may wish to allude at first to some common instances of dispute, such as legal cases, political campaigns, scientific controversies, and wars. Then elicit further examples from the students, asking them to draw on their everyday experiences.

3. Write on the board a simple declarative sentence about a physical event and then ask each of several members of the class to adopt a different physical "post of observation" toward this event. The sentence may be as simple as this one: "It rained yesterday." Then, have them briefly describe this event orally, selecting only those details which are conditioned by the point of view (and its limitations) they have assumed. It may be wise to break this exercise up into two phases, restricting the students first to a physical point of view and, later, to a mental point of view.

4. Review the techniques studied in Unit 3, "Render Sensory Experiences" and section **C.** of Unit 8, "Reveal an Idea by Example"; these materials make clear the distinctions between *showing* and *telling* and between conceptual and experiential diction.

III.   TEACHING THE UNIT

A. General Points of Interest and Emphasis

1. After the class has had sufficient time to read the passage silently, call on several students to read it aloud. Ask each student who reads to convey orally the tone he feels the selection projects.

2. Conduct a discussion in search of the narrator. Who is speaking? Where is he located in relation to the scene? Does he speak only of what he can see from his position within the boat? What attitude or range of emotions does he express? At this point you may wish to introduce the students to the important function of *voice*. Voice defines the writer's relation to his material and to his audience; it is the resonance he "hears" as he composes. And, like point of view, it is a choice a writer makes, a rhetorical stance he takes—it will bring definite advantages and limitations.

3. Call attention to the understatement so evidently at work in the unit selection. First, direct the attention of the class to the opening sentence, a masterfully succinct line of prose: "None of them knew the color of the sky." Then, ask the students to discover other examples of laconic statement in the passage. The last two sentences provide excellent illustrations of the important but often neglected strategy of understatement.

4. In order to make clear the distinction between "summary" and "scene," draw from the student's experience of camera technique in film and television media. You may also wish to describe the artistic effects created by photography in some of the great motion pictures. Orson Welles's *Citizen Kane*, Jean Cocteau's *Beauty and the Beast*, Sergei Eisenstein's *Potemkin*, and John Huston's *The Treasure of Sierra Madre* are excellent examples of point of view at work in visual art. In this connection it would be valuable to read to the students excerpts from James Agee's *Agee On Film* (Oblensky, 1958) and Sergei Eisenstein's *Film Form and the Film Sense* (Meridian, 1957).

5. What are perhaps the most definitive studies on point of view in prose fiction have been written in the 20th century. Two excellent source works, which would be helpful to the teacher preparing for this lesson, are Percy Lubbock's *The Craft of Fiction* (reissue, Viking, 1957) and Wayne Booth's *The Rhetoric of Fiction* (University of Chicago Press, 1961).

B. Special Observations for Levels A, B, and C

- **1.** *Practice 1. Level A:* Students should not have difficulty identifying Hemingway's selection as a scene and the next two items as summaries. The Thomas Wolfe sentence, however, presents more of a challenge; its opening panoramic view of the town square smears into the start of a scene "...as Grover turned into the square." This item should produce a variety of responses. Ask the students to read and to elaborate on the reasons for their choices. The Wolfe item may best be described as a combination of summary and scene, but emphasis should not be placed on a "right or wrong" answer here. You may wish to have the students compare Wolfe's sentence with the last two sentences of Crane's unit selection; there are several points of resemblance.

  Item **f.** should also produce a range of student reactions. While the subject here—the July afternoon—is treated in a summary framework, some of the words Dobrée selects are highly concrete. Throughout your treatment of this Practice, lead the students to an increasing awareness of the ways scene and summary converge. Strive for a sensitive and flexible, as well as analytical, exploration of language.

  Levels B and C: Have the students describe the feeling which each of these first four sentences gave them. Then ask them to identify the particular words or phrases which produce the most powerful sense impressions. In **b.** of the C-Level Practice, the text should lead the students to identify the last sentence as a summary. It would be well to discuss both the **a.** and **b.** papers.

- **2.** *Practice 2. Level A:* This Practice provides the student with an important step toward an increasing mastery of third person point of view. It also tests the student's grasp of the difference between summary and scene. Have some of the students read their paragraphs aloud, and call on others to make evaluative comments. All the papers should, of course, represent summaries.

  Levels B and C: See Practice 1, Level A.

- **3.** *Practice 3. Levels A and B:* Encourage the students to put themselves in the location by activating their imaginations. Prior to writing this paragraph, the student may find it helpful to make a list of those physical factors or limitations which will condition what he sees. You may wish to use the board or opaque projector to contrast some successful student paragraphs with the unit selection; by juxtaposing these distant shots of the open boat with Crane's close-ups, the students should gain a deeper appreciation of the nature of point of view.

  Level C: Encourage students to record their physiological reactions here. Some students are bound to experience a mild sense of vertigo from the beginning of this sentence: "The horizon narrowed and widened, and dipped and rose,...." Ask several students to explain the picture and the emotions this sentence produces for them.

- **4.** *Practice 4. Level A:* Call on a few students to read their paragraphs aloud and have the class attempt to detect any breach in what should be a consistently sustained *inside* point of view. Then, ask members of the class to correct one another's paragraphs, writing constructive comments concerning point of view.

Level B: It is worth taking time with this Practice because it can lead to a discussion of the pervasive influence of point of view. With each of the three questions—**a.**, **b.**, and **c.**—start by having students read their answers aloud. But in each case extend the discussion into a close analysis of the ways in which the language and point of view are intimately associated in both the altered and the original versions. Stress the fact that it is not the "content" that has been changed here but rather the angle of vision, the controls behind the language—the point of view. As point of view blurs, the language also becomes vague, fuzzy.

Level C: To help the students organize this paragraph, suggest that they list the order of objects and events that their scenes will unfold. Have some of the students read their scenes aloud and ask others to suggest ways of improving the use of the *inside* point of view.

- 5. *Practice 5. Level A:* See Practice 4, Level B. Level A students should be expected to produce criticism of a higher quality than did the Level B students.

  Level B: Joyce's passage, which concludes his great short story "The Dead," provides the student with a model that synthesizes all that this unit strives to communicate. Joyce unfolds the scene through an observer, and we see and know through his eyes and mind. The passage builds from tiny snowflakes to a universal statement, from physical point of view (a man looking out the window) to mental point of view (a man reflecting on human destiny). Throughout the passage, concrete diction expresses the sensory and emotional experience of the observer who is within the scene. Then, in the final sentence, scene merges with panorama as the observer, using broad general terms, makes a judgment that is all-inclusive. This is a rich passage, and the students should be given ample time to discuss it and to analyze it carefully. It should be made clear to the students that while their writing assignment here calls for a less dramatic, less vivid quality than Joyce's passage, they should strive for clarity and beauty in their summary statement.

- 6. *Practice 6. Level A:* See Practice 3, Level C. This Practice is purposely delayed for Level A students so they will apply the teachings of the unit to their papers.

- 7. *Practice 7. Level A:* If this passage is read in a cursory way, the total effect may be merely melodramatic. Read the passage to the students or assign this responsibility to one of your best interpretive readers. Lead the class in a close analysis of this passage. Direct the attention of the students to Flaubert's brilliant and functionally dramatic use of details. Notice, for example, how he uses the humming lathe first as a part of the physical scene but later as an objective correlative for Emma's state of mind. Encourage the student to compose his summary with care; this Practice can clearly reveal the differences between showing and telling and between scene and summary—provided the student regards it as more than a casual, perfunctory task.

- 8. **Problem 1. Level A:** As a prelude to writing, conduct a class discussion in which students recollect and recount vividly remembered experiences. This exercise may set their memories to work and trigger some authentic descriptive essays.

  Level B: Have the students reread the unit selection, the Thomas Wolfe sentence in Practice 2, and the James Joyce passage in Practice 5 in order to study the natural ways scene and summary can be blended.

  Level C: The students should revise their original paragraph before expanding it into an essay. If time permits, give the student some constructive criticism on the use he made of point of view and diction in the paragraph he wrote for Practice 4.

- 9. **Problem 2. Level A:** Request that the students reread the unit selection and the sentence by Thomas Wolfe in order to study the way these writers make a natural transition from scene to summary. Have students revise their original paragraphs for inconsistencies in point of view and weaknesses in diction.

  Levels B and C: Before the students begin to write on this Problem, ask them to make two columns on a piece of paper, one entitled "panorama" and the other entitled "close-up." Then, have them list in the appropriate columns all the appropriate physical and emotional factors which their subject and their respective points of view will require.

IV. EVALUATING THE UNIT

Emphasize the following points in your evaluation of the papers written in response to the Problems:

A. Are the writer's words helpful to his point of view?
B. Does the writer make effective use of the summary and the scene?
C. Does the writer demonstrate skill in showing and telling?
D. Is the point of view clearly established and consistently maintained?

V. ADDITIONAL WRITING TOPICS

A. Write an essay on the importance of point of view in a poem. First describe the situation, then deal with the speaker (or narrator), his relationship to the situation and to the audience. The following poems will lend themselves especially well to an analysis of point of view: "The Love Song of J. Alfred Prufrock" by T. S. Eliot; "My Last Duchess" by Robert Browning; "The Death of the Ball-Turret Gunner" by Randall Jarrell; "Birches" and "Stopping by Woods on a Snowy Evening" by Robert Frost.

B. Establish a physical point of view through an observer who is trapped. Choose the circumstances of your character's predicament and develop a tone consistent with those circumstances. Your observer may be caught between floors in an elevator, buried in a mine shaft, locked in a cell, or tottering on a window ledge. Use third person point of view and develop your scene by showing it from the inside.

C. Place a six-year-old child in an unfamiliar situation—lost in a big city, wandering through a modern art gallery, stranded in the jungle, alone in an unlighted mansion—and combine summary statements with scenes to present the experience through the mind and senses of the child.

D. Spend some time analyzing the opinions and temperament of an individual or type of person whose values and behavior you strongly oppose. Then construct a situation or series of events which will test this character's qualities. Write an essay using third person point of view and close-up technique, and present the experience through the mental attitude of the unattractive character.

Suggested Bibliography

ALL ISSUES of the following NCTE publications: *Elementary English, The English Journal, College English, College Composition and Communication.*

CRITICAL THINKING

ALTICK, RICHARD D., *Preface to Critical Reading.* New York: Holt, Rinehart and Winston, Inc., 1960.

BEARDSLEY, M.C., *Practical Logic.* Englewood Cliffs, N.J.: Prentice-Hall, Inc., 1950.

BILSKY, MANUEL, *Patterns of Argument.* New York: Holt, Rinehart and Winston, Inc., 1963.

CHASE, STUART, *Guides to Straight Thinking.* New York: Harper & Row, Publishers, Inc. 1956.

COPI, IRVING M., *Introduction to Logic,* 2d ed. New York: The Macmillan Company, 1961.

HAYAKAWA, S.I., *Language in Thought and Action* 2d ed. New York: Harcourt, Brace & World, Inc., 1964.

CURRICULUM AND METHODOLOGY

BRUNER, JEROME, *The Process of Education.* Cambridge, Mass.: Harvard University Press, 1960.

GUTH, HANS P., *English Today and Tomorrow, A Guide for Teachers of English.* Englewood Cliffs, N.J.: Prentice-Hall, Inc., 1964.

KITZHABER, ALBERT R., *Themes, Theories, and Therapy: The Teaching of Writing in College.* New York: McGraw-Hill Book Company, Inc., 1963.

LOBAN, WALTER, RYAN, MARGARET, and SQUIRE, JAMES. *Teaching Language and Literature.* New York: Harcourt, Brace & World, Inc., 1961.

NATIONAL COUNCIL OF TEACHERS OF ENGLISH, *Language, Linguistics, and School Programs: Proceedings of the Spring Institutes, 1963, of the N.C.T.E.* Champaign, Illinois, 1963.

SAUER, EDWIN H., *English in the Secondary School.* New York: Holt, Rinehart and Winston, Inc., 1961.

LANGUAGE

ALLEN, HAROLD B., *Readings in Applied English Linguistics.* New York: Appleton-Century-Crofts, 1958.

BROWN, ROGER, *Words and Things.* Glencoe, Ill.: The Free Press, 1958.

BRUNER, JEROME, GOODNOW, J.J., and AUSTIN, G.A., *A Study of Thinking.* New York: Science Editions, Inc., 1962. Copyright, John Wiley and Sons, Inc., 1956.

BRYANT, MARGARET M., *Modern English and Its Heritage*. New York: The Macmillan Company, 1962.

FRANCIS, W. NELSON, *The History of English*. New York: W. W. Norton & Company, Inc., 1963.

——, *The Structure of American English (especially Chapter 10)*. New York: The Ronald Press Company, 1958.

GLEASON, H. A., Jr. *Linguistics and English Grammar*. New York: Holt, Rinehart and Winston, Inc., 1965.

HARVARD EDUCATIONAL REVIEW: *A Special Issue—Language and Learning*, Vol. 34, No. 2. Cambridge, Mass.: Harvard University Press, 1964.

LAIRD, CHARLTON, *The Miracle of Language*. Cleveland: The World Publishing Company, 1953.

——, *Handbook for English Language and Composition*. Boston: Ginn and Company, 1964.

MENCKEN, H.L., *The American Language*, 4th ed., rev. New York: Alfred A. Knopf, Inc., 1963.

ROBERTS, PAUL, *English Sentences*. New York: Harcourt, Brace & World, Inc., 1962.

SLEDD, JAMES, *A Short Introduction to English Grammar*. Chicago: Scott, Foresman and Company, 1959.

WHITEHALL, HAROLD, *Structural Essentials of English*. New York: Harcourt, Brace & World, Inc., 1956.

RHETORIC

BAILEY, DUDLEY, *Essays on Rhetoric*. New York: Oxford University Press, 1965.

BOOTH, WAYNE, *The Rhetoric of Fiction*. Chicago: The University of Chicago Press, 1961.

GRAVES, ROBERT, and HODGE, ALAN. *The Reader over Your Shoulder: A Handbook for Writers of English Prose*. New York: The Macmillan Company, 1943.

READ, HERBERT, *English Prose Style*. Boston: Beacon Press, Inc., 1955.

BCDEFGHI   069876
Printed in the United States of America